Geographies of Post-Industrial Place, Memory, and Heritage

All industrialization is deeply rooted within the specific geographies in which it took place, and echoes of previous industrialization continue to reverberate in these places through to the modern day. This book investigates the overlap of memory and the impacts of industrialization within today's communities and the senses of place and heritage that grew alongside and in reaction to the growth of mines, mills, and factories.

The economic and social change that accompanied the unchecked accumulation of wealth and exploitation of labor as the industrial revolution spread throughout the world has numerous lasting impacts on the socioeconomics of today. Likewise, the planet itself is now reeling. The memory and heritage of these processes reach into the communities that owe the industrial revolution their existence, but these populations also often suffered adverse impacts to their health and environment through the large-scale and rapid extraction of natural resources and production of goods. Through the themes of memory, community, and place; working post-industrial landscapes; and the de-romanticization of industrial pasts, this book examines the endurance and decline of these communities, the spatial processes of industrial byproducts, and the memory and heritage of industrialization and its legacies.

While based in the traditions of geography, this collection also draws upon and will be of great interest to students and scholars of cultural anthropology, archaeology, sociology, history, architecture, civil engineering, and heritage, memory, museum, and tourism studies. Using global examples, the authors provide a uniquely geographic understanding to industrial heritage across the spaces, places, and memories of industrial development.

Mark Alan Rhodes II is Assistant Professor in the Department of Social Sciences, Michigan Technological University, USA.

William R. Price is Assistant Professor in the Department of Geography, Ball State University, USA.

Amy Walker is a PhD candidate in the School of Geography and Planning at Cardiff University, UK.

Routledge Research in Sustainable Urbanism

This series offers a forum for original and innovative research that engages with key debates and concepts in the field. Titles within the series range from empirical investigations to theoretical engagements, offering international perspectives and multidisciplinary dialogues across the social sciences.

The Experimental City
Edited by James Evans, Andrew Karvonen and Rob Raven

Imagining Sustainability
Creative Urban Environmental Governance in Chicago and Melbourne
Julie L. Cidell

Regenerative Urban Design and Ecosystem Biomimicry
Maibritt Pedersen Zari

The Politics of Urban Sustainability Transitions
Knowledge, Power and Governance
Edited by Jens Stissing Jensen, Philipp Späth and Matthew Cashmore

Ecologies Design
Transforming Architecture, Landscape, and Urbanism
Edited by Maibritt Pedersen Zari, Peter Connolly and Mark Southcombe

Planning Wild Cities
Human-Nature Relationships in the Urban Age
Wendy Steele

Games and Play in the Creative, Smart and Ecological City
Edited by Dale Leorke and Marcus Owens

Geographies of Post-Industrial Place, Memory, and Heritage
Edited by Mark Alan Rhodes II, William R. Price and Amy Walker

www.routledge.com/Routledge-Research-in-Sustainable-Urbanism/book-series/RRSU

Geographies of Post-Industrial Place, Memory, and Heritage

Edited by Mark Alan Rhodes II,
William R. Price and Amy Walker

Routledge
Taylor & Francis Group
LONDON AND NEW YORK

First published 2021
by Routledge
2 Park Square, Milton Park, Abingdon, Oxon OX14 4RN

and by Routledge
52 Vanderbilt Avenue, New York, NY 10017

Routledge is an imprint of the Taylor & Francis Group, an informa business

British Library Cataloguing-in-Publication Data
A catalogue record for this book is available from the British Library

Library of Congress Cataloging-in-Publication Data
Names: Rhodes, Mark Alan, II, 1990– editor. | Price, William R., editor. | Walker, Amy, 1993– editor.
Title: Geographies of post-industrial place, memory, and heritage / edited by Mark Alan Rhodes II, William R. Price and Amy Walker.
Description: Milton Park, Abingdon, Oxon ; New York, NY : Routledge, 2021. | Includes bibliographical references and index. | Summary: "This book investigates the overlap of memory and the impacts of industrialization within today's communities and the senses of place and heritage which grew alongside and in reaction to the growth of mines, mills, and factories."—Provided by publisher.
Identifiers: LCCN 2020026240 (print) | LCCN 2020026241 (ebook) | ISBN 9780367440909 (hardback) | ISBN 9781003007494 (ebook)
Subjects: LCSH: Industrialization. | Cultural geography. | Human geography. | Collective memory.
Classification: LCC HD2329 .G46 2021 (print) | LCC HD2329 (ebook) | DDC 338.09—dc23
LC record available at https://lccn.loc.gov/2020026240
LC ebook record available at https://lccn.loc.gov/2020026241

ISBN: 978-0-367-44090-9 (hbk)
ISBN: 978-1-003-00749-4 (ebk)

Typeset in Goudy
by Apex CoVantage, LLC

Contents

Figures

Tables

Contributors

Pablo Arboleda is Urban Studies Foundation Postdoctoral Fellow at the School of Geographical and Earth Sciences, University of Glasgow. Trained as an architect, his interdisciplinary work focuses on the heritagization of modern ruins through collaborative practices of reactivation.

John Baeten is an interdisciplinary social scientist with a background in archaeology, geography, and environmental history. Baeten directs the Historical Landscapes Laboratory at Indiana University and is researching the interrelated histories of subsurface tiling and swamp drainage in the Cornbelt.

Santanu Banerjee is Assistant Professor in and Coordinator of the Department of English, Faculty of Arts, Kazi Nazrul University, Asansol, West Bengal, India. He is also one of the founding members of the Asansol Heritage Research Group.

Rosa Cerarols is a geographer at the Humanities Department of Universitat Pompeu Fabra, Barcelona. Her research deals with cultural geographies, gender studies, and geohumanities. She is currently working on the founded project "Dialogues between art, landscape and territory in non-urban environments." She is also a founding member of the Konvent Cultural Association.

Suvojit Chatterjee is Assistant Teacher of English at Asansol North Point School, Asansol, West Bengal, India. He is also Founder Member and Independent Research Associate of Asansol Heritage Research Group.

Alex R. Colucci is a geographer working in the areas of political and economic geography with interests in state violence and the philosophy of science and technology. He earned his PhD from Kent State University.

Leila Dawney is a cultural geographer and theorist of authority, affect and embodiment at the University of Exeter. Her research concerns the forms of experience and subjectivity produced in and through spaces of late capitalism

Edward Hollis is Professor of Interior Design at Edinburgh College of Art at the University of Edinburgh, with particular research interests in the relationships between creative writing and the continuing evolution of the historic built environment.

Hayden Lorimer is Professor of Human Geography in the School of Geosciences, University of Edinburgh. He writes about past places and living landscapes, in Scotland and elsewhere.

Antonio Luna is Professor of geography at the Universitat Pompeu Fabra de Barcelona. His research is oriented toward cultural critical geographies and geohumanities.

Hemonta Mondal is an independent assistant teacher, fiction writer, and essayist. He is also an independent researcher and co-founding member of Asansol Heritage Group, Asansol, West Bengal, India.

William R. Price is Assistant Professor in the Department of Geography at Ball State University. His research focuses on the intersection of tourism and cultural heritage, with an emphasis on interpretation and development plans associated with industrial tourism.

Mark Alan Rhodes II is Assistant Professor of Geography at Michigan Technological University where he advises industrial heritage and archaeology MS and PhD students. His research critically examines the intersections of memory, identity, and landscape, particularly in Wales.

Stian Rice is a food systems geographer and a visiting research scientist at the University of Maryland, Baltimore County. His work examines structural violence within food systems and the origins of historical famine.

Carolyn F. Thompson is from New Haven, Connecticut. She earned a BA in urban studies at Eugene Lang College – part of The New School in New York City – and received her PhD in human geography from Macquarie University in Sydney, Australia.

James A. Tyner is Professor of Geography at Kent State University and Fellow of the American Association of Geographers. He is the author of numerous books, including *Dead Labor: Toward a Political Economy of Premature Death.*

Amy Walker is a PhD candidate in the School of Geography and Planning at Cardiff University. Her research focuses on everyday legacies of industrial life and work in post-industrial communities and landscapes, using ethnographic approaches and theories of affect and memory.

Acknowledgments

We would like to thank all of those involved in the series of sessions at the Annual Meeting of the American Association of Geographers in 2019 who sparked these discussions and whose effort makes this volume possible. Support from our departments and institutions – The Department of Social Sciences at Michigan Technological University, The Department of Geography at Ball State University, The School of Geography and Planning at Cardiff University, and Kent State University's Department of Geography – has also been appreciated. We offer a special thank you to Environmental and Energy Policy PhD student Shardul Tiwari at Michigan Technological University whose meticulous labor compiled an elaborate yet practical index. We are thankful for the time of the reviewers and editors who have pushed to ensure the highest quality, and we are thankful for each other, as we could not have asked for a better editorial team, particularly during these challenging times. Finally, we are most appreciative of the authors in the volume whose labor, during a pandemic nonetheless, highlights multiple and new perspectives from geography in the contexts of post-industrial place, memory, and heritage.

1 Introduction

Geographies of post-industrial memory, place, and heritage

Mark Alan Rhodes II, William R. Price, and Amy Walker

Whilst living in the Black Country, an area of industrial heritage and smoke that so granted the region its name, I had come to think of post-industrial as being defined by networks of canals, abandoned warehouses and red-brick glass cones. Small villages have run together into an endless urban sprawl of small commercial centres and many industrial estates, but each are known for their own historical trade. The Jewellery Quarter on the way into central Birmingham. My own hometown was known for glass and crystal.

Yet, in the valleys of South Wales, especially the smaller villages I find myself in, these networks are beneath ground, invisible and absent-minded. I consider that most of the people here will never have entered a mine, despite the fact that they almost all have family that were coal miners. I have never entered a foundry, even though many of my family worked in them, one as an apprentice even now.

Perhaps it is a more effective metaphor that these valleys seem to veil their own history. The oft-travelled passages to the coal face beneath my feet as I walk along a footpath that used to be a railway line. The trained eye, the informed walker, the historian, the local; they know the legacies in this landscape. The ghosts of the miners themselves might walk beneath me, their own routes so entrenched in daily routine, in mass numbers, in years of repetition, that they continue even after the carbon monoxide and time takes over the tunnels.

– Amy Walker

The legacy of industrial places and practices lives on within geographies of post-industrial heritage. As the previous anecdote illustrates, we, the editors of this book, each have our own stories behind what engrossed us in the geography and history of industry. Walker was raised on the outskirts of a region called the Black Country in England, so named for the coal seams and the smoke of foundries, now defined by deindustrialization. Price grew up amidst the oil landscapes of Oklahoma and touring industrial heritage sites on visits with family in Wales. Rhodes was born in the Rust Belt surrounded by the struggling river cities of Central Illinois who have long lost their moniker as the nation's assay yet continue on with dwindling hubs of manufacturing and increasingly corporatized industrial agriculture. We imagine that many of you can point to similar experiences in launching your passions.

Figure 1.1 View over Wordsley canal and red-brick glass cone from Stuart Crystal Factory, 2012

Source: David Walker

This book concerns the overlap of memory and impacts of industrialization within the communities that grew alongside factories, mines, power stations, warehouses, and railways. The associated infrastructure dominates the landscape of many regions around the world, whether still functioning, memorialized, adapted to other uses, or abandoned. The unchecked accumulation of wealth and exploitation of labor has lasting economic and social influences. Likewise, the acceleration of environmental degradation that began during the industrial revolution continues to have widespread ramifications.

The consequences of these processes reach both into the communities that owe their existence to the industrial revolution and those whose health, environment, and population were severely impacted through the large scale and rapid extraction of natural resources and production of goods. We examine these communities, the spatial processes of industrial byproducts, and the memory and heritage of industrialization and deindustrialization. In so doing, we assert the important role of geography in considering post-industrial places.

A geographic approach

As industrial activity – and therefore the experiences of deindustrialization and post-industrialism – impacts all areas of life, geography as a discipline is arguably best situated amongst the humanities and social sciences to address the multiplicity and complexity of these legacies. Fundamentally, industrial development and decline happen in place. These transitions occur within communities, tied into multiscalar and complex networks.

We do not downplay the invaluable contributions of other academic disciplines, including history, anthropology, sociology, urban studies, and heritage studies. Indeed, as will be evident throughout this book, geographers draw heavily on their work for inspiration and guidance. Rather, we seek to highlight that geographers are ideally positioned, through our understanding of place, spatial techniques, and the inherent integrative quality of the field, to add insights.

There are many avenues for geographers to broaden understanding of community engagement with deindustrialized and post-industrialized places. Economic geographers debate the transitions from traditional industrial work and Fordism to more diverse forms of business across development models and analyze the associated interventions from policymakers (Malmberg 1997). Historical geographers consider the patterns of industrial life and society using archival materials and oral history, drawing on the long-standing contributions of historians and archeologists to these debates (Gregory 1988). Tourism geographers investigate how communities preserve and promote their industrial heritage, translating processes and memories to visitors (Jonsen-Verbeke 1999). Planners grapple with the impacts of industrialization on the environment (Whitehead 2014).

Geographers also engage with the broader social theory surrounding these transitions, reflecting on the conceptualization of post-modern society (Bauman 2000; Beck 1992). Feminist geography provides a key contribution to these investigations, addressing issues of gendered work, inequalities of experience for those enrolled in or adjacent to industrial work, and changes from the decline of industry (Nelson and Seager 2005). Existing work on post-industrial societies focuses disproportionately on countries that were the traditional focus of models of modernity (Simon 1998). Yet, industrialization has always been international and imbued with the power relations of colonialism (McEwan 2008). Post-colonial geographers have considered this underrepresentation and acknowledged experiences beyond large Western economies and the extensive and problematic histories of these structures (Henry, McEwan, and Pollard 2002; Jacobs 1996).

Contextualizing industrialization and deindustrialization

In this section, we provide a brief overview of the historic and geographic context of industrialization and deindustrialization. Many of the topics that we raise here are revisited within place-specific circumstances across the chapters of this book.

The industrial revolution

Humans have been engaging in manufacturing for millennia, based out of homes ("cottage industry") and small professional enterprises ("guild industry"). Many common English surnames dating back more than a millennium are testaments to the longstanding influence of industrial occupations, such as Smith, Weaver, and Cooper. Indeed, the revolution that took place between the 18th and early 20th centuries is an era characterized not by the emergence of industry, but by a rapid increase in the scale of production.

The growth of the English textile industry from the 1730s is generally acknowledged as the beginning of the industrial revolution (Allen 2009; Hobsbawm 1999; Deane 1979). The first textile mills set in motion profound social, economic, and environmental changes worldwide (see Figure 1.2). Production of larger quantities of goods at lower costs accelerated demand, generated wealth, and led to a rapid expanse of the middle class. Numerous other impacts that accompanied industrialization have been well documented (Allen 2017), including mechanization of equipment, technological advances, and environmental damages at the global scale.

As geographers, we investigate many of these impacts, but our focus in this book is primarily concerned with the legacies of industrialization for communities. Perhaps the most important accompanying change in this regard has been the exponential population growth that began during the industrial revolution; a rise from less than one billion humans globally in the 1700s to 7.8 billion in 2020. Another lasting influence is an alteration in where humans live and work.

Figure 1.2 The Moser Raiser finishing machine in the National Wool Museum (Wales). The museum connects mechanized textile finishing as a particular impetus for the early 19th-century Luddite Movement

Source: Mark Alan Rhodes II

Fewer than 10% of humans lived in urban areas in 1800; now, that number is over 50%. Much of this ongoing urbanization has been driven by the association between cities, industry, and employment. The invention of the steam engine uncoupled manufacturing dependency from physical geography, allowing for the creation of power to drive machines anywhere (Allen 2009). Consequently, factories were concentrated in cities, and large numbers migrated in pursuit of economic opportunities.

In industrializing countries, communities expanded – and were sometimes founded – in response to the demands of industry, including transportation, communication, energy production, and resource extraction. Factories, mines, and other elements of industry dominated employment in many areas. Other enterprises were founded alongside industries, with businesses catering to the needs of companies, workers, and families. In some areas, "company towns" dominated, with corporations providing nearly all jobs and shaping communities' way of life.

However, not all people and areas benefited from industrialization (Allen 2017). Many places associated with agriculture and prior forms of industry suffered high unemployment and outmigration. Industrialization was fiercely resisted in some places, as underscored by the Luddites in early 19th-century England, who sought to protect their livelihoods by sabotaging machines. Industrial cities often had large numbers of impoverished people, with many rural to urban migrants not finding the economic opportunities they sought. Industrialization accelerated colonization and vice versa, driven by demand for power, raw materials, and luxury items. Among the many legacies of industrialization is its association with slavery. As World Systems Theory articulates, wealth in one area of the globe is often predicated on marginalization in another (Wallerstein 1974).

Industry also served as a center of social and political activity. Successive generations often worked in the same factory or mine. Sporting clubs, bands, educational institutes, and other elements of social life revolved around industry. Difficult, often unsafe, working conditions and low wages united workers and their communities in common cause, with industrial areas becoming some of the largest fomenters of union activity (Featherstone 2012; Francis and Smith 1980; Winterton and Winterton 1989). The products and tools of industry became symbols around which communities based their identity, whether it was the miner's lamp, the steam locomotive, or enduring nicknames such as "Steel City."

Amidst the many changes to peoples' lived experiences, the role of industry in shaping the landscape was vital. Tremendous growth in infrastructure often accompanied industrialization: for example, large factories, mines, canals, train tracks, roads, and worker housing. In addition to these direct influences, the wealth generated by industry led to the establishment of stores, theaters, parks, museums, schools, and other elements that came to define place for many communities (Cowie and Heathcott 2003). Pollution also became a common aspect of day to day life, with industrial centers becoming synonymous with smog and poor water quality.

Deindustrialization

For the countries in Europe, North America, and East Asia that defined the first industrial revolution, the era since World War II has been one of deindustrialization (Cowie and Heathcott 2003; Martin and Rowthorn 1986). As the world economy became more interconnected, the service sector – banking, insurance, healthcare, education, communications, retail, and other producer- and consumer-oriented enterprises – supplanted industrial activity as the primary source of income and employment (see Figure 1.3).

There are many reasons for deindustrialization, including further automation of machines and declining demand for particular products. Among the most important, however, is the tendency of capitalism to maximize profit through the reduction of production costs. Driven by the pursuit of large labor pools, lower labor costs, cheaper real estate, tax incentives, and other cost saving strategies, transnational corporations relocated their industrial assets, often producing what are termed commodity chains (Gereffi and Korzeniewicz 1994). Beginning with the "Tigers" of Southeast Asia in the 1960s and continuing to the growth of countries

Figure 1.3 The former coal-fired Pratt Street Power Plant is a focal point of Baltimore's Inner Harbor commercial district, among the most well-known global examples of post-industrial redevelopment and gentrification

Source: William R. Price

such as Mexico, Indonesia, Nigeria, and Turkey today, the centers of global industrial production have shifted. The rise to economic prominence of China, India, and other countries has encouraged industrial development in regions that are closer to these markets. Many of the trends that impacted the first industrializers are repeating in the world's fastest growing economies.

The many paths taken by places around the world in the aftermath of deindustrialization is a primary focus of this book. The process of deindustrialization is rooted in place, with countless factors influencing the extent, impacts, and pace (Cowie and Heathcott 2003). Many communities were devastated by the loss of industry, losing not only their primary employers and sources of income but also the unifying factor at the core of the places' identity (Wicke, Berger, and Golombek 2018).

The transition from prosperity to marginalization manifests in tangible and intangible ways. In the United States, for example, the ascribed moniker of "Rust Belt" to the once national pride "Steel Belt" references both the decay of infrastructure and the perception that the region's best days are in the past. Many areas, however, have thrived following deindustrialization. While some found new economic directions, such as those offered by the service sector, others have transformed post-industrial spaces into new working landscapes (Hobor 2013).

Capital in the conversation

Inescapable from the cycles of industrialization and deindustrialization are the explicit geographies of capital central to boom-bust communities. While the centrality of capital to fluctuating demand is obvious, geographers pull these tendrils apart in search of a deeper understanding. Whether through the privatization of space, the production of nature, or the primitive accumulation or extraction of wealth and labor through colonial practices, many connections point to industrialization, particularly the legacies of the industrial revolution.

Especially in Anglo-American contexts, privatization of space preceded heavy industrialization, but nonetheless primed both place and labor for the mechanization and production necessary for industrial practice. Via the state and the individual, privatization throughout North America followed the expansion of the settler colonial states increasingly dependent on "frontier industry." Though the 1800s are not generally considered ripe for the corporatization of the family farm, they were already channeling the majority of their production into livestock feed and driving the historic meat processing centers and stockyards of Chicago, Cincinnati, and Fort Worth.

This stripping of common land for large-scale agriculture, mining, processing, and manufacturing served the primary purpose of primitive accumulation. Influential social theorist Karl Marx clearly ties early industrialization into the act of primitive accumulation and how capitalism as we see it today runs rampant. From the Highland Clearances in Scotland to the global slave trade, this combination of privatizing land, displacing people from sustainable subsistence practices, forcing out cottage industry, and ensnaring and enslaving displaced individuals into forced labor generated these early processes. As Marx ([1867] 2019, 823) writes,

> The discovery of gold and silver in America, the extirpation, enslavement, and entombment in mines of the aboriginal population, the beginning of the conquest and looting of the East Indies, the turning of Africa into a warren for the commercial hunting of black-skins, signalised the dawn of the era of capitalist production.

These acts, and their continued repercussions, when added to "modern industry" (i.e., machines) drive the legacies of industrial heritage (de Peuter and Dyer-Witheford 2010; Harvey 2003).

A further necessity in wide-scale industrialization is the reorganization of values, particularly in terms of nature and the environment. Capitalism redefines and reaffirms human-environment relationships, whereby nature is produced, consumed, and discarded for the maximization of profit and production of goods (Smith 2008). This process, whether gold mining, shipbuilding, or weaving, leaves scars upon both land and people. The production of waste through these processes is a fundamental aspect of industrialization, and the abandoning of waste is equally central to deindustrialization. As explored by chapters within this text, the memory, landscape, and heritage of industry includes the wastelands left behind. Whether through a process of surplus labor or resources or other "free" market economic drivers, post-industrial place, memory, and heritage rest upon these reassigned values.

Questions of waste in post-industrial contexts have not escaped the spatial view of geographers. In these contexts, waste reorders not only space but time, while also navigating the false dichotomies of conservation and ruination in industrial heritage contexts. Edensor's (2005, 101) *Industrial Ruins* identifies the power of waste to break the linear production of industrialization, and as DeSilvey (2017) argues in *Curated Decay*, accepting post-industrial geographies as circular processes allows for alternative narratives to emerge (see Figure 1.4). On one hand, the concept of "human-as-waste" takes particular precedent in post-industrial processes as surplus labor renders industrial workers "useless" within the hyper capitalist systems of industrial production and gentrification (Yates 2011). Scholars such as Dillon (2014) or Cowell and Thomas (2002) make the necessary connections between race, class, and space in post-industrial contexts. On the other hand, drawing from Hollis (2010; and author of Chapter 3 in this volume) and work from *Industrienatur* (Lange 2005), DeSilvey (2017) asks how a "positive passivity" in heritage contexts may allow for more-than-human agency to rewrite these landscapes. Similarly, readers will notice work within this volume asks how we might reconsider "waste as artifact" or "waste as heritage."

Industrial communities

During the early 20th century, many sociologists conducted research into the "stereotypical" working-class communities that existed across the United Kingdom

Figure 1.4 One of the many weathered ruins dwelling within the newly formed ecosystems of the former Dinorwig Slate Quarry

Source: Mark Alan Rhodes II

and United States. Industrial communities such as Muncie, Indiana became the idealized "Middletowns" that typified the population (Lynd and Lynd 1929). Subsequent work on community as a concept, much of which spans far beyond these industrial contexts, has been based extensively on these projects. Many of the contemporary models are therefore rooted, to varying extents, on the constructions seen in literature on the "working class community" (Day 2006).

Prior to these projects, however, many scholars focused on the loss of community that occurred through the industrial revolution, as agricultural communities were diminished by programs of industrialization across Europe and Northern America. The notion of "gemeinschaft," which is often mobilized in the postmodern work addressing the "loss" of community and life-long stability, is based on the idea that the rural community is the model of "authentic" connection (Tonnies 1955). However, many of the images of industrial communities that are apparent in these works are now mobilized as constructions of lasting, close-knit, and interconnected societies (see Figure 1.5). Ideas of "everyone knows everyone" and "taking care of each other" are reinforced as key values of these lost industrial communities. The mining village, the dock workers, the industrial towns, are frequently subject to collective nostalgia (O'Brien 2018; Loveday 2014; Strangleman 2007, 2013; MacDonald 2018; Jones 2010).

Figure 1.5 View over miners' cottages in ex-coal mining village in the Ebbw Fach Valley, South Wales

Source: Amy Walker

Of course, many of these constructions are Western-centric, focusing on the waves of industrialization that occurred in Europe and North America throughout the 18th and 19th centuries. Additionally, the colonial networks that enabled these vast economic and societal transformations are often overlooked. In the context of this book, we think it pertinent to highlight the interconnected history of both industrial place and the concept of community itself, however problematic.

Constructing post-industrial communities: place, memory, and practice

Though work on postindustrial spaces has focused largely on the process of "moving on" from the industrial past, we highlight ways that industrial pasts endure. Many places labeled as "postindustrial," such as the aforementioned Black Country or the Welsh valleys in the UK, still have significant rates of manufacturing work. As Strangleman (2013), Linkon (2018), Edensor (2005) and others have explored, the images of industrial worlds endure in the imagination, through engagement with film, literature, and tourism.

It is not our aim to provide comprehensive definitions of place, memory, and heritage. We intend the book chapters to illustrate the multitude of ways in which geographers may engage with these terms, acknowledging the overlaps and slippages between the concepts themselves. Instead, we highlight the key ways in which geographers and other social scientists have engaged with these ideas, to situate the contributions of this book within a wider conversation on the relationship between contemporary (post-industrial) places and (industrial) pasts and how these are embedded in the practices of realizing imagined futures. We do not present places as static case-studies but as illustrations and frameworks of this multitemporal relationship.

Place

The plurality of place is fundamental to many of the chapters presented in this edition. For geographers, engaging with community is interwoven with work on place attachment, place-identity, and sense of belonging, drawing on humanist approaches stemming from the 1960s and 1970s (e.g., Relph 1976; Tuan 1977). Through an engagement with phenomenology, it is via this work on place-attachment that the role of memory is made apparent (Lewicka 2013). Senses of belonging, to a place or to a community, are rooted in connections of shared and collective memory (Tomaney 2015; Emery 2018; Lovell 1998; Degnen 2016) or through practices of formal and informal heritages. Memory and heritage serve to position an individual within the collective, illustrating their own relationship with place through their personal experiences and the accepted construction of "the way things were." Communities may also experience a foreboding sense of loss for what has not yet disappeared, as poignantly discussed in the context of Glasgow in the chapter by Arboleda and Lorimer.

We recognize that these forms of memory are heterogenous, complex, and often contested. Yet, for many geographers it is through the construction of shared memory and heritage that a community is perhaps best understood (Dicks 2000; Emery 2018). To draw on Massey (1995, 184), we argue that these histories can be, and often are, mobilized to invent "a coherence of place." Anderson's (2006) work on "imagined communities" is perhaps the most notable to acknowledge how these constructions of shared pasts, traditions, and identities are coalesced and mobilized, providing structure and apparent legitimacy to ideas of nationhood (see also Hobsbawm 1999; Legg 2005).

The importance of place is especially relevant in the postindustrial context, where communities have experienced significant transformation, through the processes of deindustrialization described earlier. Walker's chapter illustrates the varied ways that such legacies manifest in the lives of post-industrial communities in South Wales. These communities have endured dangerous working conditions (MacKenzie et al. 2006); pollution (Mah 2009); industrial action (Winterton and Winterton 1989); economic marginalization (Byrne 2002; Fahmy et al. 2011); changes to gender roles (Delamont 2001; McDowell 1991, 2011; Walkerdine and Jimenez 2012); increased rates of depression, anxiety, and substance addictions (Draus, Roddy, and Greenwald 2010; Gans 1996; Thomas 2016); population decline (Sampson and Goodrich 2005); and the rise of populist movements that often focus on the nostalgic image of the working-class past (Thorleifsson 2016; Emery 2019).

Memory

Memory is an area of vibrant geographic research (Rhodes 2020). Jones and Garde-Hansen's (2012) edited collection on "Geography and Memory" is an excellent example that uses the large pre-existing literature on memory to consider the relationship between self, place, and histories. Beyond geography, memory has been an expansive area of interest for social and natural scientists for as long as there has been scholarship, especially within philosophical inquiry. Henri Bergson's ideas of memory, in particular, are popular within poststructuralist approaches, considering the emergent experience of remembering as reconstituted in the contemporary, rather than simply "replaying" a memory as "pure" and unaltered (see Waterton 2014, 11; Douglas 1980). Yet, social scientists, of course, have sought to reconfigure these ideas to understand the fundamentally social aspect of memory. The power of storytelling in contextualizing the complex past and present of India's industrial and colonial heritage is considered in the chapter by Hollis et al.

Work on collective memory, from Halbwachs (1992), rooted closely in the structuralist ideas of Durkheim, has been of interest to geographers considering shared and collective identities in place, such as Foote and Azaryahu (2007), Muzaini (2015), and Johnson (2005). Similarly, the work of Pierra Nora (1989) on *milieux* and *lieux de memoire* has been influential, particularly for geographers engaging with ideas of nationhood. Many have considered how the individual may be situated within these wider structures of collective, collected, shared, and cultural memory (see for example Legg 2005; Narvaez 2006; Hoelscher and Alderman 2004; Assmann and Livingstone 2006; Bal, Crewe, and Spitzer 1999). Additionally, scholars have addressed questions of inequality and power within these nexuses of memory. To reiterate, we do not seek to provide clear definitive answers to these debates but instead to illustrate how the postindustrial context is a key site within these discussions.

Post-industrial working landscapes

Many post-industrial areas have turned to tourism to operationalize their heritage. Industrial tourism arose in the United Kingdom following World War II out of consumer interest in visiting industrial archaeology sites. Since that time, many attractions have been founded based on factories, mines, railroads, power plants, worker houses, and other elements of industry (Edwards and Llurdes i Coit 1996; Xie 2015a). Tourists are commonly drawn by nostalgia for the industrial era, interest in processes and technology, or personal connections to the sites; though, like all tourists, their motivations are personal and variable (Beeho and Prentice 1997; Prentice, Witt, and Hamer 1998). Such attractions take many forms, ranging from museums to adventure parks to heritage districts.

For communities, industrial tourism offers many potential benefits. While industry has declined in the world's wealthiest countries since the 1950s, tourism has boomed. Tourism creates an opportunity to generate employment and attract outside income (Pretes 2002), though the economic benefits of tourism are often below that generated by the prior industry (Hospers 2002). Tourism offers an incentive to clean up and renovate abandoned industrial sites, thereby moderating some of the ongoing aspects of industrial pollution. Some attractions have been great successes, drawing hundreds of thousands of visitors per year. Many industrial sites have been inscribed on the UNESCO World Heritage List, recognized alongside other "outstanding" global landmarks. Importantly, tourism may allow places to counter negative perceptions that may be associated with them due to deindustrialization (Bramwell and Rawding 1996).

Crucially, tourism also provides communities a way to formally remember their industrial heritage (Cole 2004); as considered for Great Britain's coal mining industry in the chapter by Price. Many industrial attractions are built via consultation with community members and former industrial workers (Vargas-Sanchez et al. 2009). The resultant interpretation allows communities to tell their stories and preserve artifacts of significance. Some attractions hire former industrial workers as tour guides, providing visitors with firsthand accounts of the sites.

Tourism is not a viable option for all postindustrial areas, however (Ballesteros and Ramirez 2007; Del Pozo and Gonzalez 2012); successful sites tend to be those that are accessible to large markets, have public sector support, and possess qualities that set them apart (such as size, distinctive historical or other connections, or condition). Furthermore, not all places wish to pursue tourism (Edwards and Llurdes i Coit 1996). In addition to the many impacts inherent to tourism of any kind, some communities prefer to forget or otherwise disassociate from their industrial legacies.

Tourism is by no means the only form of adaptive reuse for industrial landscapes. Industrial infrastructure has been converted into housing, retail spaces, breweries, and offices, amongst other purposes. In their chapter, Cerarols and Luna engage with the emergence of an art colony in the ruins of a textile factory in Spain. Elsewhere, new forms of industry have replaced the old; this includes the emergence of "technopoles," with industry focused on high-end technology. Operationalizing an industrial landscape does not always center on the tangible, as illustrated in Dawney's chapter considering a play inspired by a decommissioned nuclear power plant in Lithuania.

Redevelopment of post-industrial spaces is not without controversy. Such projects are often associated with gentrification (Lees 2000; Lees, Slater, and Wyly 2010). Converting waterfront industrial warehouse districts into mixed-use areas has been a hallmark of many high-profile urban redevelopment projects, from Baltimore's Inner Harbor to Darling Harbour in Sydney. While many such projects have generated significant revenue, they have also led to displacement of low-income and working-class residents (Smith 1996). It has been well documented that minority populations are disproportionately affected (Wyly and Hammel 2004).

The memory of industry in these working landscapes is at the forefront in some places and obscured in others. Redevelopment projects echo processes of deterritorialization and reterritorialization (Xie 2015b). Yet, as Baeten's chapter on wastescapes in Minnesota contextualizes, geographers may help illuminate and preserve forgotten industrial pasts. There are many countering perspectives on how industrial sites should be conserved and remembered, balancing community, professional, governmental, and many other stakeholders (Oevermann and Mieg 2015).

De-romanticizing industrial heritage

While significant previous works stress industrial heritage as "assets" (Xie 2015a), transformed cultural resources (Oevermann and Mieg 2015), new spaces of cultural consumption and production (Holt and Wergin 2013), or caught within the false dichotomy of preservation and tourism (Colin and Jolliffe 2011), we take a different approach. Though there are certainly questions of preservation, tourism, development, and transformation to address, we see continuations in unclear places and spaces. Thompson's chapter on a Connecticut power station highlights the great complexities inherent to industrial sites, often valorized and reviled simultaneously. We see the role of the spatial fix driving boom-bust "frontier" production and the "need" for development often relying on similar cycles of tourism and consumerism. We find parallels in the primitive accumulation of a global working class. We observe many "post"-industrial communities still reliant on manufacturing and industry. Following Muzaini and Minca (2018), we address these "romanticized alternative heritage formations." As such, this book gives perspective upon the role of capital, violence, and empire in industrial heritage.

In the romanticization of industrial heritage, certain narratives fall silent, and the social formations that leave communities ravaged by the scourge of deindustrialization remain intact and unchallenged. What Muzaini and Minca (2018, 5) describe as "authorized heritage discourse" shapes the telling of these narratives, as this discourse is often "forged out of the mills of politicians, archaeologists, and historians who are 'speaking for' rather than 'speaking from' the platform of the masses." As shown in Rhodes' chapter, concerning the relationship between the slate quarries of North Wales and Jamaican plantations, contemporary narratives of industry often omit controversial and uncomfortable aspects of the past.

Though not innocent of colonial, neoliberal, and romanticizing work, geography offers alternative perspectives upon industrial heritage, whereby spatial formations of social relations; layers of environmental, colonial, and historical entanglement; and power of place and community-based practice provide a framework of a post-industrial geography (Tyner, Alvarez, and Colucci 2012). Whether in the context of Tyner and Rice's consideration of industrial agriculture during the Cambodian Genocide or the connection between capital punishment and industrialization explored by Colucci, this book shows how industrial heritage is as much about the memory of violence, exploitation, and ruin as it is about community, identity, and place.

Asserting a "Place" for geography

As demonstrated throughout this introduction, recent work at the intersection of historical, cultural, environmental, economic, community, and tourism geographies has revealed the rich significance of post-industrial place, memory, and heritage. Much has been accomplished in the last decade toward understanding processes of intangible heritage and the affect of the spectral geographies of post-industrial landscapes (Hill 2013). Likewise, the intersection of gentrification, heritage, and the environment emerges in post-industrial geographic research (Mathews and Picton 2014; Kern 2015; Stehlin 2016). The impact of industrial practices on regional identities further situate the recent prominence of industrial heritage to geographers (Wicke, Berger, and Golombek 2018).

We build upon these discussions by incorporating a greater range of geographical locations and considerations into this growing body of literature. How do memory work, memorialization, and collective memory engage with labor, trauma, and community, past and present? How do spaces that were once materialistically productive and environmentally destructive transition into places of (un)sustainable tourism and environmental education? How can sense of place and community operationalize these post-industrial landscapes? And how might we trouble the idea of the (post-)industrial itself, which too often positions conversation in a "past," rather than any form of present or continuity?

This volume combines empirically and theoretically framed works in a critical engagement with industrial landscapes. Using global examples, the authors provide a distinctly geographic understanding of industrial heritage across the spaces, places, and memories of industrial development.

References

Allen, Robert C. 2009. *The British Industrial Revolution in Global Perspective*. New York: Cambridge University Press.

———. 2017. *The Industrial Revolution: A Very Short Introduction*. New York: Oxford University Press.

Anderson, B. 2006. *Imagined Communities: Reflections on the Origin and Spread of Nationalism*. New York: Verso Books.

Assmann, J., and R. Livingstone. 2006. *Religion and Cultural Memory: Ten Studies*. Stanford: Stanford University Press.

Bal, M., J.V. Crewe, and L. Spitzer. 1999. *Acts of Memory: Cultural Recall in the Present*. Dartmouth: University Press of New England.

Ballesteros, Estaban Ruiz, and Macarena Hernandez Ramirez. 2007. "Identity and Community – Reflections on the Development of Mining Heritage Tourism in Southern Spain." *Tourism Management* 28: 677–87.

Bauman, Z. 2000. *Liquid Modernity*. Cambridge: Polity Press.

Beck, Ulrich. 1992. *Risk Society: Towards a New Modernity*. London: Sage.

Beeho, Alison J., and Richard C. Prentice. 1997. "Conceptualizing the Experiences of Heritage Tourists: A Case Study of New Lanark World Heritage Village." *Tourism Management* 18 (2): 75–87.

Bramwell, Bill, and Liz Rawding. 1996. "Tourism Marketing Images of Industrial Cities." *Annals of Tourism Research* 23 (1): 201–21.

Byrne, D. 2002. "Industrial Culture in a Post-Industrial World: The Case of the North East of England." *City* 6 (3): 279–89.

Cole, Denise. 2004. "Exploring the Sustainability of Mining Heritage Tourism." *Journal of Sustainable Tourism* 12 (6): 480–94.

Colin, Michael, and Lee Jolliffe. 2011. *Mining Heritage and Tourism: A Global Synthesis*. New York: Routledge.

Cowell, Richard, and Huw Thomas. 2002. "Managing Nature and Narratives of Dispossession: Reclaiming Territory in Cardiff Bay." *Urban Studies* 39 (7): 1241–60.

Cowie, Jefferson, and Joseph Heathcott, eds. 2003. *Beyond the Ruins: The Meanings of Deindustrialization*. Ithaca, NY: ILR Press.

Day, Graham. 2006. *Community and Everyday Life. Community and Everyday Life*. London: Routledge. https://doi.org/10.4324/9780203463178.

de Peuter, Greig, and Nick Dyer-Witheford. 2010. "Commons and Cooperatives." *Affinities: A Journal of Radical Theory, Culture, and Action* 4 (1): 30–56.

Deane, Phyllis M. 1979. *The First Industrial Revolution*. 2nd ed. New York: Cambridge University Press.

Degnen, C. 2016. "Socialising Place Attachment: Place, Social Memory and Embodied Affordances." *Ageing and Society* 36 (8): 1645–67. doi:10.1017/S0144686X15000653.

Del Pozo, Paz Benito, and Pablo Alonso Gonzalez. 2012. "Industrial Heritage and Place Identity in Spain: From Monuments to Landscapes." *Geographical Review* 102 (4): 446–64.

Delamont, S. 2001. *Changing Women, Unchanged Men? Sociological Perspectives on Gender in a Post-Industrial Society*. Buckingham: Open University.

DeSilvey, C. 2017. *Curated Decay: Heritage Beyond Saving*. Minneapolis: University of Minnesota Press.

Dicks, Bella. 2000. *Heritage, Place and Community*. Cardiff: University of Wales Press.

Dillon, L. 2014. "Race, Waste, and Space: Brownfield Redevelopment and Environmental Justice at the Hunters Point Shipyard." *Antipode* 46 (5): 1205–21.

Douglas, M. 1980. "Foreword." In *The Collective Memory*, edited by M. Halbwachs. New York: Harper and Row.

Draus, P.J., J.K. Roddy, and M. Greenwald. 2010. "A Hell of a Life: Addiction and Marginality in Post-Industrial Detroit." *Social & Cultural Geography* 11 (7): 663–80.

Edensor, T. 2005. *Industrial Ruins: Space, Aesthetics and Materiality*. Oxford: Berg.

Edwards, J. Arwel, and Joan Carlos Llurdes i Coit. 1996. "Mines and Quarries. Industrial Heritage Tourism." *Annals of Tourism Research* 23 (2): 341–63.

Emery, J. 2018. "Belonging, Memory and History in the North Nottinghamshire Coalfield." *Journal of Historical Geography* 59: 77–89. doi:10.1016/j.jhg.2017.11.004.

———. 2019. "Geographies of Deindustrialization and the Working-Class: Industrial Ruination, Legacies, and Affect." *Geography Compass* 13 (2): e12417. doi:10.1111/gec3.12417.

Fahmy, E., D. Gordon, D. Dorling, J. Rigby, and B. Wheeler. 2011. "Poverty and Place in Britain, 1968–99." *Environment and Planning A* 43 (3): 594–617.

Featherstone, D. 2012. *Solidarity: Hidden Histories and Geographies of Internationalism*. New York: Zed Books Ltd.

Foote, K.E., and M. Azaryahu. 2007. "Toward a Geography of Memory: Geographical Dimensions of Public Memory and Commemoration." *Journal of Political and Military Sociology* 35 (1): 125–44.

Francis, H., and D. Smith. 1980. *The Fed, a History of the South Wales Miners in the Twentieth Century*. London: Lawrence & Wishart.

Gans, H.J. 1996. "From 'Underclass' to 'Undercaste': Some Observations about the Future of the Post-Industrial Economy and Its Major Victims." In *Urban Poverty and the Underclass: A Reader*, edited by E. Mingione, 141–53. Oxford: Blackwell.

Gereffi, Gary, and Miguel Korzeniewicz, eds. 1994. *Commodity Chains and Global Capitalism*. Santa Barbara: ABC-CLIO.

Gregory, Derek. 1988. "The Production of Regions in England's Industrial Revolution." *Journal of Historical Geography* 14 (1): 50–58.

Halbwachs, Maurice. 1992. *On Collective Memory. The Heritage of Sociology*. Chicago, IL: University of Chicago Press.

Harvey, D. 2003. *The New Imperialism*. Oxford: Oxford University Press.

Henry, N., C. McEwan, and J. Pollard. 2002. "Globalization from Below: Birmingham –Postcolonial Workshop of the World?" *Area* 34 (2): 117–27.

Hill, L. 2013. "Archaeologies and Geographies of the Post-Industrial Past: Landscape, Memory and the Spectral." *Cultural Geographies* 20 (3): 379–96.

Hobor, George. 2013. "Surviving the Era of Deindustrialization: The New Economic Geography of the Urban Rust Belt." *Journal of Urban Affairs* 35 (4): 417–34.

Hobsbawm, Eric. 1999. *Industry and Empire: The Birth of the Industrial Revolution*. 2nd ed. New York: The New Press.

Hoelscher, Steven, and Derek H. Alderman. 2004. "Memory and Place: Geographies of a Critical Relationship." *Social & Cultural Geography* 5 (3): 347–55.

Hollis, E. 2010. "Anxious Care and Unsightly Aids." In *To Have and To Hold: Future of a Contested Landscape*, edited by G. Noord, 54. Glasgow: NVA.

Holt, F., and C. Wergin, eds. 2013. *Musical Performance and the Changing City: Post-Industrial Contexts in Europe and the United States*. New York: Routledge.

Hospers, Gert-Jan. 2002. "Industrial Heritage Tourism and Regional Restructuring in the European Union." *European Planning Studies* 10 (3): 397–404.

Jacobs, J.M. 1996. *Edge of Empire: Postcolonialism and the City*. New York: Routledge.
Johnson, N.C. 2005. "Locating Memory: Tracing the Trajectories of Remembrance." *Historical Geography* 33: 165–79.
Jones, B. 2010. "The Uses of Nostalgia: Autobiography, Community Publishing and Working Class Neighbourhoods in Post-war England." *Cultural and Social History* 7 (3): 355–74. Doi:10.2752/147800410X12714191853346.
Jones, O., and J. Garde-Hansen. 2012. *Geography and Memory: Explorations in Identity, Place and Becoming*. New York: Palgrave Macmillan.
Jonsen-Verbeke, M. 1999. "Industrial Heritage: A Nexus for Sustainable Tourism Development." *Tourism Geographies* 1 (1): 70–85.
Kern, L. 2015. "From Toxic Wreck to Crunchy Chic: Environmental Gentrification Through the Body." *Environment and Planning D: Society and Space* 33 (1): 67–83.
Lange, D. 2005. *Atlas der Industriekultur Ruhrgebiet*. Essen: Regionalverband Ruhr
Lees, L. 2000. "A Reappraisal of Gentrification: Towards a 'Geography of Gentrification'." *Progress in Human Geography* 24 (3): 389–408.
Lees, L., T. Slater, and E.K. Wyly, eds. 2010. *The Gentrification Reader*. London: Routledge.
Legg, S. 2005. "Contesting and Surviving Memory: Space, Nation, and Nostalgia in Les Lieux de Mémoire." *Environment and Planning D: Society and Space* 23 (4): 481–504.
Lewicka, Maria. 2013. "In Search of Roots: Memory as Enabler of Place Attachment." In *Place Attachment: Advances in Theory. Methods and Applications*, edited by L.C. Manzo and P. Devine Wright, 49–60. New York: Routledge.
Loveday, V. 2014. "'Flat-capping It': Memory, Nostalgia and Value in Retroactive Male Working-Class Identification." *European Journal of Cultural Studies* 17 (6): 721–35. Doi:10.1177/1367549414544117.
Lovell, N. 1998. *Locality and Belonging*. Edited by N. Lovell. New York: Routledge.
Linkon, S.L. 2018. *The Half-Life of Deindustrialization: Working-Class Writing about Economic Restructuring*. Ann Arbor, MI: University of Michigan Press.
Lynd, R.S., and H.M. Lynd. 1929. *Middletown: A Study in American Culture*. New York: Harcourt Brace.
MacDonald, R. 2018. "A Place for Memory: Family Photo Collections, Social Media and the Imaginative Reconstruction of the Working Class Neighbourhood." *Picturing the Family: Media, Narrative, Memory*: 151–70.
Mackenzie, R., Mark Stuart, Chris Forde, Ian Greenwood, Jean Gardiner, and Robert Perrett. 2006. "'All that is Solid?' Class, Identity and the Maintenance of a Collective Orientation amongst Redundant Steelworkers." *Sociology* 40 (5): 833–52. Doi:10.1177/0038038506067509.
Mah, A. 2009. "Devastation but Also Home: Place Attachment in Areas of Industrial Decline." *Home Cultures* 6 (3): 287–310.
Malmberg, A. 1997. "Industrial Geography: Location and Learning." *Progress in Human Geography* 21 (4): 573–82.
Martin, Ron L., and Bob Rowthorn, eds. 1986. *Geography of Deindustrialization*. London: Macmillan International Higher Education.
Marx, Karl. 2019 [1867]. *Capital: Volume One*. New York: Dove Publications.
Massey, Doreen. 1995. "Places and Their Pasts." *History Workshop Journal* 39: 182–92.
Mathews, V., and R.M. Picton. 2014. "Intoxifying Gentrification: Brew Pubs and the Geography of Post-Industrial Heritage." *Urban Geography* 35 (3): 337–56.
McDowell, L. 1991. "Life without Father and Ford: The New Gender Order of Post-Fordism." *Transactions of the Institute of British Geographers*: 400–19.

———. 2011. *Redundant Masculinities? Employment Change and White Working Class Youth*. Vol. 37. Hoboken, NJ: John Wiley & Sons.
McEwan, C. 2008. *Postcolonialism and Development*. New York: Routledge.
Muzaini, H. 2015. "On the Matter of Forgetting and 'Memory Returns'." *Transactions of the Institute of British Geographers* 40 (1): 102–12.
Muzaini, H., and C. Minca. 2018. *After Heritage: Critical Perspectives on Heritage from Below*. Northampton, MA: Edward Elgar Publishing.
Narvaez, R.F. 2006. "Embodiment, Collective Memory and Time." *Body & Society* 12 (3): 51–73. Doi:10.1177/1357034X06067156.
Nelson, L., and J. Seager, eds. 2005. *A Companion to Feminist Geography*. Malden, MA: Blackwell.
Nora, Pierre. 1989. "Between Memory and History: Les Lieux de Mémoire." *Representations*. https://doi.org/10.2307/2928520.
O'Brien, P. 2018. "'Takes You Back Even if You Were Never There Originally': Class, History, and Nostalgia in Gordon Burn's the North of England Home Service." *Textual Practice* 32 (8): 1405–23. Doi:10.1080/0950236X.2016.1201137.
Oevermann, Heike, and Harold A. Mieg, eds. 2015. *Industrial Heritage Sites in Transformation: Clash of Discourses*. New York: Routledge.
Prentice, Richard C., Stephen F. Witt, and Claire Hamer. 1998. "Tourism as Experience: The Case of Heritage Parks." *Annals of Tourism Research* 25 (1): 1–24.
Pretes, Michael. 2002. "Touring Mines and Mining Tourists." *Annals of Tourism Research* 29 (2): 439–56.
Relph, E. 1976. *Place and Placelessness*. London: Pion.
Rhodes, M. 2020. "Memory." In *International Encyclopedia of Human Geography*, edited by A. Kobayashi, 49–52. Amsterdam: Elsevier.
Sampson, K., and C. Goodrich. 2005. "We're Coasters, Why Should We Move? Community Identity, Place Attachment and Forestry Closure in Rural New Zealand." *Sites: A Journal of Social Anthropology and Cultural Studies* 2 (1): 124–49. Doi:10.11157/sites-vol2iss1id55.
Simon, D. 1998. "Rethinking (post) Modernism, Postcolonialism, and Posttraditionalism: South – North Perspectives." *Environment and Planning D: Society and Space* 16 (2): 219–45.
Smith, Neil. 1996. *The New Urban Frontier: Gentrification and the Revanchist City*. London: Routledge.
———. 2008. *Uneven Development: Nature, Capital, and the Production of Space*. 3rd ed. Athens: University of Georgia Press.
Stehlin, J. 2016. "The Post-Industrial 'Shop Floor': Emerging Forms of Gentrification in San Francisco's Innovation Economy." *Antipode* 48 (2): 474–93.
Strangleman, T. 2007. "The Nostalgia for Permanence at Work? The End of Work and Its Commentators." *Sociological Review* 55 (1): 81–103. Doi:10.1111/j.1467-954X.2007.00683.x.
———. 2013. "'Smokestack Nostalgia', 'Ruin Porn' or Working Class Obituary? The Role and Meaning of De-Industrial Representation." *International Labor and Working-Class History* 84: 23–37.
Thomas, G.M. 2016. "'It's Not That Bad': Stigma, Health, and Place in a Post-Industrial Community." *Health and Place* 38: 1–7. Doi:10.1016/j.healthplace.2015.12.001.
Thorleifsson, C. 2016. "From Coal to Ukip: The Struggle Over Identity in Post-Industrial Doncaster." *History and Anthropology* 27 (5): 555–68. Doi:10.1080/02757206.2016.1219354.
Tomaney, J. 2015. "Region and Place II: Belonging." *Progress in Human Geography* 39 (4): 507–16.

Tonnies, F. 1955. *Community and Association*. London: Routledge and Kegan Paul (first published 1887).

Tuan, Y.F. 1977. *Space and Place: The Perspective of Experience*. Minneapolis: University of Minnesota Press.

Tyner, J.A., G.B. Alvarez, and A.R. Colucci. 2012. "Memory and the Everyday Landscape of Violence in Post-Genocide Cambodia." *Social & Cultural Geography* 13 (8): 853–71.

Vargas-Sanchez, Alfonso, Plaza-Mejia, Maria de los Angeles, and Nuria Porras-Bueno. 2009. "Understanding Residents' Attitudes toward the Development of Industrial Tourism in a Former Mining Community." *Journal of Travel Research* 47 (3): 373–87.

Walkerdine, Valerie, and Luis Jimenez. 2012. *Gender, Work and Community After De-Industrialisation. Gender, Work and Community After De-Industrialisation*. Basingstoke: Palgrave Macmillan. https://doi.org/10.1057/9780230359192.

Wallerstein, Immanuel. 1974. *The Modern World System. Vol. 1, Capitalist Agriculture and the Origins of the European World-Economy in the Sixteenth Century*. New York: Academic Press.

Waterton, E. 2014. "A More-Than-Representational Understanding of Heritage? The 'Past' and the Politics of Affect." *Geography Compass* 8 (11): 823–33. Doi:10.1111/gec3.12182/abstract.

Whitehead, M. 2014. *Environmental Transformations: A Geography of the Anthropocene*. New York: Routledge.

Wicke, Christian, Stefan Berger, and Jana Golombek, eds. 2018. *Industrial Heritage and Regional Identities*. New York: Routledge.

Winterton, J., and R. Winterton. 1989. *Coal, Crisis and Conflict: The 1984–85 Miners' Strike in Yorkshire*. Manchester: Manchester University Press.

Wyly, E.K., and D.J. Hammel. 2004. "Gentrification, Segregation, and Discrimination in the American Urban System." *Environment and Planning A* 36 (7): 1215–41.

Xie, Philip Feifan. 2015a. *Industrial Heritage Tourism*. Buffalo: Channel View Publications.

———. 2015b. "A Life Cycle Model of Industrial Heritage Development." *Annals of Tourism Research* 55: 141–54.

Yates, M. 2011. "The Human-as-Waste, the Labor Theory of Value and Disposability in Contemporary Capitalism." *Antipode* 43 (5): 1679–95.

Part 1

Constructing post-industrial communities

Place, memory, and practice

2 Notes from a shrinking market

'Anticipatory nostalgia' and place-making in the midst of change

Pablo Arboleda and Hayden Lorimer

Introduction

Travel beyond the city centre's highly polished razzamatazz, under the old railway bridge, to the other side of the tracks, where shopfronts begin to look careworn and everything feels a bit "rough-and-ready". Press on along the Gallowgate, east of Glasgow Cross. Eventually you'll be met by high metal archways, brightly painted in red and gold, one on each of the site's four sides, bidding a welcome to visitors and regulars. Pass through and you enter what can seem like a place apart. The best advice we have to offer is this: take 'The Barras Market' as you find it.

Things operate a little differently here. The tight network of lanes and streets is free of traffic, giving shoppers room to roam. When the rain holds off, market traders set up their wares outdoors on trestle tables or spilling from the stall front over the pavement. There's a clutter of second-hand stuff to weave your way through. Household flotsam: standard lamps, kitchen chairs, filing cabinets, crockery, china ornaments, chests of drawers, kids' bikes, golf clubs, guitars, carpentry tools. You name it, really.

On the street corners – offering clear lines of sight in case the authorities should come nosing – hawkers bark out the stock-in-trade of the black market: "Cigarettes! Tobacco! Viagra!" If you're not too choosy about quality, there are pirated DVDs, of the latest Hollywood releases and porn films catering to male fetishes and fantasies. When hunger pangs set in, there are a few "greasy spoon" cafes, burger vans and fast-food vendors to choose from. Local drinkers loiter in the free-houses and bars, decked out in colours celebrating the green-and-white side of Glasgow's famous footballing rivalry.

Covered markets and small courtyards interconnect the lanes. Some of the stall holders deal in seasonal staples and festive decor. A few are pop-ups, surfacing only intermittently, punting heavily discounted fakes, shop-soiled stock, and stuff likely to have "fallen off the back of a lorry". Others are licensed to trade in homeware and hardware, flooring and furnishings. Some are aimed at the specialist worlds of collectibles, memorabilia and military paraphernalia dating from old wars. Plenty more deal in period pieces trawled from house clearances: antiques and curios, the odds and ends, bric-a-brac and knick-knacks of yesteryear. There are surviving scraps of the city's once-roaring rag trade: tangles of second-hand clothes and jumbles of shoes. A couple of junk traders sprawl their salvage and scrap along the length of indoor halls with fading facades that once gave the impression of an olde-world arcade. There's ample room. Things have gotten quieter than in the market's heyday. By certain measures, it is a shadow of its former self. A fair number of the stalls lie unoccupied, shuttered and locked, during the entire trading weekend. Things feel and look like they're just about hanging on, while successive waves of urban change surge and swirl in the city beyond.

'Resilience' is a concept commonly bandied about in multiple planning and policy circles today, presented as a valuable asset and estimable quality (Jha, Miner, and Stanton-Geddes 2013) and projected onto all sorts of social and cultural settings, including the domain of heritage (Holtorf 2018). Yet resilience doesn't quite capture the situation or sensibility in The Barras. Rather, it's an air of defiance that lingers on here, exhibited as a politics of endurance within a socially disenfranchised community and place (Povinelli 2011). It shows up in unfussy, sometimes proud, displays of vernacular culture. It is visible as an attitude or a way of carrying yourself. The way bargain hunters set their jaw and square their shoulders. It's akin to a siege mentality: still here, in spite of everything. "A tax haven for the poor" is how one trader describes the market's current function and significance. This description feels like a truer fit. A statement of self-determination, solidarity and social concern. Communitarian and compassionate ideals coupled with commercialism, pitted against continued structural inequalities.

Over the course of 2019, we have paid a series of research visits to The Barras, documenting change, challenge and compression, as complex cultural processes, occurring in real time. This chapter is an opportunity to report on this exercise in embedded observation and engagement and to do so conscious of how our practice falls within a long ethnographic tradition of urban inquiry, one where the act of witnessing must neither overlook research conduct as a form of social privilege nor erase the possibility that the researchers' presence can itself be a source of concern, uncertainty or suspicion (McCorkel and Myers 2003).

To begin, we provide a capsular history of The Barras place in Glasgow's industrial and post-industrial story; we then review how questions of post-industrial place-making are currently being addressed and re-theorised. We go on to offer three place-portraits, drawing on informal conversations with three members of the Barras business community, as part of fieldwork investigations encompassing site survey and observant participation as market shoppers (Gall, Gall, and Borg 2003, 239). Informality, as well as our differing identities (one Scot, one Spaniard) and accents, allowed for flexibility and responsiveness in chance conversations. The resulting descriptive vignettes are expressed, we hope, with an empathic voice. Each enables us to fuse local realities, personal memories and emerging impressions, turning stories and snatches of speech into affective narratives. Our overarching aim is to present the phenomena of 'anticipatory nostalgia' as a place-making attribute, one that explains how powerful forms of affiliation are enabling The Barras to turn towards an uncertain future.

A situated history of The Barras

There is a lively place mythology centring on The Barras – and a tendency to romanticise its history. Efforts at portraiture are seldom entirely immune from it, our own included. The market is widely regarded as a city institution and a site integral to Glasgow's modern story. Referred to conversationally with warmth and affection, local lore recalls an independence of spirit, where anything goes and punters are ever ready to "Tell it like it is". For some Glaswegians The Barras remains a "People's Republic", home to street-smart enterprise backed by quick-witted sales patter: "Take your time, but hurry up!", "See ye later gorgeous!", "Wan way in, no way oot!" Notoriety and infamy are another legacy from the past, stemming from an entrenched history of organised crime and gang violence in the city's East End (i.e., Holligan and Deuchar 2009; Jeffrey 2009; Davies 2013). This dark and difficult inheritance is now reconfigured as charismatic folk memory, personified in a dramatis personae of indigenous white Scots, associated with a collective, territorialised identity built around standards and measures of masculinity (Fraser 2013). To understand the complex fusion of place, politics and personality, this locality needs to be situated in a greater transformative urban geography of ongoing post-industrialisation.

The street market takes its name from the term 'barra'; in West of Scotland dialect, a single-wheeled hand-pushed vehicle, used by city pedlar-traders in the early days to load and transport their goods for sale. The first of the market halls opened for business in 1921. Founded by James and Maggie McIver (known as 'The Barras Queen'), the same family remain the site's proprietors today. The McIver name still appears in green and gold paintwork, alongside a bold assertion of 'World Famous' status (Figure 2.1). Claims to global renown are attributable, in large part, to the Barrowland Ballroom, an adjoining night-time venue. Opened in 1934, the ballroom was for decades a prime venue for weekend dancing, drinking and socialising (Irvine, Leslie, and Miller 2019). It continues to operate as a live indie and folk music venue today – in the main frequented by a city-wide community of gig-goers, many the descendants of white, working-class Irish migrants. If the ballroom, the neighbouring market and the neighbourhoods of the East End can be subject to broad sociological characterisation, as urbanists Gray and Mooney (2011, 8) note, they do not have 'anything approaching the ethnic concentrations of the French *banlieue* or US ghetto'.

For much of the twentieth century, the mercantile quarter of the inner East End was host to a series of outdoor and covered markets, serving a population of local labourers in shipyards, manufacturing and heavy industries and their families. Specialist merchants, brokers and stall holders traded in the Meat Market (and slaughterhouse), the Fruit Market, the Fish Market and Paddy's Market, the latter dealing in second-hand clothing (Figure 2.2). Now on the brink of significant change, The Barras is the sole survivor from that older tradition of urban mercantilism (Dudgeon 2009). Over the last fifty years, Glasgow's other great arcades and bazaars catering to the industrial working class were swept away by programmes

Figure 2.1 Origin story in blistered and peeling paint: 'World Famous McIver's Markets Est. 1921'

Source: Authors

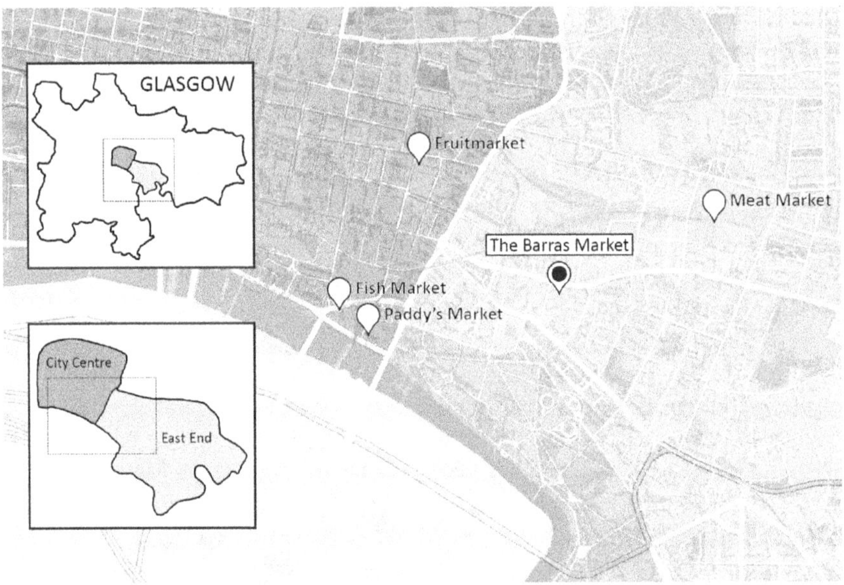

Figure 2.2 The Barras is the sole surviving trading place from a network of historic markets in Glasgow's mercantile quarter

Source: Authors

of large-scale urban redevelopment and post-industrial economic restructuring. The relic architecture and original sites of a 'City of Markets' are occupied by new residential developments, artists' studios, hotel and retail space and entertainment venues. For the immediate vicinity of The Barras, a civic narrative of investment and boosterism continues to set as its target the reversal of persistent trends of decline and decay. Abandoned industrial spaces, notable for the quality of their relic features and facades, afford multiple development possibilities and are increasingly aligned with a neoliberal configuration of urban culture (Göbel 2014). To counteract what some judge a 'shabby and underwhelming' appearance (Braiden 2016), a range of arts and music initiatives have been introduced to support East End communities where multiple indicators of social deprivation impact intergenerationally on the health and life opportunities of residents of all ages.

The changing market as post-industrial place

Within the cultural sector, the phenomenon of industrial heritage has emerged and flourished over the course of the past three decades, as a response to cycles of sectoral and regional restructuring in the economies of the Global North. The recognition and re-presentation of former factories, docklands and extractive landscapes has broken down the temporal and aesthetic barriers of early, more conservative, heritage categorisations, opening the way for more progressive, if sometimes contentious, designations (Orange 2008). With the growing significance afforded to a critical heritage agenda – led by academic debate and its dissemination into wider public programming – the labour experiences of former workers and their communities have been afforded increased prominence (High and Lewis 2007). The democratisation and diversification of narrative histories told about industrial development and decline (Mah 2012) are no longer confined to sites of labour and production. They also materialise in former domestic architectures, public spaces, sites of popular recreation and cultural consumption, such that the patterning of everyday life has come to be valued as a heritage asset (Atkinson 2008).

In the case of The Barras – located in the midst of neighbourhoods where multiple measures of social deprivation register highly – 'post-industrial' status is manifold variously. The market is an ordinary meeting place where community life occurs and social identities are affirmed, and it is an ongoing place of work, continuing to sustain (if not stimulate) the local economy. While during the late nineteenth and early twentieth centuries Glasgow could confidently claim status as Britain's 'Second City of the Empire', with economic and imperial contraction the city experienced successive decades of shrinkage (Maantay 2017). The Barras' celebrated rise to prominence overlaps with a period of steady economic decline, marked by the collapse of heavy industry along the River Clyde and the city's shift to a post-industrial condition.

Commonly, literatures on de-industrialisation and ruin studies draw from Walter Benjamin's famous *The Arcades Project* ([1982] 2002) to account for the end of an era in spectacular consumption. The German critic, writer and theorist reconstructed the glamour of fin-de-siècle Paris by musing on the shopping galleries that were abandoned in the rapidly changing world of the interwar era. In more humble terms, a comparable process of transformation is taking place in The Barras. Dramatic changes in cultures, habits and patterns of consumption have engulfed some of its original functions as a marketplace. Much of the commerce is entirely peripheral to discourses of smart urbanism, where digital and technology-driven innovation is advanced as 'a universal solution to varied urban issues in different cities' (Verrest and Pfeffer 2019, 1328). Importantly, The Barras' community is not 'falling prey' to a process of change that – combining the familiar dualism of 'local presence vs. economic progress' – might all too easily be labelled as gentrification since, at present, it is not actively being displaced.

If approaches to post-industrial dereliction often depict sites that seem to be 'frozen in time', here – it seems reasonable to contend – the site's materiality is 'melting'. It doesn't yet belong to any trending trade in retro-goods. Rather it is a space of commerce where the powerful 'aesthetics of juxtaposition' and their extremely low 'regime of value' (Cresswell 2012) are brought to the fore. They materialise in chaotic piles of poor-quality goods on sale, spiralling to the point where any likelihood of further circulation seems doubtful. It is tempting – but illusory – to read this pairing of deteriorating architecture and all-but-obsolete objects as a choreographed display (Figure 2.3).

Yet, in spite of its decline, The Barras continues to be upheld as one of the few remaining relics that properly encapsulates the city's soul, amid a greater

Figure 2.3 Marketplace aesthetics, jumble and juxtaposition

Source: Authors

recognition that for too long Glasgow has neglected – or sometimes simply obliterated – its industrial pasts (Richter 2017). Understanding heritage authenticity from a traditional point of view – centring on an awareness of original architectural fabric (Silverman 2015) – The Barras' tangible qualities are partly acknowledged. Some of its signature buildings have listed architectural status, and the area features in many promotional brochures and the routes of institutionally approved city heritage tours. The City Council's 'People Make Glasgow' website presents The Barras as the place where visitors can go to enjoy 'the real Glasgow experience'.[1] The safe-guarding of a more intangible, social authenticity is at stake. In this sense, the notion of social preservation, defined as active care for the 'presence and practices of old-timers, [who are seen] as indispensable to preserving a pristine "social" wilderness and as arbiters of authentic community' (Brown-Saracino 2004, 135), can function as a potential approach to cushion the processes of change already underway (Figure 2.4).

While the original conceptualisation of heritage value emerged as a protective response to authenticity endangered by new development, it is now generally accepted that processes of managed change are integral to heritage futures and moreover that actively inviting or generating change through a heritage site can be a means to foster acceptable forms of development. By borrowing the concept of 'anticipatory nostalgia' (Batcho and Shikh 2016) and framing it within the present discussion, it is our intention to ground social preservation's emotional aspects in the realm of ongoing geographical, heritage and urban debates. Departing from

Figure 2.4 New modular architectures in the traditional market
Source: Authors

the conventional formulation of nostalgia (as a feeling for that which has passed from experience), Batcho and Shikh define the anticipatory version of this sentiment as one born of 'missing aspects of the present before they are lost in the future [which is aligned with] a greater tendency to sadness and worry' (2016, 75). Our configuration of anticipatory nostalgia conveys a melancholic sense of loss felt for meaningful sites that are not yet gone but seem set to fade from view and then eventually disappear. Places that are cast in the twilight hour. Certainly, a review of online posts left for 'The Barras Market' in Google Maps shows how sorrow is expressed by those who first came to know the place in its heyday and feel a prick or pang from the realisation that it "is not yet gone but surely soon will be". What remains significant to our understanding is that anticipatory nostalgia does not channel feelings down a dead-end. Awareness can result in *a motivation to act* – and in this sense, is related to progressive structures of feeling such as 'productive nostalgia' (Blunt 2003), 'pre-nostalgia' (Mindlich 2016) and 'anticipatory history' (DeSilvey, Naylor, and Sackett 2011).

To give deeper texture and a degree of situated detail to our account of anticipatory feelings brought by change we now spotlight the activities of three traders from The Barras business community.

Change in the spotlight I: keeping on

Aged in her seventies, Marion has been a Barras stallholder on-and-off for many years. She sells babywear and kid's clothing. Everything is hand-made in patterns, styles, and colour schemes of her own design. There are bibs and booties, dresses, leggings and knitted cardigans, hats, mittens and baby-grows. Her stall is one of several set around the perimeter of a small covered courtyard. It is open-faced, with display items pegged and hung from the back wall. She took the pitch on a year ago, following a move caused by business closure in another of the city's cornerstone trading outlets. When Sloane's Argyll Arcade "went under", the resident makers and traders lost their rental spaces. In the past, Marion's pitch rentals at the Barras happened between spells spent on the move. She travelled the country, selling at fairs and markets, living and trading out of the van she drove. Decades of independent trading have fostered adaptability and durability. In wintertime, she keeps herself well-bundled up because the stall is unheated. Between customers, she works at the sewing machine, wearing fingerless gloves. She sees the irony in people's appreciation of her choice of striking colour-schemes, since colour-blindness means she must identify any piece by its pattern alone. With her eightieth birthday now not far off, Marion has ended up doing just what she told her family she wouldn't do: keeping at it, not letting up.

Marion's presence is a testament to persistence, where, to invoke the well-worn axiom, necessity has been the mother of invention. From a social preservation perspective, she personifies qualities understood to characterise the community pillar or elder, one of those in whom it is thought that 'authentic community belongs' (Brown-Saracino 2004, 141). In Glasgow's East End, hers is a now-ageing generation, with an accent, family ties and friendship relations that correspond, in the main, with working-class values and communities and an identity forged through its association with the Catholic Church, dating back to waves of Irish immigration. Within the homogenous population in the market area, still distinct from a more ethnically diverse one found in the rest of the globalised post-industrial city, these plain facts of belonging can accrue the status of local heritage since they are sustained by shared memories and continuity of experience.

But on Sunday afternoons when the protective shutters are drawn down, there is no certainty that they will be pulled back up the following week, since like so many of The Barras old-timers Marion has no business plan based on generational succession.

Change in the spotlight II: new designs

Fresh out of art college, Isobel is one of the few Barras new stall holders. And 'Razor' is her first tentative step into the world of independent commerce. One and a half metres deep, it's little more than a narrow strip, providing just enough room to display the latest issues of fashion and style magazines and allow sufficient browsing space for those she hopes will become her clientele: Glasgow's community of designers and artists in search of inspiration. And perhaps the occasional inquisitive passer-by, much like ourselves. Propped up in mint condition, each magazine is presented as a collectible art object in itself. As if to emphasise the point, her stock only extends to a single copy of everything. Cover models, captured in high gloss or artfully left out-of-focus, throw hard stares and strike curious poses, all sharp cheekbones and expensive hair. Most of the titles on sale are single word statements – *Plastik. Broccoli. System. Blanc. Pylot.* – promising to blaze a trail to all that's nouveau and avant-garde.

Perched behind a laptop, Isobel is generous with her time, describing how welcome she's made to feel by the established trading community. She likes the proprietors' relaxed approach, their openness to an influx of new licensees. And the peppercorn rent helps, of course. There's a strategy at work here. Generating renewal, fostering vibrancy and enabling occupancy (no-one is yet mentioning the more worrisome word 'rescue') means bringing a new, younger generation of traders and makers to the site. New businesses, it is hoped, will increase footfall, turning the market into a destination for discerning shoppers. Bigger moves are afoot across the road. The arrival on-site of BAaD ('Barras Art and Design') – a multi-purpose entertainment, dining and arts venue, equipped with units and workshops for creatives and independent business people – spells out one future: the sort that speak of investment based on the logics and language of place-making, home-grown talent, start-ups and urban connectivity. In 2020, BAaD has begun hosting its own covered Sunday market, family and dog friendly, in an indoor courtyard, promising 'true Barra style' with 'a new twist'.[2]

In the marketplace, Isobel still feels like a rarity. Her case is different, buoyed up on youthful promise, energetic and educated, the 'regime of value' (Cresswell 2012) of her stock-in-trade is considerably higher than the junk-sellers abutting her stall to the left and right. High enough in fact, that sales need only hit two or three magazines per day to cover the week's rent. Yet, the investment she has made is in more than arthouse publishing alone. Isobel is speculating with time, and the measure of her success will depend on how long she can hold on. Her confidently stated belief that 'things here are going to change' does not imply that old timers must pack up and clear out. The Barras' owners are aware that the place can only survive with a fresh breeze (Irvine, Leslie, and Miller 2019), but the ethics of saving the market without saving its people are underlying – how 'true' to the 'old' will the 'new' be? Life goes on, and heritage is something also produced in the present (Harvey 2001). For the moment, there seems room enough for happy coexistence.

Change in the spotlight III: anything goes

Gary sits in the studio's clutter, coffee in hand, the splash, splatter and spill of art-making all around. Tins, tubes and tape, brushes propped in mugs, half-drunk cans and pie-crusts. He recounts the origin story for the 'Arti Son Toi' gallery:

> "Wi started sellin' furniture. And this wis ur front office. Still is tae be fair. Then the painting started up, as a way to bring mair folk in. Mibbe it's takin over. That's the hope anyway."

Some of the pieces are finished, others partway done. There's enough wall space to mount just a few. Most of the stock is propped up around the walls, two or three canvases deep. Lots of it is figurative stuff. Life-size portraits of local legends: champion boxers, gangland leaders, star-crossed lovers. The mythology of The Barras is never too far from view. Some of the work is being done on commission, requested by other stallholders. Paintings are priced according to size, sales settled by haggling. Gary talks us around the gallery, piece by piece. The wild takes. The experimental efforts. Introducing us to the gallery's prevailing spirit where – stylistically at least – anything goes. We chat about neo-expressionism, mental health and the therapeutic value of art and the point at which drink or weed helps or hinders the creative process.

The 'Arti Son Toi Gallery' occupies the ground floor of a former pipe factory. Its practitioners are local to the area, none has formal training, all are self-taught. Some come with their issues, sensing that art might offer a way out, aware of the consolations to be found in shared company and keeping busy. Glasgow's renowned contemporary scene is a distant presence, so too the national funding landscape in support of creative arts. "We don't need to sell ourselves to them", Gary asserts. "The art world can come here and discover us". As gallery curator, he explains an alternative, permissive version of grassroots politics and arts-activism, growing in different directions, promoted with a personal touch and through the gallery's own YouTube channel. Having wandered in, without appointment, we left, immediately feeling the need to return.

In many respects, the gallery's sense of community materialises many of the intangible qualities that have given The Barras its renown. There is companionship, self-conscious happiness and wilful naivety. There are cutting jokes and elaborate anecdotes. There is modesty in ambition and soaring levels of self-confidence that function like a protective shield, guarding against the excesses of the world beyond. The collective identification with the outsider and the amateur, in art as in life, plays an essential social role, and it serves to scramble how we understand values of critical heritage being built from the bottom up (Robertson 2012). By actions as important as they are mundane – gather, paint, listen, talk, laugh – integrity, authenticity and place-making are constructed (Atkinson 2008). And mirroring this atmosphere, a transitional streetscape, which keeps original architectural materiality in place and ushers in new modular multipurpose built forms. Glasgow's lifelong idiosyncrasy in a nutshell, despite assumed aesthetic rejections where, much like in other post-industrial cities, decaying architectures become a form of identity reaffirmation (Sandler 2011).

Anticipating a centenary story

In its current guise, The Barras is a site foreshadowed by visions of its final days. That the market is also on the cusp of its centenary year makes the anticipation of cultural change all the more intense. Having arrived much too late to experience its heyday and yet too early to simply mourn its passing, for researchers, there are obvious temptations in taking sides: backing the underdog, the losing side, the wrong team, David faced by Goliath's might. These notes on the market's shrinking time-horizon emerge from having set foot at the precise moment in which an ambivalent emotional response was likely to be aroused and when the near future is complex enough to merit critical heritage inquiry. Thus, our understanding is not of a place entirely beyond help and cannot be anything else except that. This tension is one of the striking aspects of encountering post-industrial heritage.

We want to recognise that The Barras is an area that should not be imprisoned by stubborn efforts to cling on to cultural authenticity. Opting for a steadily phased transition, rather than for fast planning, means empowering the voices of a remaining and passing generation of stall holders and making them part of forms of urban coexistence that grant dignity without confrontation. This realisation can be usefully aligned with the recent efforts to exhibit greater ethical concern for the atmospheres and ambiances of deindustrialised areas (i.e., Guano 2015; Giddy and Hoogendoorn 2018; Jaffe et al. 2019). We argue that certain characteristics of informal street economies (such as barter, bargaining, deregulation and disorder), which can easily be judged undesirable aspects of urban life, can also become attributes in imaginaries of rooted authenticity. The livelihoods of pedlars and stall holders and the landscapes of the street-market are part-and-parcel of Glasgow's shift to a post-industrial condition. This version of social preservation is not in denial about rights to an improved quality of life. Instead, it acknowledges that, currently, stall-holders in The Barras' are not wholly part of or entirely commensurate with the promise of a better life in this area of the city. Rather, elements are disappearing, as a consequence of being dislocated from an increasingly normative world of consumption. To forestall (perhaps even to prevent) the community's eventual disappearance, through social preservation, its ongoing presence needs to be conceived of and cared for as a heritage value. This involves advocacy for kinds of coexistence that grant rights to the city *within the city* and resist retail-led homogenisation. In Glasgow, as well as many other post-industrial cities (Sandler 2011), anticipatory nostalgia has the potential to function as a wake-up call: a structure of feeling that, instead of making us succumb, changes people's perception, first raising awareness and then triggering action.

Notes

1 See the guide's official website at <https://peoplemakeglasgow.com/trip-inspiration/shopping/weekend-markets> (accessed March 20, 2020).
2 See BAaD's website at <https://baadglasgow.com/barras_art_and_design_east_end_glasgow/markets-shops> (accessed March 20, 2020).

References

Atkinson, D. 2008. "The Heritage of Mundane Places." In *The Ashgate Research Companion to Heritage and Identity*, edited by B. Graham and P. Howard, 381–95. Aldershot: Ashgate. doi:10.4324/9781315613031.

Batcho, K.I., and S. Shikh. 2016. "Anticipatory Nostalgia: Missing the Present Before It's Gone." *Personality and Individual Differences* 98: 75–84. doi:10.1016/j.paid.2016.03.088.

Benjamin, W. 2002. *The Arcades Project*. Cambridge, MA: Harvard University Press.

Blunt, A. 2003. "Collective Memory and Productive Nostalgia: Anglo-Indian Homemaking at McCluskieganj." *Environment and Planning D: Society and Space* 21 (6): 717–38. doi:10.1068/d327.

Braiden, G. 2016. "Glasgow's Notorious Barras Earmarked as Arts, Events and Music Quarter in £30m Plans." *The Herald*. March 4. Accessed December 5, 2019. www.heraldscotland.com/news/14320207.glasgows-notorious-barras-earmarked-as-arts-events-and-music-quarter-in-30m-plans/.

Brown-Saracino, J. 2004. "Social Preservationists and the Quest for Authentic Community." *City & Community* 3 (2): 135–56. doi:10.1111/j.1535-6841.2004.00073.x.

Cresswell, T. 2012. "Value, Gleaning and the Archive at Maxwell Street, Chicago." *Transactions of the Institute of British Geographers* 37 (1): 164–76. doi:10.1111/j.1475-5661.2011.00453.x.

Davies, A. 2013. *City of Gangs: Glasgow and the Rise of the British Gangster*. London: Hodder & Stoughton.

DeSilvey, C., S. Naylor, and C. Sackett. 2011. *Anticipatory History*. Devon: Uniformbooks.

Dudgeon, P. 2009. *Our Glasgow: Memories of Life in Disappearing Britain*. London: Headline Review.

Fraser, A. 2013. "Street Habitus: Gangs, Territorialism and Social Change in Glasgow." *Journal of Youth Studies* 16 (8): 970–85. doi:10.1080/13676261.2013.793791.

Gall, M.D., J.P. Gall, and W.R. Borg. 2003. *Educational Research: An Introduction*. 7th ed. Boston: Allyn & Bacon.

Giddy, J., and G. Hoogendoorn. 2018. "Ethical Concerns Around Inner City Walking Tours." *Urban Geography* 39 (9): 1293–99. doi:10.1080/02723638.2018.1446884.

Göbel, H.K. 2014. *The Re-Use of Urban Ruins: Atmospheric Inquiries of the City*. London: Routledge. doi:10.4324/9781315756455.

Gray, N., and G. Mooney. 2011. "Glasgow's New Urban Frontier: 'Civilising' the Population of 'Glasgow East'." *City* 15 (1): 4–24. doi:10.1080/13604813.2010.511857.

Guano, E. 2015. "Touring the Hidden City: Walking Tour Guides in Deindustrializing Genoa." *City & Society* 27 (2): 160–82. doi:10.1111/ciso.12062.

Harvey, D.C. 2001. "Heritage Pasts and Heritage Presents: Temporality, Meaning and the Scope of Heritage Studies." *International Journal of Heritage Studies* 7 (4): 319–38. doi:10.1080/13581650120105534.

High, S., and D.W. Lewis. 2007. *Corporate Wasteland: The Landscape and Memory of Deindustrialization*. Ithaca, NY: Cornell University Press.

Holligan, C.P., and R. Deuchar. 2009. "Territorialities in Scotland: Perceptions of Young People in Glasgow." *Journal of Youth Studies* 12 (6): 731–46. doi:10.1080/13676260902965298.

Holtorf, C. 2018. "Embracing Change: How Cultural Resilience is Increased Through Cultural Heritage." *World Archaeology* 50 (4): 639–50. doi:10.1080/00438243.2018.1510340.

Irvine, A., C. Leslie, and M. Miller. 2019. *Barrowland Ballads*. Glasgow: Graphical House.

Jaffe, R., E. Dürr, G.A. Jones, A. Angelini, A. Osbourne, and B. Vodopivec. 2019. "What Does Poverty Feel Like? Urban Inequality and the Politics of Sensation." *Urban Studies*. doi:10.1177/0042098018820177.

Jeffrey, R. 2009. *Blood on the Streets: A-Z of Glasgow Crime*. Edinburgh: Black and White Publishing.

Jha, A.K., T.W. Miner, and Z. Stanton-Geddes. 2013. *Building Urban Resilience: Principles, Tools, and Practice*. Washington, DC: World Bank. doi:10.1596/978-0-8213-8865-5.

Maantay, J.A. 2017. "The Collapse of Place: Derelict Land, Deprivation, and Health Inequality in Glasgow, Scotland." In *Urban Land Use: Community-Based Planning*, edited by K. Etingoff, 3–49. Oakville, ON: Apple Academic Press. doi:10.1201/9781315365794.

Mah, A. 2012. *Industrial Ruination, Community and Place: Landscapes and Legacies of Urban Decline*. Toronto: Toronto University Press.

McCorkel, J.A., and K. Myers. 2003. "What Difference Does Difference Make? Position and Privilege in the Field." *Qualitative Sociology* 26 (2): 199–231. doi:10.1023/A:1022967012774.

Mindlich, B. 2016. "Reflecting on the Past, Understanding the Present, and Controlling the Future: Pre-Nostalgia and its Impact on Memory, Temporality, and Identity as Represented in Classic Films from the 1980s." M.A. diss., Dartmouth College.

Orange, H. 2008. "Industrial Archaeology: Its Place within the Academic Discipline, the Public Realm and the Heritage Industry." *Industrial Archaeology Review* 30 (2): 83–95. doi:10.1179/174581908X347292.

Povinelli, E. 2011. *Economies of Abandonment: Social Belonging and Endurance in Late Liberalism*. Durham, NC: Duke University Press. doi:10.1215/9780822394570.

Richter, R. 2017. "Industrial Heritage in Urban Imaginaries and City Images: A Comparison Between Dortmund and Glasgow." *The Public Historian* 39 (4): 65–84. doi:10.1525/tph.2017.39.4.65.

Robertson, I.J.M. 2012. "Introduction: Heritage from Below." In *Heritage from Below*, edited by I.J.M. Robertson, 1–28. Farnham: Ashgate.
Sandler, D. 2011. "Counterpreservation: Decrepitude and Memory in Post-Unification Berlin." *Third Text* 25 (6): 687–97. doi:10.1080/09528822.2011.624343.
Silverman, H. 2015. "Heritage and Authenticity." In *The Palgrave Handbook of Contemporary Heritage Research*, edited by E. Waterton and S. Watson, 69–88. London: Palgrave Macmillan. doi:10.1057/9781137293565.0010.
Verrest, H., and K. Pfeffer. 2019. "Elaborating the Urbanism in Smart Urbanism: Distilling Relevant Dimensions for a Comprehensive Analysis of Smart City Approaches." *Information, Communication & Society* 22 (9): 1328–42.

3 Asansol

Unfinished biography of a Raj Era railway town: Explorations in heritage practice in post-India

Santanu Banerjee, Suvojit Chatterjee, Edward Hollis, and Hemonta Mondal

Introduction

From the construction of India's first coal mine in 1832 to the arrival of rail in the 1860s and steel in the late 19th century, the built heritage of the district of Asansol in West Bengal has been the product and the agent of industrial processes. At the same time, Asansol is home to religious, tribal, or precolonial heritages that tell very different stories.

Far from tourist trail or metropolis, this complex built fabric is at risk. Like many provincial Indian districts, Asansol lacks a developed heritage infrastructure. There are no public museums or libraries in which its citizens might encounter its histories, and archives are hard to access. Consequently and paradoxically, the built environment of Asansol, undervalued as it may be, may form the only accessible public history of the district.

This chapter explores three post-industrial sites in Asansol, narrated by the Asansol Heritage Research Group (henceforward AHRG). In them, the detritus of industrial and colonial 'progress' intersect with local, 'immemorial' and 'oriental' worlds, defying neat binary separations normalised by a 'modern' and orientalising historical consciousness (Said 1995).

These accounts follow Homi Bhabha in using collaborative storytelling to explore how to articulate and understand these apparent inconsistencies in:

> the writing of cultural difference in the midst of modernity that is inimical to binary boundaries: whether these be between past and present, inside and outside, subject and object, signifier and signified.
>
> (Bhabha 2004, 360)

This chapter will begin by placing these stories within three contexts: heritage practices in India; the district of Asansol; and discourses surrounding industrial and colonial heritage. The methodological approach is then outlined, before the narrative explorations are presented. The stories are followed by a discussion that explores the issues raised by their construction.

Context: heritage practices in India

The Archaeological Survey of India (ASI) is in charge of India's built heritage, setting agendas for both its own properties and those of others, which often correspond to an 'authorised heritage discourse' identified by LauraJane Smith that:

> defines heritage as material, non-renewable and fragile. It privileges aesthetically pleasing material objects, sites, places and/or landscapes. Their fragility requires that current generations must care for, protect and venerate these things so that they may be inherited by future generations. Within this framework heritage is something that is 'found'.
>
> (Smith 2015, 135)

Founded in 1861, the aims of the ASI were also imperial: to excavate, survey, classify, and preserve ancient monuments that had, according to their colonial masters, fallen victim to oriental lassitude and neglect. Indeed, in using archaeology – the excavation of (apparently) unoccupied ruins – as the dominant heritage paradigm, the ASI possessed an Orientalising slant of its own, that, Said comments:

> suggests both an enduring Oriental reality and an opposing but no less enduring Western essence, which observes the Orient from afar and from above, so to speak. What this false opposition hides is historical change.
>
> (Said 1995, 3)

That colonial regime still survives to some extent, directed towards the disencumberment of monuments and their preservation in regulated zones, separated from the detritus of everyday life (and thereby Said's 'historical change'). These practices, along with attempts to regulate them, are discussed in Sutton's (2018) account of misdemeanours at historic sites in Delhi and Dhabai's (2018) exploration of campaigns to 'disencumber' the historic walls of Jaipur, from the informal habitations that crowd them, setting heritage preservation against a right to housing.

However, recent initiatives recognise that heritage can inhabit less-exalted contexts. The UK Arts and Humanities Research Council (AHRC) and the Indian Council for Historical Research (ICHR) have run two recent calls for research projects relating heritage to rapid urbanisation, sustainability, and well-being (AHRC 2018). This initiative has generated projects that use, for example, Digital Humanities to study urban heritage (AH/R003211/1, Sutton), community-led regeneration on the Yamuna waterfront in Agra (AH/N007220/1, Orbasli), and the intangible heritages of performance on the periphery of Indian cities (AH/R003734/1, Turner). Recently the Indian National Trust for Art and Cultural Heritage (INTACH) committed 'to involve people in caring for our common heritage' (INTACH 2019a).

This new framing of the 'everyday' as heritage has opened up new areas of interest related to our study here – industrial and colonial heritage.

For example, the English and Scottish cemeteries in Kolkata have undergone extensive heritage campaigns, involving major symbolic shifts. Without colonial relatives to visit the graves and less encumbered by Christian anxieties about buried bodies, these spaces of grief have become part of the matrix of green spaces that ventilate the city, associated more with pleasure than mourning (Scottish Cemetery Kolkata 2020). The re-use (and therefore survival) of postcolonial heritage is often such a story of symbolic transformation and a breaking down of colonial binaries.

Interest in industrial heritage is also nascent. For example, former mill buildings in both Mumbai and Kolkata have sparked popular literary publications such as Neeraj Adarkar and Meena Menon's *One Hundred Years, One Hundred Voices, the Millworkers of Girangaon: An Oral History* (2004) and later, after regeneration had happened, Maura Finkelstein's *The Archive of Loss: Lively Ruination in Mill Land Mumbai* (2019). In 2019 INTACH (2019b) launched their first course for conservation professionals on industrial heritage in India.

Post-industrial ruins undermine the 'authorised heritage discourse' in India. Rather than being set apart from the detritus of everyday life, they *are* that detritus, both left behind by and representing ongoing processes of modernisation (Edensor 2006). In a country (unlike Britain, for example) that is *still* industrialising, industrial ruins are still being created: the result of modernising 'success' rather than post-imperial failure.

Second, industrial heritage in India is often associated with colonisation. Industry arrived with the British. In fact, according to historians such as Tharoor (2017). The British authorities in fact destroyed an autonomous (and therefore potentially competitive) industrial base. At the same time, parts of the Independence movement staged resistance to industrialisation – think of Gandhi's spinning wheel, for example.

Industrial heritage in India is not, to paraphrase Smith (2015, 135), 'non-renewable and fragile . . . aesthetically pleasing . . . "found",' but is, instead, in a continuous process of creation and destruction, often 'ugly', and subject to multiple contestations of value.

Heritage site below the radar: Asansol

This section will introduce the district of Asansol (Paschim Bardhaman) in West Bengal, within which our three sites are found.

Asansol is a 'modern' creation. The name does not appear in Rennell's *Bengal Atlas* of 1781 nor, a century later, in Joseph Beglar's *Report of a Tour through the Bengal Provinces* of 1878, though he must have passed through the town to reach the archaeological curiosities at Barakar and Panchakot he mentions. These ruins remain today, in zones managed by the Archaeological Survey of India (at Barakar) and the Bengal Heritage Commission (at Garh Panchakot).

They are also memorialised in poetry and myth. A local version of the Hindu epic the *Ramayana*, composed by Jagath Ram in the late 18th century, probably imagines Panchakot as the city of Ayodhya, while sonnets by Michael Madhusadhan meditate on the ruins in the Shakespearean mode (Madusadhan Dutt and Goswami 2016). But that, one might say, is all just poetry and myth.

The name 'Assensohe' appears in the memoirs of the engineer George Turnbull (Turnbull 1893), who led the construction of the East Indian Railway in the 1850's. A neo-gothic station was built in 1863 and, at the same time, a 'European Colony', separated by the Grand Trunk Road from the original (now 'native') town. This, our second site, remains under the single ownership of the railway, resulting in a remarkable state of preservation. Buildings recently received an enthusiastic facelift from the recent Divisional Railway Manager Mr P.K. Mishra after, he claims, a business visit to Europe convinced him of the importance of heritage preservation.

The initial purpose for the railway had been the transportation of coal from the collieries of Raniganj at the eastern end of the district to the markets of Calcutta. Until the railway, this supply chain was dependent on the seasonal whims of the river Damodar and its ferrymen – and, it transpires, the goddess Mathurachandi, who was worshipped on the loading jetty, our first site. Mathurachandi is sacred to the local 'bawri' forest dwellers who were also the primary source of labour for the coalmines. Their experience has been documented in *Gin Girls to Scavengers: Women in Raniganj Collieries* (Lahiri-Dutt 2001).

Finally, at the other end of the district, the plants of the Steel Authority of India at Burnpur and Kulti, accompanied, like the railway, by residential and social colonies – our third site – were the result of a later, 20th-century, process of colonisation and post-colonial nationalisation.

Asansol is now the second largest city in West Bengal and one of its fastest growing – a growth that produces and casts aside a complex heritage ecology along the way.

The story of Asansol is seemingly straightforward: a semi-mythical oriental realm is mapped, mined, re-named, excavated, and modernised – each phase forming a neatly defined 'unit' of heritage, several of which become, as industry itself changes, post-industrial. It would be a neat story to tell – and one that universalising Western sciences have often been accused of telling, in accounts such as Gregory's (1994) *Geographical Imaginations*.

Methodology

Yet, there are just enough exceptional details within this story to suggest something more complicated. This section will explore how and why we might examine these 'exceptional details' with more attention.

The AHRG is interested in connecting stories and places. Its co-founder, Santanu Banerjee, is head of English Literature at Kazi Nazrul University in Asansol, while co-authors Suvojit Chatterjee and Hemonta Mondal are schoolteachers and graduates from the department.

Their work began in 2015. Scholars of literature and cultural studies, they believe that:

> new narratives can be produced by our heritage, and [that] destruction of heritage would end narratives. . . .
>
> Heritage is not a dead thing. It is always a living thing which has been made alive by human beings who infuse life into it. The conservation of heritage is in no sense restriction of human participation, but a means of furthering life and health.
>
> (Mondal and Chatterjee 2019)

The AHRG encountered Hollis through his book of folk tales about historic buildings, *The Secret Lives of Buildings* (Hollis 2009), in which he argues that both buildings and stories are iterated, hybrid artefacts, handed down from one generation to another, both preserved and transformed in the retelling or rebuilding.

The combination of storytelling and heritage activity is not unique in India. It has been used recently in the work of Kamalika Bose in celebrating *A People Called Kolkata* (Bose 2019) through community storytelling and by Neeta Das, a conservation architect who has written children's stories about the built heritage of Lucknow (Das 2007).

It is unusual, however, for this approach to be taken to a provincial industrial town like Asansol, where, as well as building on the literary predilections and interests of the AHRG, it has helped them to understand and share their heritage anew.

First, through telling locally gathered, specific stories, self-generated rather than elicited by 'outsiders', the AHRG have sought what Gregory has called:

> sense-making without universals or absolutes, one that questions grand modernist narratives in favor of more grounded and contextual cultural theory.
>
> (Gregory 1994, quoted in Pickles 2008,)

Doing so challenges an 'authorized heritage discourse', which might preserve ruined temples and palaces but ignores coal mines or railway stations. As Tolia-Kelly, Waterton, and Watson (2016, 5) write:

> Before being canonized, authorized or, indeed, made material in the public domain, memory is at heart inclusive, accessible and a way of 'doing' heritage from below.

Second, the register(s) of these 'stories' enables them to go beyond 'objective' accounts of 'found' heritage to consider, instead, buildings and environments as participants in, as well as settings for or objects of, heritage creation. LauraJane Smith (2015, 133) argues that 'the dichotomy between tangible and intangible heritage needs re-thinking' and here myth, gossip, the results of archival research, and personal introspection are mixed: their apparent incompatibilities obviated by the frame of 'story' in itself: a framed and multiple representation rather than a transparent and consistent account in which 'affective registers, atmospheres, emotional contours . . . are about pluralizing the terms of engagement'. (Tolia-Kelly, Waterton, and Watson 2016, 4).

No longer transparent but 'thickened', the *form* of the texts provide data about how heritage is framed in multiple, particular ways. These stories have been written in English – a language that functions on the one hand as an (apparently) universal currency and on the other as a synecdoche of the heritage of Asansol itself – the relic of global Empire, fragmented into local idiosyncrasies.

The production of these stories involves, as Sather-Wagstaff (2017, 21–22) writes in *Making Polysense of the World*:

> analytical attention to how individuals attempt to narrate the sensorium of their experiences. . . . This approach necessitates implementing a form of critical discourse analysis that attends to the minutiae of the narrative.

Thus the 'data' presented here makes no claim to any universalising theory of heritage, industry, or place or to provide any objectivity but, instead, to share a milieu that is as complex and contradictory as the form in which it is narrated.

3 Stories about Asansol

Narankoori

Hemonta Mondal

Rather like Abraham Darby, the industrialist of Coalbrookdale, Prince Dwarkanath Tagore, grandfather of the poet Rabindranath, successfully ran his coal mining

Figure 3.1 The ruins of the house of Prince Dwarkanath Tagore, Narankoori

Source: Photograph by Edward Hollis, 2020

business from Narankoori, two kilometres away from the railway town of Raniganj, by the banks of the river Damodar, in the name of Carr Tagore and Co. between 1834 and 1843.

In this place, so far away from Calcutta, Dwarkanath's business could not be successful without divine aid – or so the local people believe. Though born in the Vaisnavite Brahmin faith, Dwarkanath became almost an atheist, yet, in popular imagination he had to pray to the deity Mathurachandi in her temple on this spot, many a time, for prosperity.

It is an ancient place of worship. The people say that a cow boy called Mathura Bawri used to worship some stones under a Tamarind tree in this spot in pre-colonial times. The stones signified the goddess; 'Chandi' being the word for a local goddess eventually given a place in the Hindu pantheon. Later the coal miners followed the rituals, and with the help of the Prince the temple became a shrine for the people of these areas.

In order to protect the goddess and the remains of the original Carr Tagore mine, the people of Narankoori founded a committee in 1998 and reconstructed the temple. They have been quite successful in convincing the West Bengal State Heritage Commission to declare the old coal jetty ghat, the haulage house, the office building, the bungalow, and also the shrine of Mathurachandi as heritage sites associated with Dwarkanath's memory. They have also been victorious in restraining Eastern Coalfields Ltd. from razing to the ground those structures for open cast mining. People there have been trying to save whatever they have by arranging a fair in mid-January every year, which increases the value of the area and brings the people to this historical place, knowingly or unknowingly.

It was the month of November in 2017 when I got a call to do something on the field of heritage in Raniganj, and I was excited that the work would allow me to procure many beautiful stories; I had no idea of the possible hazards of executing this task.

Industrialists had earned money by exploiting the common people: either by excavating the villagers from the mining areas or by paying them little wage and taking huge profits. This led to the destruction of forests and those people who were fully dependent on the resources collected from the forest, making them homeless. Many industrial authorities did not care about the lives of local people or about the ecology of these underground resources. After the colonial period, people somehow managed to occupy these industrial sites without any authorisation, and they live in fear of eviction if the buildings where they live are brought to public attention. Making information about them unavailable prevents this from happening.

It is not easy to search for data and get information about any significant building or place when people make it invisible. We went from door to door, but nobody replied properly. Some even threatened us. We eventually went to the local authorities, but they also showed us the door to get out before even entering their offices.

'Heritage means what?' they said, 'Why should people care for it? Forget about the people at Narankoori'.

'They have thousands of tales from pre-colonial times to the present', I thought, 'but who shall listen to them?'

Now people stop me and ask, 'What do you think about the fate of Narankoori?'

I am really not ready for the question. Perhaps the fate of the people lies in their own hands or perhaps the deity would come for the rescue of their heritage.

A European institute?

Dr Santanu Banerjee

Established as the European Institute in 1878 by the Mechanical Engineers of the East Indian Railway, this hall was renamed in 1925 to honour Sir Mortimer Durand, the architect of the line between Afghanistan and modern-day Pakistan. It was rechristened as the Vivekananda Institute in 1984 and finally re-dedicated on 15 August 2018 as the Durand Vivekananda Institute.

The name of the building has caused much worry. Durand brings to mind territories lost long ago to the partition with Pakistan, while Vivekananda is simultaneously a Hindu revivalist and a progressive and spiritual-humanist Bengali icon – a figure whose legacy is dear to – and potentially critical of – both the Hindu religious nationalists in Delhi and the Bengali nationalists in Kolkata.

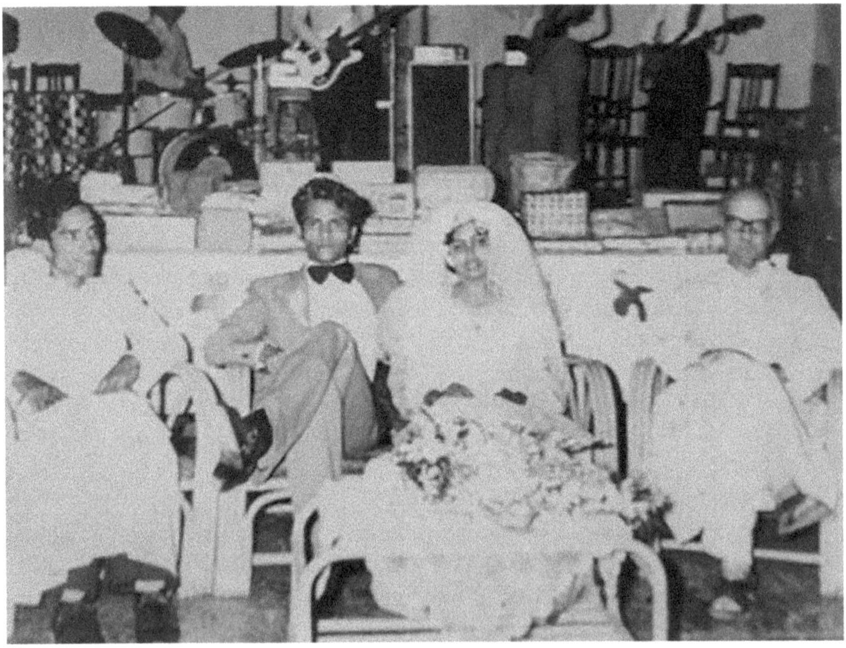

Figure 3.2 The Vivekananda Durand Institute, Asansol: then, and now

Source: Santanu Banerjee, 2020

Located in the erstwhile European Colony of Asansol, it has a sprawling campus where lawns and old mahogany, margosa and chhaatim trees still remind one of the late 19th- or early 20th-century village. The splendour of its pointed arches and the squared columns of the Durand Institute, its tower, the rose-windows and other Gothic architectural designs, speak loudly of the glory of Victorian urban planning and railway engineering.

The bell tower of the Institution is a unique structure. Once the tallest construction in the whole Asansol-Raniganj Coal Field, it was added much later to the portico of the old building. The copper plate fixed to a well-carved granite niche on its inner wall contains the names of the officers and men of the East Indian Railway who sacrificed their lives for the British Empire in the Great War.

The Durand Institute was popular among the high officials of East Indian Railway (E.I.R.), right from Calcutta to Saharanpur, and during Christmas they would join in fortnight-long celebrations in the elegant dance hall. Other amenities available were the billiards and cards room, the bar, the lawn-tennis and the badminton courts, the library, the projection room, the spacious wash rooms separately built for both ladies and gentlemen and a swimming pool.

The legacy of the Durand Institute was continued till the 1980s by Anglo-Indian members of the Eastern Railway family. Though native Indians were not allowed to enter the premises even after Independence, gradually they took over and eventually renamed it the Vivekananda Institute.

This takeover had a new consequence. The elitism of the Europeans and their legacy carried forward by the Anglo-Indians helped preserve cultural practices that became redundant after the 1980s. After then, the Durand Institute turned into a cinema hall, a community centre for trade union meetings and other political gatherings, and a place of access for all. Too much use and too little care caused damage to the building and also erased a great deal of its colonial significance from people's memory.

The attempt taken by the Asansol Divisional Railway in renovating it with the help of the AHRG was a major turning point of the railway's interest in heritage in this district.

Bhoot

Suvojit Chatterjee

In Bengali, there is a word for 'ghost', bhoot, *which also means 'the past'. This is a 'bhoot' story, in both senses, about a house, how it got transformed into a hospital in 1972 and how now the ghosts of its patients roam the building.*

There was a time when the Director's Bungalow at Kulti near Asansol boasted the residence of the illustrious father of Bengali engineers and industrialists, Sir Rajendranath Mukherjee, and his equally famous son Sir Birendranath Mukherjee. But browse YouTube now and one would find ample videos of this building describing it as a horror house: a spooky place that asks only daring visitors.

Figure 3.3 The staircase hall of the Director's Bungalow, Kulti

Source: Photograph Edward Hollis 2020

There were efforts to produce iron in various parts of Bengal by 1855, and in 1870, Mr James Erskine came from England and set up the 'Bengal Iron Works' in Kulti, 214 kilometres away from Kolkata. Mr Erskine set up a blast furnace and a power house, but nine years later his works had to be closed down, and Marillier and Edwards, a large engineering company, took over the management of the firm, also failing to run it successfully. Around 1880, the British government took a 999-year lease from the Secretary of State for India the works. After a decade Stirling and Co. bought the plant for 50,000 pounds, and in 1892 they handed over the management to Martin and Company.

In 1918, Sir Rajendranath Mookherjee took over this company and transmuted it into the Indian Iron and Steel Company. By that time, the Kulti Plant was the country's largest production unit of pig iron.

His son, Sir Birendranath Mookerjee was born on 14 February 1899. He took the Indian Iron and Steel Company (IISCO) on to commercial success between 1939 and 1952. Lady Ranoo Mookherjee, Sir Birendranath's celebrated wife, made memorable contributions in the establishment of the famous Academy of Fine Arts at Kolkata.

Rajendranath built a large mansion at Harrington Street at Kolkata in 1910. It had 37 rooms and two kitchens catering separately for Indian and Western culinary tastes and a large dining hall to accommodate 150 guests at a time. The house had a domed skylight, terracotta tiles, chandeliers and expensive carpets.

The Director's Bungalow at Kulti was built seven years later in a similar style, though on a smaller scale. The house had a front entrance facing the golf course of Kulti, and from the Grand Trunk Road one could view this majestic mansion. The building is in a style of Roman architecture largely meant for the Europeans working in the company at Kulti.

In 1975, just three years after the government of India took over the management of the steelworks, the Director's Bungalow was transformed into a hospital. A lot of changes were made, and nobody knew where all those expensive chandeliers, carpets and furniture went. The skylight was covered, the wooden staircases blocked, some servants' quarters at the back were added, a ramp was constructed and the beautiful veranda was partitioned into rooms. The front side of the building now serves as the entry of the hospital, and the back side bears the year of its establishment.

Currently, some of the bungalows at Kulti are occupied by remaining company officers; but others are also encroached upon (illegally occupied) by idol makers and craftsmen: in one bungalow, 20 to 30 people live in a house built for approximately four.

One can easily imagine perhaps, Sir Birendranath Mukherjee watching a golf match from his first floor veranda with his wife Lady Ranoo Mukherjee, but those days are gone now. Their garden is now fully covered with bushes.

Discussion

The third story may be most familiar to post-industrial scholars: an industrial site is made redundant by industrial progress (see, for example, Edensor 2006). This situation is, however, inflected by its Indian context. Although the site itself was founded as a British-owned concern, it reached its apogee under a local family – the Mukherjees – until the independent state of India took it away from them, suggesting that traditional binaries between a rapacious industrial empire and a passive, primitive orient might be a simplification.

The second story will be familiar to postcolonial scholars, narrating negotiations around identity and ownership. For whom was the 'Institute' built, and, consequently, to whose heritage does it belong? This is not just a matter of naming: in this case, a particular industry (the railway) is associated with particular populations (Europeans and Anglo Indians) and cultural practices (public drinking, ballroom dancing, public swimming). Postcolonial occupants and occupations disrupt the original architecture of the building as well as its name, blurring distinctions between tangible and intangible heritage.

In the first story, the post-industrial intersects with religious and tribal concerns. It might appear to narrate the straightforward exploitation of the latter by the former, but, in fact, the villagers have leveraged the newly fashionable mantle of 'industrial heritage' to rebuild their temple, and, conversely, have used the temple fair to raise the profile (and hence the protection) of their village from subsequent mining. They have successfully operationalised two different discourses against one another.

These stories demonstrate ways in which individual sites cannot neatly be categorised as 'heritage' or not, 'industrial' or not, 'colonial' or not but that – like many stories – they represent complex meeting places between many of these discourses and multiple retellings.

'Doing Heritage from Below'

Mondal in the first story writes that 'It is not easy to search for data and get information about any significant building or place when people make it invisible'. Indeed, most archives in India have not been digitised, and there is little concept of open public access to information. In many cases, the information has quite simply been mislaid – the entire archives of the Asansol municipal area, for example, are missing following a district boundary change. But often, as Mondal goes on to explain, this mislaying is sometimes deliberate, motivated by a fear that historic documents will be operationalised in property disputes or that their publication will lead to government or municipal interference in sites of informal or illegal occupation.

In a neo-colonial twist, obtaining a meeting with an official at the local coal board and government offices, for example, was impossible until the production of letters of recommendation from Hollis, the collaborator from the British University of Edinburgh, who was, of course, (despite himself) doing Heritage 'from above', as an 'expert'.

Thickening discourses

In this context, it cannot be surprising that the elision of fact and fiction through stories is sometimes used to make connections or provide interpretations.

Like many stories these texts have themselves been through multiple retellings, being initially researched and drafted by Mondal, Banerjee et al. (2008), and Chatterjee in India. They were subsequently edited by Hollis in the UK.

First, Hollis used comments and questions to draw out what might interest an international readership but which was obvious to a local audience. As Gregory, quoting from the historian E.P. Thompson, reflected in *Geographical Imaginations*, being inside our own history makes us:

> part-subjects, part-objects, the voluntary agents of our own involuntary determinations . . . ever-baffled and ever-resurgent human agents.
>
> (Pickles 2008, 3)

Next Hollis proposed textual edits. This was a delicate task: on the one hand, questions of word limit or syntactical meaning preponderated. On the other, to 'smooth' the language in which these tales are written into some lingua franca would be to lose a key part of their import: most notably their affect. We hope that the stories do *not* read as if they were written by an Englishman.

The power relations of this process will be evident and are only partly mitigated by their mention here and evidence retained of every edit in track changes. They raise a question: who (and therefore what) are these stories about the heritage of Asansol actually for?

'None of the Orientalists I write about' reflected Said (1995, 5), 'seems ever to have intended an Oriental as a reader. The discourse of Orientalism, its internal consistency and rigorous procedures, were all designed for readers and consumers in the metropolitan West.' By the same token, are we, for all our postcolonial pleadings, Orientalists?

Conclusion

Nevertheless, this isn't just a story written in the UK, for the UK, about an exotic foreign land. Bhabha argues that

> The Western metropole must confront its postcolonial history . . . as an indigenous narrative internal to its national identity; and the reason for this is made clear in the stammering, drunken words of Mr 'Whisky' Sisodia from The Satanic Verses: 'The trouble with the Engenglish is that their hiss hiss history happened overseas, so they dodo don't know what it means.'
>
> (Bhabha 2004, 9)

Conversely, these stories and their construction have had an agency on the ground in Asansol. For example, research by the AHRG into the Dwarkanath Tagore connection and a public visit by Hollis to Narankoori in early 2019 have contributed to the decision of the local development authority to grant the Narankoori heritage group funding for heritage activities. Similarly, AHRG research into the social history of the Durand institute has supported the rationale of the Divisional Railway to restore the building.

These stories narrate ways in which a post-industrial geography is interwoven with a (post) colonial one and in which lenses including archaeology, (neo)colonial control, modernisation, appeals to religious tradition and literary heritage intersect (Hill 2013).

Why would they not? Said (1995, 2) wrote that 'Orient and Occident correspond to no stable reality that exists as a natural fact' and Ashish Nandy in 'The uncolonized mind: Postcolonial India and the East' envisages an India that is neither, in the words of Bhabha 'modern nor anti-modern but non-modern'.

Nandy places the binary somewhere else, writing:

> in every situation of organized oppression the true antonyms are always the exclusive part versus the inclusive whole. . . . [N]ot the past versus the present but either of them versus the rationality which turns them into co-victims.
>
> (Nandy 1983, 99)

We have attempted here to narrate parts of that 'inclusive whole': a millowner's mansion becomes a ghost story. Once there are no Europeans left to use it, a European institute is restored. A disused coal wharf becomes a shrine to an ancient goddess.

In India, discussions about heritage often exclude places like Asansol, and yet is it in places like these that 'doing' heritage can perhaps have useful effect on the lives of ordinary people. These places offer an almost inexhaustible fund of folk memory, and also opportunities to explore how storytelling can provide a new way of dealing with our continually re-industrialising environment across the globe.

References

Adarkar, N., and M. Menon. 2004. *One Hundred Years, One Hundred Voices, the Millworkers of Girangaon: An Oral History*. Kolkata: Seagull.

AHRC. 2018. *Cultural Heritage and Rapid Urbanisation in India*. Accessed January 2020. https://ahrc.ukri.org/funding/apply-for-funding/archived-opportunities/cultural-heritage-and-rapid-urbanisation-in-india/.

Banerjee, D., S.K. Chakraborty, S. Bhattacharyya, and A. Gangopadhyay. 2008. "Evaluation and Analysis of Road Traffic Noise in Asansol: An Industrial Town of Eastern India." *International Journal of Environmental Research and Public Health*, ISSN 1661-7827. Accessed March 2019. www.ijerph.org.

Bhabha, Homi K. 2004. *The Location of Culture*. Abingdon, UK: Taylor & Francis Group.

Bose, K., ed. 2019. *People Called Kolkata: Stories of a Resilient City*. Kolkata: The People's Place Project.

Das, N. 2007. *Hap'pant Meets Asfu Dadu, Slowly Down the Rajpath, Where's My Mother*. New Delhi: Mansara + INTACH.

Dhabai, G. 2018. "The Purusharthi Refugee: Sindhi Migrants in Jaipur's Walled City." *Economic and Political Weekly* LIII (4).

Edensor, T. 2006. *Industrial Ruins: Space, Aesthetics, and Materiality*. Oxford and New York: Berg.

Finkelstein, M. 2019. *The Archive of Loss: Lively Ruination in Mill Land Mumbai*. Durham, NC: Duke University Press.

Gregory, D. 1994. *Geographical Imaginations*. Cambridge, MA: Blackwell.

Hill, L. 2013. "Archaeologies and Geographies of the Post-Industrial Past: Landscape, Memory and the Spectral." *Cultural Geographies* 20 (3): 379–96. Sage.

Hollis, E. 2009. *The Secret Lives of Buildings*. London: Portobello Books.

INTACH. 2019a. "Mission Statement." Accessed January 2020. www.intach.org/about-mission.php.

———. 2019b. "Industrial Heritage." Accessed January 2020. http://heritage.intach.org/event/industrial-heritage/.

Lahiri Dutt, K. 2001. "From Gin Girls to Scavengers: Women in Raniganj Collieries." *Economic and Political Weekly* 36 (44): 4213–21. Accessed March 2019. www.jstor.org/stable/4411329.

Madusadhan Dutt, M., and D.K. Goswami, eds. 2016. *Panchakot O Manbhumer Sabhyata*. Purulia: Vajrabhumi Prakashani.

Mondal, H., and S. Chatterjee. 2019. *Presentation to Interior Design Research Themes Seminar Series*. Edinburgh: University of Edinburgh unpublished.

Nandy, Ashis. 1983. *The Intimate Enemy: Loss and Recovery of Self under Colonialism*. Oxford: Oxford University Press.
Pickles, J. 2008. "Geographical Imaginations (1994): Derek Gregory." In *Key Texts in Human Geography*, edited by Phil Hubbard, Rob Kitchin, and Gill Valentine. London: Sage.
Said, Edward W. 1995. "Orientalism, an Afterword." *Raritan* 14 (3) (Winter): 28, 32.
Sather-Wagstaff, J., 2017. "Making Polysense of the World." In *Heritage, Affect and Emotion: Politics, Practices and Infrastructures*, edited by D. Tolia-Kelly, E. Waterton, and S. Watson, 12–31. Abington, UK: Routledge.
Scottish Cemetery Kolkata. Accessed March 2020. https://scottishcemeterykolkata.wordpress.com/.
Smith, L., 2015. "Intangible Heritage: A Challenge to the Authorised Heritage Discourse?" *Revi'ta d'etnologia de Catalunya* 40: 133–42.
Sutton, D. 2018. "Inhabited Pasts: Monuments, Authority, and People in Delhi, 1912–1970s." *The Journal of Asian Studies* 77 (4): 1013–35.
Tharoor, S. 2017. *Inglorious Empire: What the British Did to India*. London: Hurst and Co.
Tolia-Kelly, D., E. Waterton, and S. Watson, eds. 2016. *Heritage, Affect and Emotion: Politics, Practices and Infrastructures*. Oxon: Routledge, 4.
Turnbull, G. 1893. *The Autobiography of George Turnbull with Added Extracts from His Diary*. London: Cooke and Co.

4 Everyday resonances of industrial pasts

Considering lived and affective memories in ex-coal mining landscapes in a South Wales valley

Amy Walker

In 1988 a huge coal-mining complex based at Marine colliery, known as a 'super pit', stretching across the valleys of Ebbw Vale and Ebbw Fach, was closed by the National Coal Board (see Burns, Newby, and Winterton 1985). This was typical of many mine closures across the UK following the Miners' Strike of 1984–85 and the Coal Industry Act of 1987. This large complex was made up of several merged collieries, many of which had been operating in the area since the late 1800s, and they had been gradually merged in an effort to keep the pits as profitable as possible. In the case of the South Wales coalfield, the closures were endemic of several decades of decline in the industry, which had drastically transformed the nature of everyday life for mining communities in the area.

A considerable amount of literature, including within the discipline of geography, has addressed the discontinuities that are associated with the massive structural changes that resulted from processes of deindustrialisation (see for example Martin and Rowthorn 1986; Turner 2000; Strangleman 2007; Strangleman and Rhodes 2014). However, I am concerned in this chapter with highlighting instead the continuities present in so-called post-industrial communities. This approach builds on existing work on the conditions of communities following processes of deindustrialisation. Instances of continuity often emphasise the instances of discontinuity and loss. In this chapter I argue that by attending to these instances of continuance and endurance we can perhaps engage in greater detail with the abiding importance of these industrial heritages, especially when considering the everyday lives of people who live within these communities.

Engaging with the legacies of industrial heritage is not difficult, especially when dwelling in a state such as the UK, where most places have been significantly impacted by the transformative power of the industrial revolution. Throughout this research, I was based at Cardiff University, in a city that developed as a key port – at one time the world's largest coal port – for the export of coal from the neighbouring South Wales coalfield (as detailed by Pinder 2003). Historical geographies more broadly have focused on considering the various legacies of history that can be traced in our contemporary world, and this project builds on much of this existing work (Darby 2000; Nash 2002).

In this chapter, I will start by briefly outlining the theoretical approaches that inform my fieldwork practices and then introduce both the research area of Ebbw Fach and the methods that I employed. Following this, I will identify four ways in which registers of industrial pasts endure in the contemporary lives, practices and landscapes of Ebbw Fach. First, I will discuss the ways in which the continuing reliance on manufacturing can be understood as enduring industrial heritage in both the forms of bodies and in the experience of the surrounding landscape. I will then engage in detail with the role of community, in terms of shared pasts and local networks and then outline practices of belonging that are fundamentally related to these constructions of both historical and contemporary community. Finally, I will introduce the ideas of material continuity in the traces of industry, which endure in the local infrastructures and landscape more broadly.

Theories of heritage and memory

The term industrial heritage is used throughout this chapter to describe an instance whereby an area has a past that is related to manufacturing industries and working-class people. This is not to suggest that industrial heritage is, or industrial pasts are, homogenous or uncontested; it is intensely subjective, localised and political (Harvey 2001, 2008). Indeed chapters from both Price (2021) and Rhodes (2021) within this collection consider the interpretive and contested nature of industrial heritage in the Welsh and UK contexts. I use the term instead to refer to an undefined past that is tied to the established identity of these communities as 'coal-mining' towns and villages (Bulmer 1975; Frankenberg 1966; Day 2006). Prevailing discussions on post-industrial places generally consider the process of moving from industrial society, through deindustrialisation to a state of post-industrialisation as a linear process, particularly within economic and development disciplines but also within traditional sociological investigations into working-class communities (Krzysztofik et al. 2016; Day 2006). However, some work has troubled these ideas, by engaging with reindustrialisation (Krzysztofik et al. 2016), 'industrial structures of feeling' and societal norms (Byrne 2002), gender roles (Walkerdine and Jimenez 2012), infrastructure (Dawney 2020), or landscape 'scars' (Storm 2014), to provide but a few examples. This chapter seeks to address the relative gap at the intersection of these ideas; what can be revealed if we trouble the past/present binary of an industrial/post-industrial place?

Theoretically speaking, I draw more heavily on theories of memory than on heritage. The multiplicity of memory is central to my research in this area, as I seek to engage with the many ways in which industrial pasts endure in the presence. This draws on a wide array of work, including Halbwach's (1992) concept of collective memory and Nora's (1989) work on the *milleux* and *lieux de memorie*, which both highlight the importance of collective ideas of the past as well as the role of place in the establishment of these ideas (c.f. Atkinson 2007; Alderman 1996; Buciek and Juul 2008; Johnson 2005; Legg 2005; Terranova-Webb 2012). Additionally, many scholars have argued that the preoccupation with memory and heritage is symptomatic of the growing sense of insecurity associated with various forms of contemporary society, such as Beck's (1992) 'risk society' and Bauman's (2000) concept of 'liquid modernity'. However, much of the work on memory has tended to focus on particular registers of memory, such as narrative memory, material memory, curated or heritage, personal memory, collective memory and so on. Attending to these individual registers of memory can be advantageous, such as by highlighting overlooked histories or considering the complex nature of social remembering. Yet I suggest that it is within a landscape that exists as a cumulation of these forms of memory that people live their everyday lives (drawing on Mah 2012; Wylie 2005). Therefore, I seek to engage with these multiplicities, and I therefore draw at various stages on ideas of collective and shared memory, as well as memory as discursive, embodied, material, affective and emotive.

The works of Desilvey (2012), Stewart (2007) and Hoskins (2016) are useful in order to conceptualise how these multiple registers of memory may be encountered within the landscape. For instance, I employ Hoskins (2016) model of 'memory ecologies', whereby we can negotiate multiple scales and forms of memory throughout our interactions and experiences. Memory is understood as emergent, drawn into comprehension as we engage with these narrative, material, absent, emotive pasts (Hoskins 2016). Additionally, Desilvey (2012, 48), drawing on Stewart's (2007) concept of 'ordinary affects', describes moments where there are 'residues of resonance' that we encounter in landscape. These moments are difficult to articulate; they are rooted in a sense that *something* needs to be attended to; they are often amorphous, connective, emergent, sometimes imaginative and fundamentally moving, as an assemblage of bodies, materials and atmospheres (Desilvey 2012, 48; Stewart 2007, 3–5; Merriman and Jones 2017). It is in these moments of 'resonance' – or affective intensity – I argue, that it is possible to engage with different registers of memory, which, in turn, makes some aspects of industrial pasts legible in the contemporary landscape.[1]

The South Wales Coalfield, Ebbw Fach and coal mining communities . . .

Ebbw Fach is a valley that is situated on the eastern side of the South Wales coalfield, an area of steep-sided valleys with rich coal deposits that became the main site of coal mining in Wales (see Figure 4.1). Much of my research was focused in the town of Abertillery and the adjoining village of Six Bells. However, due to the process of travelling in and out of the valley, my research often extended beyond these communities to include Llanhilleth, Aberbeeg and Cwmtillery (see Figure 4.1).[2] The development and character of these areas were typical of much of the South Wales coalfield. Following the sinking of the first coal mine in the area in 1884, the population of the Ebbw Fach valley boomed, reaching 40,000 people living in the area of Abertillery by 1931. During these years of high population and coal export, the town included cinemas, local businesses and miner's institutes that provided support and social organisations for the local community (Dennis, Henriques, and Slater 1969; Frankenberg 1966; Bulmer 1975).

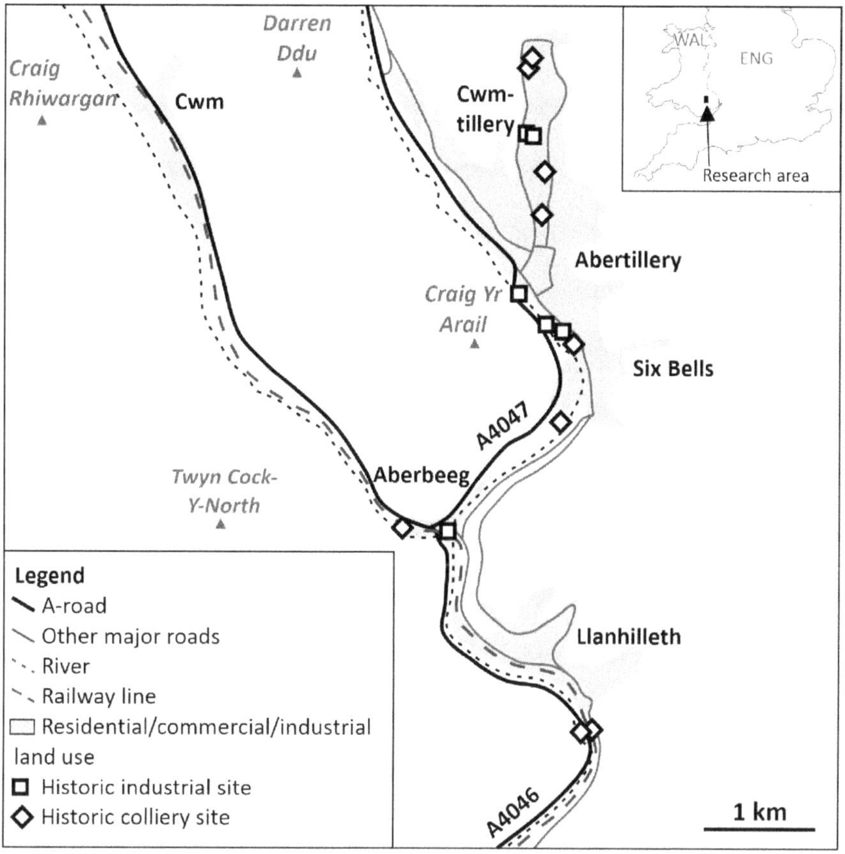

Figure 4.1 Ebbw Fach Research Area and notable historical sites

Source: George Guice

Similar to many other industrial areas of the UK, decline and closures of the mines and related industries were prolific in the second half of the 20th century, with coal mining ceasing finally in 1988, as discussed in the introduction. As such, the area of Ebbw Fach, like much of "the Valleys" area of South Wales, is now associated with high rates of unemployment, low educational attainment, low average wages and low house prices, as well as poor transport connections, isolation and limited social mobility (Beatty, Fothergill, and Powell 2007; Beatty and Fothergill 1996; Rees 1978; Walkerdine and Jimenez 2012; NOMIS 2010).

The findings of this chapter are based on ethnographic research in the Ebbw Fach area, which I conducted throughout 2018, mostly in the town of Abertillery and the neighbouring village of Six Bells. The fieldwork was informed by approaches of "going-along" (Kusenbach 2003) and "hanging out" as ethnographic method (Trivelli 2016; Bernard 2013), meaning I spent a large amount of time in the area with participants in an informal context. This was most commonly the case at community groups; I regularly attended 4 social groups in the area and visited many others, such as groups for carers, craft groups and church coffee mornings. Key figures in these groups became my main participants, numbering around 12 individuals, who I would sometimes meet separately to discuss their own family history and engagement with narratives of the coal-mining history (Allen and Montell 1981). At other times the ethnography involved conversations or sometimes informal interviews with locals in cafés in the area, having a cup of tea in someone's front room, quick chats with locals at bus stops, being given a "lift" to the train station or being invited to a local event. I would commonly "run into" someone I had come to know or catch snippets of interesting conversations at bus stops, in shops, and at community group meetings; the ethnographic practice was not clearly delineated in place or time (Mannay and Morgan 2014; Stebbins 1991).

As such, whilst some of the information presented is from transcribed interviews, most is from collected fieldnotes and reflections, often frantically jotted down as people spoke or as I sat on the bus after a visit to the area, sometimes recorded in a quick audio note to myself whilst walking (Hammersley and Atkinson 1995). I also drew on principles of auto-ethnography throughout, using a fieldwork diary to reflect on my own experiences (Haynes 2012; Browne 2013). This was also helpful due to my own background of growing up in the Black Country, another area of the UK with extensive industrial heritage and subsequent decline. At times, meaning is ascribed and imaginaries are invoked within these fieldnotes, which draw on my own pre-existing ideas and experiences of post-industrial heritage, highlighting the key role of my own positionality in this case (Collins and Gallinat 2010; Waterston and Rylko-Bauer 2006).

I suggest that by engaging with these "messy" or "live" methods, it is possible to consider the complexity and multiplicity of memory in these post-industrial contexts (Back and Puwar 2012; Law and Urry 2004). The choice to engage with ethnographic practices, rather than relying primarily on interviews, was also made to allow for the engagement with memory beyond accounts from residents of the past (drawing on Fuchs 2002). Meaning is not based only on singular accounts, but becomes emergent and interconnected across stories, practices, everyday conversations and embodied experiences (Hoskins 2016). By engaging with participants' everyday lives, it was possible to engage with understandings of industrial heritage beyond the most common understandings, such as through museums and statutes. Instead I was able to observe and engage in everyday conversations and interactions, in mundane and unremarkable settings, highlighting relationships to industrial pasts that may otherwise be overlooked. I sought to develop an embodied and experiential sense of place, rooted in my own experiences of the community and my own affective responses to the multiplicity of memory within the landscape, which were simultaneously rooted in the accounts of local people.

Industrial bodies

> One overcast day in August, I am meant to be meeting the local walking group to walk around Cwmtillery lakes, but have been confused by the local buses and am therefore walking what I hope is the route in the hope that I catch up to them. As I walk along the valley side towards the lakes, according to google maps, there is a large industrial estate on the valley floor to my right. I realise, from its size and the stories I have heard, that this is Tillery Valley Foods, the largest employer in the area, which produces food for hospitals. It's made up of a series of large sheds, green and oddly luminous amongst the lines of brick cottages and the pale yellow fields of grass. There are a series of metal-sounding bangs emanating from the site, and a scent of savoury, perhaps gravy, in the air. I wonder what sounds or smells would have seeped into the villages and hillsides around Cwmtillery when this was not a food factory but instead an operational pit. The pit didn't close completely until 1982.
>
> (Excerpt from fieldnotes and reflections, walking along a footpath on a valley-side above Cwmtillery, August 2018)

The most obvious instances of continuance of industrial society in the area is in the continuing reliance on manufacturing as a source of employment. Employment levels in manufacturing in the borough of Blaenau Gwent, which includes the Ebbw Fach valley, was significantly higher than in other parts of the country. In 2018, 22.2% of working people were employed in manufacturing, compared to an average of 8.1% across the UK (NOMIS 2010).[3] However, the dependence of the communities on this form of work was reinforced, as Tillery Foods, a food-production factory based on the site of the Cwmtillery colliery, was the largest employer in this area of the Ebbw Fach valley. Many of the other colliery sites had been redeveloped as industrial estates housing small unit-based industries and companies. As one participant, Lloyd, stated: 'there's no work here, unless you want to work in the factories'. Walkerdine and Jimenez (2012) discuss the ways in which traditional ideas of masculinity shape attitudes to work. They explore how many ideas of acceptable work for working-class men still relate to industrial work, even following the closure of the predominant sites of employment in these industries. They explain that a loss of manufacturing was 'difficult' for young men to accept, so in instances of Tillery Valley Foods and other forms of manufacturing that endured in Ebbw Fach, it is of importance to not only the continuation of industry but also the continuation of industrial and working-class masculinities that are embedded with these practices.

The bodies that are enrolled in this work are of great significance. Butler's (2013) work has engaged in detail with the ways in which identity is embodied, and this can be considered through the physical impacts labour has on the working-class body. Contemporary manufacturing, often due to mechanisation, does not have the same physical impacts of historical industrial work, especially that of coal mining, which was defined by its physicality and risk (Dicks 2000; Selway 2016). However, the men that are employed in these manufacturing jobs continue to embody their work; their bodies are physically engaged in ways which, to varying degrees, echo the physicality of the coal mining, to which many of those employed in the area would have familial links.[4] In terms of identity, again, the continuation of a working-class masculinity, tied to their repeated bodily behaviours and movements, is reinforced through these practices.

This work itself provides other ways to engage with instances of continuance in the area. Whilst the endurance of practices can clearly illustrate a continuity of industrial pasts, I also seek to consider the affective sense of endurance, drawing on Desilvey (2012) and Stewart (2007). By attending to moments of affective intensity, 'resonance' or 'transversal flashes' (Renold and Ivinson 2014), I suggest it is again possible to engage with ideas of continuity. In the previous vignette, I am moved to reflect on the multi-sensory experiences of industry, for those who are not enrolled in the work – but who dwell in varying degrees – in the area. The scent of gravy, a smell that is somewhat out of place on the fringe between a village and an undeveloped hillside, is still comforting; the scents I associate with mining, of dust and fire and even gases that carry imaginaries of risk and fear, are invoked. These are imaginaries, drawn from depictions of mining from my own experiences, the stories of participants, and the painting of a coal mine I saw in the hallway of one ex-miners home. They are uncertain, yet they continue to highlight both the continuances – how industry permeates beyond the site in multi-sensory ways – and the discontinuities of a relatively safe and clean place of employment.

Community as continuity

In order to identify some instances where aspects of industrial life endure into contemporary contexts, it is also necessary at times to engage with recollections of these industrial pasts. An aspect of mining communities that is often central to discussions for both residents and academics is that of the nature of the mining community; that is, the interconnections between families, friends and acquaintances in these close-knit areas. Much of the literature concerning mining towns and villages focuses on the intense bonds between miners and the families of miners in light of difficult working conditions, risk of injury and even death and experiences of poverty and hardship (Westergaard 1975; Warwick and Littlejohn 1992; Selway 2016). Many of the residents I engaged with expressed aspects of this as part of their own experiences living in the area whilst the coal industry was operational:

> We all went down the pit together, and the men, they were always your butty. You made sure he was alright, he made sure you were.
>
> (Interview with Joe, an ex-miner, during an interview at his home with his wife, Jane, April 2018)

> Everyone you was at school with, they all had their . . . their fathers down the pit, and you, you grew up and most stayed nearby.
>
> (Comments from a local resident on a Walking Group outing, May 2018)

> You really had to look after one and other. And people did.
>
> (Comments from local residents at a Ty Ebbw Fach community event, March 2018)

> People talk about how you didn't lock your doors because it was so friendly . . . we didn't lock our doors because we had nothing worth stealing. . . . No one did.
>
> (Comment from Brenda, whilst we were having a cup of tea in her living room in Aberbeeg, September 2018)

Quotes here from older participants, many who had been born in the 1930s and 1940s, display how these pasts are discursively constructed. It is possible here to not only appreciate the intense community that these people recount but also the ways in which there is a construction of a "shared past". Through the previous comments, it is possible to perceive the ways in which they establish a collective experience, that *everyone* was poor, for example. Although it was evident throughout the fieldwork that experiences varied for everyone, this idea of having a shared past was pervasive. These recollections were often focused around working identity, with family members, or the participants themselves, involved in coal mining. This is to be expected, as the population of these communities boomed as the coal mines opened; the vast majority of individuals who lived in the area had relatives who had migrated to the valleys in order to work in the coal pits. This similar familial trajectory across different families further reinforced these shared experiences; as Marilyn said 'everyone around here, their families came here for the coal'.

These ideas of shared pasts are not only important in the recollection of such pasts, but these perceptions of shared experiences also serve to reinforce ideas of community in the present. As Amit (2002) explains, a sense of shared experiences is fundamental in the development of a sense of community and belonging. I argue that these shared historical experiences, however dissimilar they may have been when experienced by individuals, are the basis for many of the social interactions and community practices that continue. The historical sense of solidarity that is discussed in literature and was expressed by many participants recalling the coal-mining years was reinforced in the contemporary practices and beliefs of residents. For example, Gwen explained her choice to return to the area after living in Germany for some years:

> It's a really special place. The people, the people here are just wonderful. Everyone takes good care of you, and will help you out if you need anything. They're just so friendly.
>
> (Interview with Gwen in Ty Ebbw Fach cafe, June 2018)

This was not only expressed by Gwen – who could remember the area whilst the mines were operational – but also by younger participants, Rebecca and Emma.[5] Emma, for instance, said 'like, living here, I've got so many people I could call or just knock on their door if I was in a mess'. This sense of community support was often positioned as being 'at-odds' with the way of life in more cosmopolitan areas, such as London.

Joe: 'I was in London, visitin' my son, and I saw the undertakers come and take out a body, like in a bag like, from next door. . . . And I told my son, and he said "oh he must have died." And I was so surprised that he didn't know, and I asked if he'd been ill. And my son said he didn't know. And I can't imagine being somewhere where you don't know that, about your next door neighbour. It's such, so strange

Me: 'So you'd never live in London then?'

Joe: 'I'd never live anywhere but here. I know everyone here

(Interview with Joe and his wife Jane, in Joe's home in Six Bells, April 2018)

'Everyone knows everyone'

These senses of shared pasts also highlighted the role of shared knowledge for belonging in the community. Many residents used localised knowledge to situate their stories and recollections, assuming I would be aware of these places and events. For example, in the vignette presented earlier, I was unable to find the meeting place of the walking group and was 'confused by the local buses'. Whilst this highlighted my own lack of belonging in the area, it was possible to perceive these uses of local references as also being a performance[6] of belonging in itself. These references were often both historical or contemporary but, again, were reminiscent of a sense that everyone shared the same experiences, histories, geographies and social networks.

> Do you remember Adam, used to work in the butchers down on Llanhilleth?
>
> (Fieldnote, question asked at Care Group, June 2018)

> 'My dad, he used to own that shop'. 'I remember there, I used to get my hair cut there.
>
> (Conversation between group members, at a local pub after a Walking Group outing, August 2018)

> Have you met Eleri? Oh you have!
>
> (Comment to me at Ty Ebbw Fach cafe in Six Bells by local resident, April 2018)

> She's my cousin, I heard you'd been talking to her.
>
> (Comment to me from a member of the Craft Group, June 2018).

It is difficult here to convey the affective sense of importance that is embedded in these practices, almost rituals, of belonging. In the sheer number of times I was enrolled in or witness to discussions of these interconnections between people, places, and histories, it became more apparent that *something* in these discussions was of great significance to those who engaged with them. An affective sense of belonging, of expressing one's own knowledge and history in the community, was evident, even in the relief and emotional satisfaction I felt when I too could successfully engage in these exchanges.

These accounts may also suggest a sense of romanticism about the community, yet others did express feelings of claustrophobia and insularity that related from these sorts of performances and practices of belonging. For instance Lloyd, who had grown up in Abertillery and since moved to Bristol, the USA and then to Cardiff, expressed: 'It's such a bubble up there'. Whilst Emma, who was hoping to move away to attend university expressed 'everyone knows everyone and after a while you just get bored of the same people'. This feeling echoes similar perceptions in literature, such as in Hudson's (1995) work, addressing communities transitioning from mining employment (see also Samuel, Bloomfield, and Boanas 1986).

The example of community and the ways in which belonging is established and experienced are complex and far beyond the scope of this chapter. Yet it is evident that many of the defining features that are associated with mining communities endure in varying forms into the contemporary 'post'-industrial context, despite narratives and experiences of community decline. This continuity can be perceived in many other cases, such as the enduring presence of various community organisations and in families remaining in close proximity to each other, with many instances of children living adjacent to their parents' homes. The community is, of course, transformed from the days when 'everyone' worked at the pit, yet these ideas of shared knowledges and networks endure. By attuning to the historical roots of these interconnections and how they may be rooted in ideas of shared pasts, it is possible to again perceive the legacies of industrial life that extend beyond that of the physical work into the realm of the social life of the community itself.

Infrastructures and traces of coal as continuity

> 'We start to walk back up the hill towards the baths, the sky is white cold. My breath rises in front of my face. I think about how many times the miners here would have trudged up here, as we would have, but black from coal, and presumably shattered, even wet from working on their bellies in the mine, to get to the baths at the top of this incline A shift-load at a time, the path underneath as muddy as now but with miners boots, heavier than mine, made muddier each day, after each man, Back and forth. . . .
>
> As we walk I notice that the gullies of water that run alongside the paths are orange. I ask Meg why, and she explains it's because of everything that the mines left underground when they shut. The streams run through the old passages, conveying

> the drams, props, rail lines, lift shafts, pulleys and cables that sit entombed in the hillsides out into the fresh air in rusted particles.
>
> (Excerpt from fieldnotes, Walking on the hills around Aberbeeg with Meg, January 2018)

Dawney's (2020) work discusses an example of the legacies of industry in the context of post-atomic communities and the remaining infrastructure. By engaging with similar ideas and other ideas of landscape as fundamentally enrolled in processes of remembering and encountering pasts (Wylie 2005; Hoelscher and Alderman 2004; Jones 2007), it is possible to consider the ways in which mobilities and infrastructures in the Ebbw Fach area can also be understood as instances of continuity for industrial pasts. As I moved through the area, I used footpaths that trace the route of closed railway lines and paths to old industrial hubs that are now absent and demolished. At times, old tram-lines were visible in the undergrowth, long disused. Even the trees that made up dense woodland along the valley sides, as one participant explained to me, were planted for fuel and timber. The rust described in the previous vignette often ran beneath my feet, in the abandoned tunnels.

Many of these routes were once well-travelled, serving as the commute for miners walking between the baths and the pits. I argue that, in keeping with the ideas of Merriman and Jones (2017), that my understanding of these sites was facilitated by being in these spaces; as they state: 'these forces and affects *circulate between* and are only partially *apprehended by* bodies inhabiting and moving through particular spaces and sites' (ibid, 600). Walks with local groups followed similar paths around lakes that were once feeder ponds, yet these histories remained undiscussed within the group.

This again highlights the way in which bodies are enrolled in these continuities, echoing in physical movement how workers would have once moved through the landscape. Even to the bodily sensations of fatigue as I climbed the steep hillsides that Joe talked about: 'the valley and the hills . . . they're the reason the coal was so easy to get down to'. Whilst the mining is now gone, the hills remain. In light of Joe's comment, the relationship between the history of mining and the landscape through which I walk and the miners would walk is continually reinforced. The absent miners and the absent buildings are made only more affectively present as the infrastructure endures.

> Back and forth, they would have walked day after day. Breathy conversations that they would have had together on their walk, on days as cold and damp as this, their breaths as mist, I feel like the silence now is made deafening by their absence.
>
> (Further excerpt from fieldnotes, walking on the hills around Aberbeeg with Meg, January 2018)

Conclusions: troubling the 'Post'-industrial

> "Amy, I was on a train and met some people from the valleys . . . they were ex-miners . . . I was telling them about your research, and one was like 'what's she researching all that stuff about the mines for? They closed years ago' ".
>
> (Quote from a colleague, January 2018)

This chapter has sought to highlight a number of ways in which we can engage with the traces of industrial pasts in the present, rather than relegating the importance of mining and the associated way of life to the past. The previous quote, from a colleague to myself during my fieldwork period, indicates the tendency to assume that meaning and continuities are diminished as the history of mining becomes temporally distant, even from people within these communities. There are many other examples of continuity than those I outline; this is, of course, not an exhaustive discussion, as even in these presented cases it is possible to draw on more traces than are considered in depth here. Working bodies, gender identities, multisensory experiences of landscape, material traces, community practices and performances of belonging can all be interwoven with ideas and constructions of what the area 'was once like' when mining was operational. By engaging with the multiplicity of memory and moments of affective intensity, the temporal binary of industrial pasts and post-industrial presences can be troubled and blurred.

Again, it is not my aim to suggest that these presences diminish the vast changes associated with the decline of the coal industry and the associated ways of life, which are widely reported and discussed in geographical literature. Instead, I argue that attuning to these continuities can expand our understanding of the post-industrial condition and the overlooked vestiges of these pasts that remain pervasive in these areas. Discontinuities can be understood alongside these continuities; the absences and changes are punctuated by that which does remain. By looking beyond museums and formal heritage and engaging with memory in its multiple forms, which ebb and flow yet remain present, we can attempt to understand how these histories endure throughout the everyday lives of those who lived and live within and with legacies of coal mining.

Notes

1 These ideas of affective resonance and intensity draw on theoretical models of affect, based significantly on the work of Deleuze and Guattari (2004 [1987]) and Stewart (2007). Whilst this chapter is not the place to provide an expansive reading on the many conceptualisations of affect – nor its place within heritage work – readers may wish to read the work of Renold and Ivinson on gender, identity and affect (2014), Merriman and Jones (2017) on affect and national identity, Wateron on affect and heritage (2014) and Desilvey on post-industrial mining landscapes (2012) as excellent examples of the application of these ideas in related contexts.

2 Throughout this chapter I refer to the research area as Ebbw Fach. I do not mean to suggest that I have spent equal time in each area of the valley, just that the term is applicable to the areas in which I spent time.
3 The industries that have filled the vacuums of the coal pits in the valleys do not provide the community-defining reach or perceived long-term security of coal mining and other work that typified the 'modern era' (which itself has been studied and debated extensively, see Bauman 2000 on these ideas of security, Strangleman 2007; Milkman 1997 on these trends around industrial work, and Power 2008 specifically on coal mining).
4 Of course many women are also employed at Tillery foods. However, in the interest of continuities, the industrial work of men is most relevant here.
5 This was, of course, not a sentiment that was held universally by the participants and residents I spoke to and spent time with. Many did express a belief that people had become more selfish and less integrated in community life, in keeping with ideas of the 'loss' of community that resulted from deindustrialisation.
6 Drawing on the work of Butler (2013), the term 'performative' is not to suggest any lack of authenticity or falsity to their experience or belief in their own belonging.

References

Alderman, Derek H. 1996. "Street Names and the Scaling of Memory: The Politics of Commemorating Martin Luther King, Jr within the African American Community." *Area* 35 (2): 163–73. doi:10.1111/1475-4762.00250.

Allen, Barbara, and William Lynwood Montell. 1981. *From Memory to History: Using Oral Sources in Local Historical Research*. Nashville, TN: American Association for State and Local History.

Amit, Vered. 2002. *Realizing Community: Concepts, Social Relationships and Sentiments*. London: Routledge.

Atkinson, David. 2007. "Kitsch Geographies and the Everyday Spaces of Social Memory." *Environment and Planning* A 39 (2): 521–40.

Back, Les, and Nirmal Puwar. 2012. "A Manifesto for Live Methods: Provocations and Capacities." *Sociological Review* 60 (1): 6–17. doi:10.1111/j.1467-954X.2012.02114.x.

Bauman, Zygmunt. 2000. *Liquid Modernity*, Cambridge: Polity Press.

Beatty, Christina, and Stephen Fothergill. 1996. "Labour Market Adjustment in Areas of Chronic Industrial Decline: The Case of the UK Coalfields." *Regional Studies* 30 (7): 627–40.

Beatty, Christina, Stephen Fothergill, and Ryan S. Powell. 2007. "Twenty Years on: Has the Economy of the UK Coalfields Recovered?" *Environment and Planning* A 39 (7): 1654–75.

Beck, Ulrich. 1992. *Risk Society: Towards a New Modernity*. Vol. 17. London: Sage.

Bernard, H.R. 2013. *Social Research Methods: Qualitative and Quantitative Approachs*. London: Routledge.

Browne, Brendan Ciaran. 2013. "Recording the Personal: The Benefits in Maintaining Research Diaries for Documenting the Emotional and Practical Challenges of Fieldwork in Unfamiliar Settings." *International Journal of Qualitative Methods* 12 (12): 420–35. https://doi.org/10.1177/160940691301200121.

Buciek, Keld, and Kristine Juul. 2008. 'We Are Here: Yet We Are Not Here': The Heritage of Excluded Groups." In *The Ashgate Research Companion to Heritage and Identity*, edited by B. Graham and P. Howard, 105–23. Aldershot: Ashgate.

Bulmer, Martin. 1975. *Working-Class Images of Society*. London: Routledge. https://doi.org/10.1093/sf/55.2.566.

Burns, Alan, Martin Newby, and Jonathan Winterton. 1985. "The Restructuring of the British Coal Industry." *Cambridge Journal of Economics* 9 (1): 93–110. https://doi.org/10.1093/oxfordjournals.cje.a035568.

Butler, Judith. 2013. *Excitable Speech: A Politics of the Performative. Excitable Speech: A Politics of the Performative*. https://doi.org/10.4324/9780203948682.

Byrne, David. 2002. "Industrial Culture in a Post-Industrial World: The Case of the North East of England." *City* 6 (3): 279–89.

Collins, Peter, and Anselma Gallinat. 2010. "The Ethnographic Self as Resource?" In *The Ethnographic Self as Resource: Writing Memory and Experience into Ethnography*, edited by Peter Collins and Anselma Gallinat, 228–45. New York: Berghahn Books.

Darby, Wendy Joy. 2000. *Landscape and Identity: Geographies of Nation and Class in England*. London: Bloomsbury.

Dawney, Leila. 2020. "Decommissioned Places: Ruins, Endurance and Care at the End of the First Nuclear Age." *Transactions of the Institute of British Geographers* 45 (1): 33–49.

Day, Graham. 2006. *Community and Everyday Life. Community and Everyday Life*. London: Routledge. https://doi.org/10.4324/9780203463178.

Deleuze, Giles, and Felix Guattari. 2004 [1987] *A Thousand Plateaus: Capitalism and Schizophrenia*. Translated by B. Massumi. London: Continuum.

Dennis, Norman, Fernando Henriques, and Clifford Slater. 1969. *Coal Is Our Life: An Analysis of a Yorkshire Mining Community*. 2nd ed. London: Tavistock Publications. https://doi.org/10.2307/2798864.

DeSilvey, Caitlin. 2012. "Copper Places: Affective Circuitries." In *Geography and Memory: Explorations in Identity, Place and Becoming*, edited by Owain Jones and Joanne Garde-Hansen, 45–57. London: Palgrave Macmillan.

Dicks, B. 2000. *Heritage, Place and Community*. Cardiff: University of Wales Press.

Frankenberg, Ronald. 1966. *Communities in Britain: Social Life in Town and Country*. Harmondsworth: Penguin.

Fuchs, Anne. 2002. "Towards an Ethics of Remembering: The Walser-Bubis Debate and the Other of Discourse." *German Quarterly* 75 (3): 235–47.

Halbwachs, Maurice. 1992. *On Collective Memory. The Heritage of Sociology*. Chicago, IL: University of Chicago Press.

Hammersley, Martyn, and Paul Atkinson. 1995. *Ethnography: Principles in Practice*. 2nd ed. London: Routledge.

Harvey, David C. 2001. "Heritage Pasts and Heritage Presents: Temporality, Meaning and the Scope of Heritage Studies." *International Journal of Heritage Studies*. https://doi.org/10.1080/13581650120105534.

———. 2008. "The History of Heritage." In *The Ashgate Research Companion to Heritage and Identity*, edited by B. Graham and P. Howard, 19–36. Aldershot: Ashgate.

Haynes, Kathryn. 2012. "Reflexivity in Qualitative Research." In *Qualitative Organizational Research: Core Methods and Current Challenges*, edited by C. Cassell and G Symon, 72–89. London: Sage.

Hoelscher, Steven, and Derek H. Alderman. 2004. "Memory and Place: Geographies of a Critical Relationship." *Social and Cultural Geography* 5 (3): 347–55. https://doi.org/10.1080/1464936042000252769.

Hoskins, Andrew. 2016. "Memory Ecologies." *Memory Studies* 9 (3): 348–57. https://doi.org/10.1177/1750698016645274.

Hudson, Ray. 1995. *Coming Back Brockens: A Year in a Mining Village*. London: Vintage.

Johnson, Nuala C. 2005. "Locating Memory: Tracing the Trajectories of Remembrance." *Historical Geography* 33: 165–79.

Jones, Owain. 2007. "An Ecology of Emotion, Memory, Self and Landscape." In *Emotional Geographies*, edited by J. Davidson, L. Bondi, and M. Smith, 205–18. London: Routledge.

Krzysztofik, Robert., M. Tkocz, Tomasz Spórna, and I. Iwona Kantor-Pietraga. 2016. "Some Dilemmas of Post-Industrialism in a Region of Traditional Industry: The Case of the Katowice Conurbation, Poland." *Moravian Geographical Reports* 24 (1): 42–54.

Kusenbach, Margarethe. 2003. "Street Phenomenology: The Go-Along as Ethnographic Research Tool." *Ethnography*. https://doi.org/10.1177/146613810343007.

Law, John, and John Urry. 2004. "Enacting the Social." *Economy and Society* 33 (3): 390–410.

Legg, Stephen. 2005. "Contesting and Surviving Memory: Space, Nation and Nostalgia in Les Lieux de Memoire." *Environment and Planning D: Society and Space* 23 (4): 481–504.

Mah, Alice. 2012. *Industrial Ruination, Community, and Place: Landscapes and Legacies of Urban Decline*. Toronto: University of Toronto Press.

Mannay, Dawn, and Morgan, Melanie. 2014. "Doing Ethnography or Applying a Qualitative Technique? Reflections from the 'Waiting Field'." *Qualitative Research*. doi:10.1177/1468794113517391.

Martin, Ron L., and Bob R. Rowthorn. 1986. *Geography of Deindustrialization*. Basingstoke: Palgrave Macmillan.

Merriman, Peter, and Rhys Jones. 2017. "Nations, Materialities and Affects." doi:10.1177/0309132516649453.

Milkman, Ruth. 1997. *Farewell to the Factory: Auto Workers in the Late Twentieth Century*. Los Angeles: University of California Press. https://doi.org/10.2307/3343136.

Nash, Catherine. 2002. "Cultural Geography: Postcolonial Cultural Geographies." https://doi.org/10.1191/0309132502ph365pr.

NOMIS. 2010. Accessed January 23, 2020. www.nomisweb.co.uk/reports/lmp/la/1946157401/printable.aspx.

Nora, Pierre. 1989. "Between Memory and History: Les Lieux de Mémoire." *Representations*. https://doi.org/10.2307/2928520.

Pinder, David. 2003. "Seaport Decline and Cultural Heritage Sustainability Issues in the UK Coastal Zone." *Journal of Cultural Heritage* 4 (1): 35–47. https://doi.org/10.1016/S1296-2074(03)00006-2.

Power, Rosemary. 2008. "'After the Black Gold': A View of Mining Heritage from Coalfield Areas in Britain." https://doi.org/10.1080/00155870802056977.

Price, William R. 2021. "Unearthing Community Identities at the National Coal Mining Museums of Great Britain." In *Geographies of Post-Industrial Place, Memory, and Heritage*, edited by M. Rhodes, W. Price, and A. Walker. Abingdon: Routledge.

Rees, Teresa L. 1978. "Population and Industrial Decline in the South Wales Coalfield." *Regional Studies* 12 (1): 69–77. https://doi.org/10.1080/09595237800185061.

Renold, Emma, and Gabrielle Ivinson. 2014. "Horse-Girl Assemblages: Towards a Post-Human Cartography of Girls' Desire in an Ex-Mining Valleys Community." *Discourse: Studies in the Cultural Politics of Education* 35 (3): 361–76.

Rhodes, M. 2021. "Amgueddfa'r Gogledd: Slate, slavery, and transatlantic labor in the National Slate Museum." In *Geographies of Post-Industrial Place, Memory, and Heritage*, edited by M. Rhodes, W. Price, and A. Walker. Abingdon: Routledge.

Samuel, Raphael, Barbara Bloomfield, and Guy Boanas. 1986. *The Enemy Within: Pit Villages and the Miners' Strike of 1984–85*. London: Routledge.

Selway, David. 2016. "Death Underground: Mining Accidents and Memory in South Wales, 1913–74." *Labour History Review* 81 (3): 187–209. doi:10.3828/lhr.2016.10.

Stebbins, Robert A. 1991. "Do We Ever Leave the Field? Notes on Secondary Fieldwork Involvements." In *Experiencing Fieldwork: An Inside of Qualitative Research*, edited by W. Shaffir and R. Stebbins, 248–55. London: Sage.

Stewart, Kathleen. 2007. *Ordinary Affects*. London: Duke University Press. https://doi.org/10.1215/9780822390404-001.

Storm, A., 2014. *Post-Industrial Landscape Scars*. Aldershot: Palgrave Macmillan.

Strangleman, Tim. 2007. *The Nostalgia for Permanence at Work? The End of Work and Its Commentators Introduction-an End of Work?The Sociological Review* 55 (1): 81–103.

Strangleman, Tim, and James Rhodes. 2014. "The 'New' Sociology of Deindustrialisation? Understanding Industrial Change." *Sociology Compass* 8 (4): 411–21. https://doi.org/10.1111/soc4.12143.

Terranova-Webb, Ariel. 2012. "Moving through Memory: Notes from a Circus Lot." In *Geography and Memory: Explorations in Identity, Place and Becoming*, edited by O. Jones and J. Garde-Hansen, 199–215. New York: Palgrave Macmillan.

Trivelli, Elena. 2016. "Exploring a 'Remembering Crisis': 'Affective Attuning' and 'Assemblaged Archive' as Theoretical Frameworks and Research Methodologies." In *Affective Methodologies: Developing Cultural Research Strategies for the Study of Affect*, edited by Britta Timm Knudsen and Carsten Stage, 119–39. https://doi.org/10.1057/9781137483195_6.

Turner, Royce. 2000. *Coal Was Our Life: An Essay on Life in a Yorkshire Former Pit Town*. Sheffield: Sheffield Hallam University Press.

Walkerdine, Valerie, and Luis Jimenez. 2012. *Gender, Work and Community After De-Industrialisation*. *Gender, Work and Community After De-Industrialisation*. Basingstoke: Palgrave Macmillan. https://doi.org/10.1057/9780230359192.

Warwick, Dennis, and Gary Littlejohn. 1992. *Coal, Capital and Culture: A Sociological Analysis of Mining Communities in West Yorkshire*. London: Routledge.

Waterston, Alisse, and Barbara Rylko-Bauer. 2006. "Out of the Shadows of History and Memory: Personal Family Narratives in Ethnographies of Rediscovery." *American Ethnologist* 33 (3): 397–412. doi:10.1525/ae.2006.33.3.397.

Waterton, Emma. 2014. "A More-Than-Representational Understanding of Heritage? The 'Past' and the Politics of Affect." *Geography Compass* 8 (11): 823–33.

Westergaard, John. 1975. "Radical Class Consciousness: A Comment." In *Working Class Images of Society*, edited by M. Bulmer. London: Routledge and Kegan Paul.

Wylie, John. 2005. "A Single Day's Walking: Narrating Self and Landscape on the South West Coast Path." *Transactions of the Institute of British Geographers* 30 (2): 234–47 https://doi.org/10.1111/j.1475-5661.2005.00163.x.

Part 2

Post-industrial working landscapes

5 Unearthing community identities at the National Coal Mining Museums of Great Britain

William R. Price

A century ago, Great Britain was the world's largest producer and exporter of coal. "Black Gold," as the resource was nicknamed, was an essential driver of the Industrial Revolution that vaulted Britain to the dominant political and economic force of the nineteenth and early twentieth centuries. Coal fueled iron and steel factories; powered trains, ships, and steam engines; and provided the energy to keep Britons' homes warm during the winter. For these and many other reasons, the resource was a cornerstone of the British Empire.

Successive generations of Britons were dependent on coal mines for their livelihoods. In addition to thousands directly employed at the pits, many businesses provided services to miners and their families, as well as the mines. The mines formed the basis for communities' social and political lives, providing the impetus for celebrations, sports leagues, and education. Many communities fiercely resisted the rapid closure of collieries between the 1960s and 1990s, with Wales and Scotland for a time becoming synonymous with union actions.

The days of "King Coal" in Great Britain are gone. In 2015, the last deep pit coal mine in the island closed, and in 2019 Britain had its first week since the 1880s without any power in the country provided by coal (Arnold 2018; BBC 2019). The decline of coal mining led to immense changes to the communities that grew based on the resource extraction (c.f. Walker 2021, this collection). Many communities have experienced prolonged periods of economic and demographic decline ever since.

Reflecting the significance of coal to the heritage of Great Britain, national museums preserve the legacy of the resource. This chapter investigates representation of the wider social impacts of coal within and across Wales' Big Pit National Coal Museum (hereafter Big Pit), National Mining Museum Scotland (NMMS), and National Coal Mining Museum for England (NCMME). As arguably the most prominent faces of the once regionally dominant industry, these museums play an essential role in influencing memories of coal and associated communities in present and future generations (see Figure 5.1).

Industrial heritage tourism in Great Britain

Great Britain has been a leading destination for industrial heritage tourism since the 1950s. Attractions rooted in former factories, mines, railroads, canals, and other tangible and intangible aspects of industrial heritage exist across the island

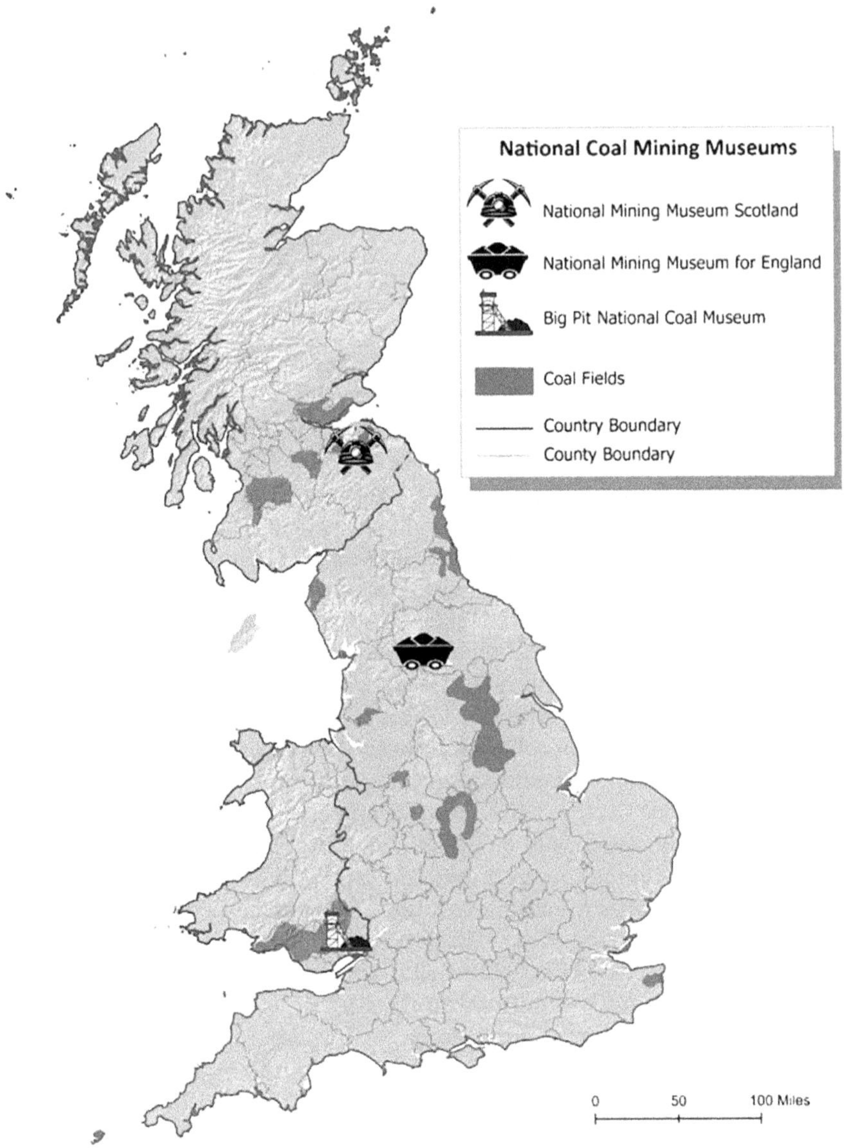

Figure 5.1 Map of British coal fields and research sites

Source: Reuben Allen

(Goodall 1993; Edwards and Llurdes i Coit 1996; Beeho and Prentice 1997; Cole 2004; Palmer, Nevell, and Sissons 2012). Industrial heritage tourism is part of the larger cultural heritage tourism product that serves as a key driver of tourism demand to the island (Hooper 2016).

Wales is among the most researched areas regarding industrial heritage tourism. Attractions in the coal valleys of South Wales have been investigated for tourist motivations (Prentice, Witt, and Hamer 1993), tourist typologies (Prentice, Witt, and Hamer 1998), interpretation and authenticity (Pitchford 1995; Dicks 2003; 2008), and development (Edwards and Llurdes i Coit 1996; Powell, Thomas, and Thomas 2011), with Big Pit a primary study arena (e.g., Light and Prentice 1994; Wanhill 2000; Coupland and Coupland 2014; Price and Rhodes 2020). The slate quarries of North Wales have also been a focus of research (Wanhill 2000; Price and Ronck 2019), as highlighted by Rhodes' (2021) chapter on the National Slate Museum in this collection. In England, the most researched area has been the former tin mines of Cornwall (Hale 2001; Coupland and Coupland 2014). Griffin (2006) analyzed the National Coal Mining Museum of England regarding the interpretation of labor history. To date, industrial heritage tourism in Scotland has received comparatively little scholarly attention, with a concentration on the development of tourism resources (Oglethorpe 1987; Ewing 1989; Lennon 2016) and New Lanark (Beeho and Prentice 1997). No known prior studies have compared the interpretations presented at the three national coal mining museums.

Tourism attractions have the potential to shape the perceptions that visitors hold toward the associated industries (Barthel 1996; Dicks 2008). Hence, interpretation is challenging to design and frequently contested within communities (Xie 2015). For some tourists, the attractions may be their only source of information about the industry. The perceived authenticity of attractions, with displays often rooted in equipment, buildings, and tour guides directly linked to industry, is conducive to visitor engagement with the interpretation (Coupland and Coupland 2014). This impact on perception is particularly relevant to the analyzed coal mining attractions, which also carry the legitimacy ascribed to nationally endorsed museums (Kaplan 1994). Museums play an important role in reinforcing the "imagined community" at the heart of national identity, providing unifying narratives that connect people of diverse backgrounds (Anderson 2006).

Big Pit is the most visited of the coal mining attractions in Wales, while the other two coal museums of interest are the only museums in England and Scotland that are located at former collieries. With free admission, access to government funds, and a large collection of infrastructure and artifacts, the national coal mining museums are prominent industrial heritage tourism attractions within Great Britain.

Methods

To gather the necessary qualitative data for this research, fieldwork was conducted between 2017 and 2019 at the following sites (see Table 5.1):

Big Pit was a working mine from 1860 to 1980, opening as the Welsh national museum in 1983. NMMS was founded in 1984 at the Lady Victoria Colliery, which ceased operation in 1981. NCMME opened in 1988 at the site of the Caphouse and adjoining Hope collieries, which closed in 1985. The museums have buildings expressly created to accommodate exhibit space and former mine infrastructures adapted for visitors. Big Pit and NCMME provide visitors the opportunity

Table 5.1 Fieldwork sites (visitation data provided by National Museum Wales and the annual reports for NMMS and NCMME)

Industrial Attraction	*Location*	*Visitation (2018–2019)*
Big Pit National Coal Museum (Big Pit)	Blaenavon, Wales	149,000
National Mining Museum Scotland (NMMS)	Newtongrange, Scotland	48,000
National Coal Mining Museum for England (NCMME)	Overton, England	111,000

to descend underground with ex-miner tour guides. Notably for this collection, many of the tour guides at Big Pit were previously employed in the collieries in and around Abertillery and Six Bells, the communities discussed in Walker's (2021) chapter. NMMS gives tourists the option of accompanying an ex-miner tour guide on a walk through the colliery surface facilities or a self-led tour with an audio guide.

All interpretive content at the museums was documented using a camera and field notes. The interpretation at the museums primarily encompasses informational signs, pictures, videos, artifacts, hands on displays, and tours. Information presented by the live and audio guides was documented immediately at the end of the tours to aid recollection of the presented content. At the conclusion of the fieldwork sessions, the pictures and field notes were converted into a systematic account of the interpretive content of each museum.

Interpretive content in the museums was evaluated using a discourse analysis methodology (Dunn and Neumann 2016; Hay 2016). Rooted in a postmodern perspective, discourse analyses involve identification of common uses of language and representation within texts and other forms of media such as photographs, videos, and artifacts. Discourse analysis is based on the presumption that there is no single, objective way to represent knowledge. Humans frame knowledge in a way that coincides with, or reinforces, their objectives or worldviews; these different representations are referred to as *discourses*. In a discourse analysis, the researcher seeks to identify how knowledge is being characterized and to what purpose. Acknowledging researchers' positionality is an important aspect of postmodern research; identification of discourses was influenced by my perspective as a tourism geographer with personal connections to both England and Wales.

When studying interpretation, the identification of discourse involves looking for recurring themes across media and museums – referred to as intertextuality (Fairclough 1992) – and areas where the provided content is conspicuously absent on certain issues, termed discursive silences (Rose 2016). The spatial organization of attractions is also an indicator of narrative prioritization (Azaryahu and Foote 2008). Given the scope of this study, only information related to community-scale impacts in the interpretation and discursive themes that were common across all museums are included in the analysis. There remain many possibilities for future research projects comparing different aspects of interpretation at the museums.

Interpretive discourses at the national coal museums

In the investigation of the interpretation at the national coal mining museums, four primary discourses concerning the social impacts of coal are identified. This section discusses these discourses in depth, drawing on examples from the museums.

Economic benefits of coal

Among the most prominent discourses across the interpretation is a demonstration of the economic importance of coal to Great Britain during and after the Industrial Revolution. As highlighted in the museums, for the better part of two centuries, coal was central to the economies of large areas of England, Wales, and Scotland. NCMME notes in a sign on "The Coal Revolution," that "by 1913 national output had reached 290 million tonnes and over 1.1 million workers were employed in the industry." Large mines employed several thousand people and numerous businesses relied on providing services to mines and the miners and their families. As the Big Pit alludes with the interpretive sign entitled "Klondyke Cymru,"[1] referencing the famous nineteenth-century gold rush in northwest Canada, the coal boom had a profound economic influence.

Tellingly, the first room in the main exhibit at NCMME is largely devoted to explaining the economic consequences of coal. Large figures on the wall display the declining total production of coal, coal mining jobs, and the number of mines between 1913 and 2016. Visitors see the outcomes of the disappearance of coal mining with, for example, a graph showing the decline of employment from 1.1 million in 1913 to 0 in 2016.

The national museums present the numerous occupations associated with collieries. At Big Pit, interpretive signs throughout the museum explain positions such as safety officer, shotsman, haulier, and engineer that were necessary for the functioning of the mine. The museums in England and Scotland likewise describe numerous occupations in primary interpretive displays corresponding to machines and buildings throughout the complexes. At all museums, the ex-miner guides describe their roles in the mines and the essential jobs needed for the mine to function.

Large displays at each museum are devoted to explaining the role of women and children. In the early Victorian Era, coal mining was a family affair; wives and children assisted the husband miner as he worked the coalface. Women were primarily responsible for transporting the coal, while children minded the ventilation doors that led to the coalfaces. At each museum, firsthand accounts collected during an 1840 Royal Commission tell the horrors of the working conditions, with early miners compared several times to slaves at NMMS. This Royal Commission would lead to the banning of women and small children from mines in 1842; an outcome not universally celebrated by communities, with families deprived of a portion of their income. Underground, ponies and succeeding transportation technology largely replaced women, but they continued to work on the surface. As noted at

NCMME, the law forbade women to mine underground in the country until passage of the *Employment Act of 1989*.

The museums consider the end of coal mining in Great Britain through different lenses. NMMS recognizes that the "subject is still fiercely debated with no neat historical perspective." A display at Big Pit concerning "The Reasons Why" argues that: "British mines were the most economic in Europe. But despite this, and unprecedented public protests, the closures were carried out pit by pit." Numerous interpretive signs at Big Pit point out that the closure of pits in Wales led to the loss of 20,000 jobs. NCMME explains "The End of Mining" as a result of advancements in other forms of energy generation and increased government emphasis on environmental protection. At NMMS, the explanation is also primarily economics: "competition from abroad was a chief reason for the decline, as were efforts to find cleaner ways of generating electricity." Big Pit presents the decision to close mines as a political rather than economic one, assigning blame to the Conservative political party (led by Prime Minister Margaret Thatcher) that controlled Great Britain during the era of peak mine closures in the 1980s. As Wales was the most actively unionized mining region (Curtis 2013), this emphasis is expected.

The fates of former mining communities are painted in unflattering terms. NCMME describes how, "although there have been coalfield regeneration schemes, business developments, new jobs and retraining, many miners and their families have experienced deprivation and poverty." Considering the aftermath of the 1981 closure of the Lady Victoria colliery, the NMMS states "the homes were boarded up, people left to find other work, shops closed, and empty houses were infested with rats."

Significantly, the final message of the Big Pit's main display is a large wall covered with the names of closed Welsh collieries below the words "We'll be Back." This proclamation underscores a belief clung to by many communities that the mines will one day reopen, and the economic prosperity will be returned. This perspective also discursively privileges jobs and income generated by industry over those created by other sectors in the aftermath of mine closure; economic activities that may be more accessible to wider segments of the population than male-dominated coal mines (Oberhauser et al. 2017).

Coal mining communities

The museums prominently demonstrate the role of coal mines in shaping their associated communities. At Big Pit, a section of the museum is devoted to the "People of Coal." Interpretive material lays out the different aspects of life in the coal communities, from education, religion, and leisure, to hardship. In a panel on "Coal Communities," NCMME argues, "Coalmining was always more than just a job – it took miners and their families from the cradle to the *grave*" (emphasis added).

The museums effectively illustrate the impact of coal mines on infrastructure development across geographic scales. Given the remote, rural location of many mines, owners often created the community foundations, including miners' houses, stores, schools, and roads. The development of such "company towns" was commonly associated with coal, as owners sought to ensure that miners' wages were spent at other company holdings, thereby maximizing their profits (Freese 2003). NMMS places the most emphasis on the link between coal mining communities and their wider regions; displays discuss the creation of barge networks and railways to carry the coal to cities and ports.

As Big Pit argues, "as each coal mine was developed a vibrant community grew around it." Interpretation and a model village at Big Pit illustrate the structures found in the archetypical coal mining community, including terraced housing, stores, churches, public houses, schools, roads, police stations, and Workmen's Institutes. Recognition of the wider influence of coal mines was a primary reason behind the inscription of the Blaenavon Industrial Landscape – of which Big Pit is an important component – on the UNESCO World Heritage List in 2000, as well as other heritage designated industrial regions (Palmer, Nevell, and Sissons 2012). A laminate at NMMS entitled "Miners Housing" describes the development of the company owned Newtongrange community that surrounds the museum, while a stop on the guided tour allows visitors to glimpse the landscape of the town for themselves. All museums incorporate numerous pictures showing the different buildings that comprised mining communities, and NMMS and NCMME have recreated miners' houses for visitors to inspect (see Figure 5.2)

Figure 5.2 Representation of a miners' home at National Coal Mining Museum for England
Source: William R. Price

The museums discuss creation of the Miners' Welfare Fund in 1920 at length. In addition to improvements at the mines themselves, such as pithead baths, medical facilities, and canteens, funds were invested in the communities. As described in a sign on "Colliery Welfare" at NCMME:

> the Miners' Welfare Fund was financed from a levy made on all saleable coal. The money was used for 'purposes connected with the social well-being, recreation and conditions or living for workers in or about coal mines, and with mining education and research.'

The museums cite the creation of diverse amenities including community halls, recreation facilities, convalescent homes, and holiday camps. After Nationalisation, responsibility for miner welfare transferred to the Coal Industry Social Welfare Organisation, which continues in operation, aiding ex-coal miners and their families.

The opportunities generated by coal mines and the supporting service industries made them beacons for migration from within and outside of Great Britain. The cultures, impacts, and challenges associated with immigrants are a noteworthy aspect of interpretation at the museums. The most prominent such representation is at NCMME, which notes in a display accompanied by pictures and Caribbean flags that:

> After World War II there was a shortage of workers in the UK and many Afro Caribbean men emigrated from the West Indies. These men had no experience of deep coal mining and many experienced discrimination and racism including pay variation, negative references to skin colour and refusal to wash their backs in the showers.

NMMS describes the arrival of Irish and Lithuanian immigrants in search of opportunity and the prejudice they faced from the mining communities.

Coal mines served as the basis of numerous social activities. A prominent example mentioned by the museums are the gala days, during which parades, speeches, and assorted entertainment would take place for families. A center point of the gala days, as described in all museums, was the crowning of Coal Queens. As NCMME explains in a detailed display accompanied with pictures and a tiara, a National Coal Queen competition was held from 1969–1983, with all competitors coming from coal mining families. Some former mining communities in Great Britain continue to hold galas, a strong testament to their place in the annual social calendar. The annual Durham Miners' Gala in England, for example, is attended by more than 100,000 visitors. NCMME describes the significance of colliery brass bands in several displays. The museum notes the wider recognition of the bands' importance to community identity with mentions of "Brassed Off!," a 1996 movie about a fictionalized band inspired by Grimethorpe colliery band in Yorkshire. NMMS also recounts the role of colliery bands in parades and gala days.

As described in the museums, sports formed the heart of leisure time in mining communities. Football (soccer), cricket, and rugby were important team sports, and the museums note the fervor with which the public cheered on favorite teams and players from among the miners. NCMME describes the role of "The Beautiful Game":

> Football was well established in mining communities before the Football Association (FA) accepted rules were implemented in 1863. As a team sport it was suited to miners who were used to working as a team underground. Institutes often used to set up football clubs and were able to provide the space for the pitches.

Activities such as quoits, fishing, and bicycling were also popular. Regional differences are evident in the museums, with Bit Pit identifying several champion boxers from among the Welsh miners and NMMS discussing miners' passion for pigeon racing.

The museums lament the loss of the coal mining communities and landscapes, highlighting the disappearance of pitheads and rows of terraced housing. Though some communities continue the traditions begun during the mining era, much of the associated culture has been lost. At Big Pit, the coal miners' lamp is likened to the Scottish thistle, serving as a symbol of national identity that recalls a past remembered but gone.

Coal mining tragedies

The many dangers associated with coal mining are a recurrent interpretive thread woven through the museums. Interpretive signs, displays, and photographs tell the harm of roof falls, suffocation, fire, and injury. Being located at former collieries, the museums explain the connections between machines and buildings and the technology intended to improve safety, such as roof supports, pump houses, and ventilation. A laminate called "Death's Steady Toll" at Big Pit highlights that "the annual death toll in British mines did not drop below 100 until the 1970s." The long-term adverse health consequences of coal mining, born from years of working in darkness, the deafening noise of cutters, and the daily inhalation of coal dust are described in depth. While weight is placed on the threats facing miners, the museums make it clear that the scale of the associated impacts stretched far beyond the individual. Each museum is replete with stories of community tragedy.

Though only a relatively small percentage of overall coal mining deaths occurred in large-scale accidents, it was these that would capture public attention and linger in the memories of impacted communities. NMMS describes the devastation of mining accidents in a sign on "Disaster and the Community":

> When the siren blew to indicate a disaster, people converged on the pit in great numbers. Men willingly volunteered to assist in the rescue, but women

> and children were stranded between agony and hope. To have loved ones in peril, not far away, but underground and out of reach, was terrible.

To portray the scale of loss, each museum contains multiple timelines that identify major mining accidents, associated causes, and the number of lives lost. Yet, the museums do not lose themselves in these numbers, also striving to bring the personal scale of these accidents home to the visitor. Big Pit accomplishes this personalization with objects associated with individuals lost in these incidents, while at NCMME quotes of associated individuals and poetry add poignancy.

To further illustrate the wide-reaching impacts of the mining tragedies, each museum tells stories concerning the most prominent accidents from each of their respective countries. Big Pit gives most attention to the horrific accident at the mining community of Aberfan in a dedicated display:

> On 21st October 1966, 116 children died when an avalanche of waste from a colliery tip buried part of the village of Aberfan. Torrential rain brought the tip down onto several buildings. The waste engulfed Pantglas Junior School, where morning lessons had just begun. Most of the victims were children or teachers at the school. 144 people were killed, with a further 28 children and 6 adults seriously injured.

Big Pit also incorporates nearby displays on the 1877 flooding at Tynewydd that resulted in five deaths and a heroic rescue and the 1913 Senghenydd explosion that claimed the lives of 439, the deadliest mining accident in British history. At NCMME, the most discussed tragedy is that which occurred at Hartley Colliery in 1862. Despite a valiant rescue effort, 204 people died, predominantly from carbon monoxide poisoning.

At NCMME and NMMS, memorials are specifically included in the museum design. NCMME incorporates both a small memorial garden and the Kellingley Colliery Miners Memorial with a plaque to 17 individuals that died between 1960 and 2011. At NMMS, the National Mining Memorial Centre houses a poignant gallery of photographs showing mining memorials from throughout the country.

Unionism and political identity

A major interpretive theme across the museums is the important role of unionism in the history and identity of mining regions in Great Britain. Big Pit and NMMS place great symbolic emphasis on unions, devoting the last rooms of their primary exhibit spaces to the discussion of unions. NCMME discusses unions, but they are not given privilege of placement; associated displays are interspersed among other exhibits or isolated in less trafficked areas of the museum.

In the museums, the peak of coal mining is linked with the Miners Federation of Great Britain ("The Fed"), founded in 1889 and soon thereafter reaching unprecedented influence. As noted in a designated sign at Big Pit, "In 1914 'The Fed' was the largest single trade union in Britain, with 200,000 members." Big Pit describes the poor conditions facing miners prior to unionization and their struggles to affect meaningful concessions from coal owners over many decades of isolated efforts. All museums clearly explain the primary ambitions of "The Fed": increased wages, improved safety, and care for miners and their families in times of adversity. The successes and failures of "The Fed" are considered, including the swift decline in membership following a failed 1926 labor action.

Following Nationalisation, "The Fed" was replaced by the National Union of Mineworkers (NUM) in 1945. NMMS argues, "Miners fought for it (Nationalisation) in the 1945 General Election," eager to divorce control of the mines from coal owners viewed as self-serving. As the Big Pit points out in a sign titled "On Behalf of the People," Nationalisation was accompanied by improvements in equipment and safety implemented by the newly formed National Coal Board (NCB). However, the declining fortunes of coal would result in the beginning of government endorsed pit closures from the 1960s.

The museums all provide descriptions and timelines of labor victories and defeats, with narratives complemented by photographs and artifacts such as strike pins and banners. Discussions consider labor actions of, for example, 1912, 1926, 1972, and 1974, but the largest amount of related interpretive content is devoted to the Strike of 1984–1985; each museum has a labeled display that describes the causes, events, and outcome of the strike. NUM leadership called the 1984–1985 strike after the NCB announced the planned closure of 20 pits. The British government had prepared long in advance for the strike, stockpiling large reserves of coal. After a year without pay, coal miners returned to work with no concessions from the government. With the strength of the NUM broken, the British government proceeded with an accelerated policy of pit closures, resulting in the end of the coal industry.

The museums strongly assert the support given by communities to the striking miners, highlighting picket lines, soup kitchens, and many other actions. The important role played by women is also a central aspect to the interpretation. All museums display pictures of women participating in protest marches during the 1984–1985 strike, providing a strong illustration of their vital role in advocating for coal miners. A central idea presented at Big Pit is that coal strikes provided many women with their first opportunity to participate in politics.

The title of the exhibit space at Big Pit references the challenges of representing labor issues that remain controversial in former mining regions: "Heroes or Villains?" Unions were deeply intertwined in the rise and fall of coal mining. Big Pit presents differing opinions on closures via a panel of quotes from former miners, some mourning the loss of jobs and identity, others happy to leave the life of a miner behind. Interestingly, NCMME points out several times across the exhibits that NUM never held a national ballot of members to approve the strike. The museum notes that in "the bitter divisions of that time still linger, with resentment enduring to the present day," going on to say that "the time has come to face up to these divisions, and to try and avoid the paralyzing chasm that exists between and within communities continuing into the future." This distinct reconciliatory and apologetic tone for those who opposed or broke the strike early is singular to the English museum.

Conclusion

The national coal mining museums of England, Wales, and Scotland share four principal interpretive themes regarding the social impacts of the resource: economic benefits of coal, coal mining communities, coal mining tragedies, and unionism and political identity.

The most emphasized social impacts of coal across the museums are the benefits of mining. The museums laud coal for the comparative economic prosperity that it represents, with a spotlight on job generation. The accompanying discussions of the ongoing struggles facing former mining communities serve to reinforce this message. The central part that coal played in community building and fostering shared identity is stressed, with all museums describing the creation of infrastructure, the cohesion produced by galas, and the benefits of the Miners' Welfare Fund. This focus may be construed as aligning with the interests of those wishing for a return of coal mining to Great Britain, consistent with previous research observing emphasis on positive impacts in industrial tourism interpretation (Rudd and Davis 1998; Price and Ronck 2018).

Displays on tragedies caused by coal mining accidents are among the most poignant in the museums, with interpretation including artifacts associated with victims and personal accounts. The museums emphasize these tragedies, in part, for the role they played in uniting the affected communities. Yet, importantly, the museums acknowledge that mining communities were not harmonious to all residents, with references to discrimination faced by immigrant miners. All museums also reference the deep divisions that continue to exist within mining communities due to the 1984–1985 strike and the resultant difficulty in interpreting that chapter of mining history in a way that will appease all visitors

Though most interpretive focus is shared across the museums, there are several noteworthy differences. Perhaps most significant is the contrasting approach used to tell the story of union activity. In Wales and Scotland, the interpretation and representation of unions has discursive priority, being the final exhibits in the narrative space of the museums. The focus at Big Pit is on the unjust closure of the coal mines and the possibility of a return; in NCMME, signs call for reconciliation within the communities and a common path forward. It is noteworthy too that only Big Pit expressly draws a link between coal mining and national identity, submitting the miners' lamp as an icon for Wales.

Note

1 Cymru is the name for the country of Wales in the Welsh language.

References

Anderson, B. 2006. *Imagined Communities: Reflections on the Origin and Spread of Nationalism*. New York: Verso.

Arnold, J. 2018. "'Like Being on Death Row': Britain and the End of Coal, c. 1970 to the Present." *Contemporary British History* 32 (1): 1–17.

Azaryahu, M., and K.E. Foote. 2008. "Historical Space as Narrative Medium: On the Configuration of Spatial Narratives of Time at Historical Sites." *Geojournal* 73: 179–94.

Barthel, D. 1996. "Getting in Touch with History: The Role of Historic Preservation in Shaping Collective Memories." *Qualitative Sociology* 19: 345–64.

BBC. 2019. "Britain Goes a Week without Coal Power for the First Time Since the Industrial Revolution." May 8. www.bbc.co.uk/newsround/48190269.

Beeho, A.J., and R.C. Prentice. 1997. "Conceptualizing the Experiences of Heritage Tourists: A Case Study of New Lanark World Heritage Village." *Tourism Management* 18 (2): 75–87.

Cole, D. 2004. "Exploring the Sustainability of Mining Heritage Tourism." *Journal of Sustainable Tourism* 12 (6): 480–94.

Coupland, B., and N. Coupland. 2014. "The Authenticating Discourse of Mining Heritage Tourism in Cornwall and Wales." *Journal of Sociolinguistics* 18: 495–517.

Curtis, B. 2013. *The South Wales Miners: 1964–1985*. Cardiff: University of Wales Press.

Dicks, B. 2003. "Heritage, Governance and Marketization: A Case-study from Wales." *Museum & Society* 1 (1): 30–44.

———. 2008. "Performing the Hidden Injuries of Class in Coal-Mining Heritage." *Sociology* 42 (3): 436–52.

Dunn, K.C., and I.B. Neumann. 2016. *Undertaking Discourse Analysis for Social Research*. Ann Arbor: University of Michigan Press.

Edwards, J., and J.C. Llurdes i Coit. 1996. "Mines and Quarries. Industrial Heritage Tourism." *Annals of Tourism Research* 23 (2): 341–63.

Ewing, R.G. 1989. "Industrial Museums in Scotland: Development and Prospects." *Scottish Geographical Magazine* 105 (3): 178–81.

Fairclough, N. 1992. *Discourse and Social Change*. Malden, MA: Polity Press.

Freese, B. 2003. *Coal: A Human History*. New York: Basic Books.

Goodall, B. 1993. "Industrial Heritage and Tourism." *Built Environment* 19: 92–104.

Griffin, C. 2006. "'Instead of Manufacturing Goods, We Are Manufacturing Heritage': The National Coalmining Museum for England." *Labour History Review* 71 (3): 289–302.

Hale, A. 2001. "Representing the Cornish: Contesting Heritage Interpretation in Cornwall." *Tourist Studies* 1 (2): 185–96.

Hay, I. 2016. *Qualitative Research Methods in Geography*. 4th ed. Oxford: Oxford University Press.

Hooper, G., ed. 2016. *Heritage and Tourism in Britain and Ireland*. London: Palgrave Macmillan.

Kaplan, F.S., ed. 1994. *Museums and the Making of "Ourselves": The Role of Objects in National Identity*. London: Leicester University Press.

Lennon, J.J. 2016. "Transforming Waterways: The Tourism-Based Regeneration of Canals in Scotland." In *Heritage and Tourism in Britain and Ireland*, edited by G. Hooper, 85–97. London: Palgrave Macmillan.

Light, D., and R.C. Prentice. 1994. "Market-Based Product Development in Heritage Tourism." *Tourism Management* 15 (1): 27–36.

Oberhauser, A.M., J.L. Fluri, R. Whitson, and S. Mollett, eds. 2017. *Feminist Spaces: Gender and Geography in a Global Context*. New York: Routledge.
Oglethorpe, M.K. 1987. "Tourism and industrial Scotland." *Tourism Management* 8 (3): 268–71.
Palmer, M., M. Nevell, and M. Sissons. 2012. *Industrial Archaeology: A Handbook*. New York: Council for British Archaeology.
Pitchford, S.R. 1995. "Ethnic Tourism and Nationalism in Wales." *Annals of Tourism Research 22* (1): 35–52.
Powell, L., S. Thomas, and B. Thomas. 2011. "Innovation and Heritage Entrepreneurship Development in the South Wales Valleys." *Annals of Innovation & Entrepreneurship* 2 (1): 7371.
Prentice, R.C., S.F. Witt, and C. Hamer. 1993. "The Experience of Industrial Heritage: The Case of Black Gold." *Built Environment* 19 (2): 137–46.
———. 1998. "Tourism as Experience: The Case of Heritage Parks." *Annals of Tourism Research* 25 (1): 1–24.
Price, W.R., and M.A. Rhodes. 2020. "Coal Dust in the Wind: Interpreting the Industrial Past of South Wales." *Tourism Geographies*. DOI: 10.1080/14616688.2020.1801825.
Price, W.R., and C.L. Ronck. 2018. Gushing about Black Gold: Oil and Natural Gas Tourism in Texas. *Journal of Heritage Tourism* 13 (5): 440–54.
———. 2019. "Quarrying for World Heritage Designation: Slate Tourism in North Wales." *Geoheritage* 11 (4): 1839–54.
Rhodes, M. 2021. "Amgueddfa'r Gogledd: Slate, slavery, and transatlantic labor in the National Slate Museum." In *Geographies of Post-Industrial Place, Memory, and Heritage*, edited by M. Rhodes, W. Price, and A. Walker. Abingdon: Routledge.
Rose, G. 2016. *Visual Methodologies: An Introduction to Researching with Visual Materials*. London: Sage.
Rudd, M.A., and J.A. Davis. 1998. "Industrial Heritage Tourism at the Bingham Canyon Copper Mine." *Journal of Travel Research* 36: 85–89.
Walker, A. 2021. "Everyday Resonances of Industrial Pasts: Considering Lived and Affective Memories in Ex-Coal Mining Landscapes in a South Wales Valley." In *Geographies of Post-Industrial Place, Memory, and Heritage*, edited by M. Rhodes, W. Price, and A. Walker. Abingdon: Routledge.
Wanhill, S. 2000. "Mines – A Tourist Attraction: Coal Mining in Industrial South Wales." *Journal of Travel Research* 39: 60–69.
Xie, P.F. 2015. *Industrial Heritage Tourism*. Toronto: Channel View Publications.

6 Contamination as artifact

Waste and the presence of absence at the Trout Lake concentrator, Coleraine, Minnesota

John Baeten

How does the world's largest iron ore concentrator become invisible and forgotten? From 1910 to 1960, the Trout Lake concentrator operated as the world's largest iron ore processing plant, churning out more than 160-million tons of iron ore concentrates and paving the way for other iron ore concentrating plants throughout the Lake Superior Iron Mining District. Despite the Trout Lake concentrator's historical importance, the legacy of the facility has faded from memory, owing to both post-mining reclamation coupled with an absence of heritage recognition. Today there is a tussock-filled meadow where the concentrator once stood, and to both untrained and trained eyes, there are nary signs of the massive industrial facility that once operated there (see Figure 6.1). However, while the Trout Lake concentrator remains visually absent from this landscape, its legacy remains present on-site, found in the abundance of mine waste dwelling both above and below the surface. This chapter explores how the legacy of an internationally important industrial site can become lost to history and how we might once again discover it. To reestablish the site's historical and cultural importance, I first develop a theoretical approach, *contamination as artifact*, a materialist perspective that extends the spatiotemporal framework in which post-industrial sites are framed and expands the focus of industrial heritage scholarship that has been overwhelmingly centered on technological and economic nostalgia. Next, I utilize a methodological approach developed in Historical Geospatial Information Systems (HGIS) to both uncover the environmental legacies that remain at the site and as a tool to articulate these findings to the public through the use of story maps.

The Mesabi Iron Range and washable ore technologies

The iron mines of the Lake Superior district have been the United States' principle source of iron ore since the 1890s, and among these, the Mesabi Range has been the most productive. Situated on the south shore of Lake Superior in Northern Minnesota, the Mesabi Iron Range was North America's most important source of iron ore (See Figure 6.2). From 1893 to the present, Minnesota's iron mines have yielded economic benefits at both local and national scales – evident in jobs, schools, and commercial opportunities for Mesabi Range communities and the

Figure 6.1 Overview of site
Source: John Baeten

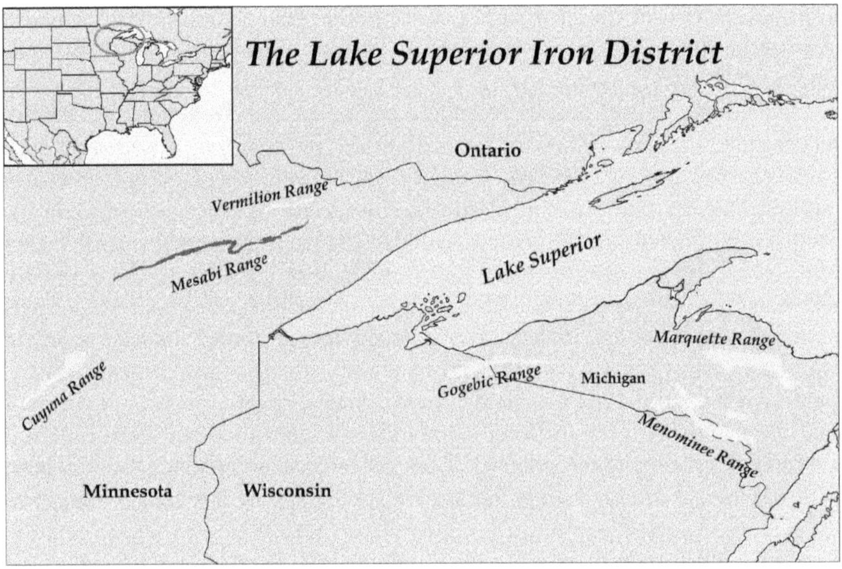

Figure 6.2 Overview of study area
Source: John Baeten

abundance of steel used throughout the United States. Iron mining in the Mesabi Range underwent three overlapping technological phases:

1 The mining of high-grade direct shipping ores (1893–1950s)
2 The mining of low-grade washable ores (1905–1980)
3 The mining of lower-grade taconite ores (1957-today).

Each phase of mining required specific technologies to transform these mineral deposits into profitable ore, and each of these technological systems resulted in various landscape-scale impacts – evident in the Range's many open-pit mines, overburden piles, and mine waste. However, the mining of low-grade ores differed from high-grade direct shipping ores, as low-grade ores required processing before they could be profitably smelted and converted into steel – a process called beneficiation. While beneficiation increased the iron content in these low-grade ores, it also produced a new and mobile form of mine waste in the Mesabi Range, called tailings.

The mining of low-grade ores in the Mesabi Range began in 1905 with the construction of an experimental beneficiation plant constructed by U.S. Steel's mining branch, the Oliver Iron Mining Co., who built the plant on the north shore of Trout Lake near Coleraine, Minnesota. At this plant, Oliver Iron ran tests on washable ores, which proved favorable, and owing to this success, Oliver Iron began developing plans to construct a permanent beneficiation plant on the Mesabi Range. By 1907, U.S. Steel had purchased property on the eastern side of Trout Lake and began developing plans to erect their flagship industrial plant in the Mesabi Range. The location at Trout Lake was important, as waterbodies, particularly inland lakes, provided mining companies with two beneficial uses: first, the beneficiation of low-grade ores required tremendous amounts of water, which Trout Lake provided, and second, beneficiation also produced tailings, which mining companies needed to dispose of. In Minnesota, the tailings produced by beneficiation plants were originally dumped directly into lakes, as these waterbodies provided mining companies with a sink where their waste could be stored out of sight and often out of mind (Melosi 1973; Tarr 1996).

By May of 1910, the Trout Lake concentrator was operational and was at once the first beneficiation plant on the Mesabi and also the largest iron ore concentrator in the world. The Trout Lake concentrator (see Figures 6.3, 6.4, and 6.5), was massive, measuring 162 ft. in width, 225 ft. in length, and 91 ft. in height. While the footprint of the concentrator building was massive, so too was the plant's associated infrastructure constructed to both bring ore to the plant and to ship iron ore concentrates out. These included a 4,000 ft. long 120 ft. tall earthen ramp for trains to deliver the ore directly to the plant's seventh-floor classifying and crushing level and a 650 ft. long steel trestle that connected the Trout Lake concentrator to the earthen ramp (Soper 1910).

In 1910, the first shipments of washable ore concentrates were sent from the Trout Lake concentrator to ports in Duluth, setting off a flurry of development among other Mesabi Range mining companies seeking to profit off washable ores (Soper 1910, 1911). For nearly five decades the Trout Lake concentrator remained the largest iron ore concentrator in the world, and owing to its success, the washable ore industry in the Mesabi Range boomed. By 1920, more than 30 beneficiation plants were located across the Mesabi Range, and by 1950 that number would nearly double (Landis 1934; Baeten, Langston, and Lafreniere 2016). By 1940, the Trout Lake concentrator had produced nearly 50-million tons of iron

Figure 6.3 Overview of the Trout Lake Concentrator, 1940s

Source: Courtesy of Todd Monroe: Personal collection from the Iron Range Research Center

ore concentrates, resulting in the production of more than 75-million tons of tailings, all of which were deposited directly into Trout Lake (Trout Lake Ore Washer Improvements 1940).

From 1910–1960, the Trout Lake concentrator operated as the world's largest iron ore concentrator. However, by the late 1950s, mining companies began to shift their focus to taconite ores, ultimately abandoning the mining of washable ores by the early 1970s (Manuel 2015). In October of 1973, the Trout Lake concentrator processed its last carload of washable ore, marking 63 years of continual production. In total, the Trout Lake plant processed more than 160 million

Figure 6.4 Overview of the Trout Lake Concentrator, 1940s

Source: Courtesy of Todd Monroe: Personal collection from the Iron Range Research Center

tons of washable ores and paved the way for the 78 other washable ore plants that operated on the Mesabi Range. In 1974, U.S. Steel began the process of dismantling the Trout Lake concentrator, a process that would take eight years to complete. In 1982, Western Steel Cutting Inc. was contracted to finish dismantling the remaining shell of the Trout Lake concentrator, ultimately removing its physical remains from the landscape (U.S. Steel to Dismantle Three Mesabi Facilities 1981).

The closure and dismantling of the Trout Lake concentrator are emblematic of the larger post-1970s economic landscape of the Mesabi Range, one that depended on an industry-backed tax system for continual taconite mining, the consolidation of industrial operations, and the loss of jobs to automation (Manuel 2015). These processes led to the Mesabi's transition to a largely post-mining economy, a transition that was met by concerted efforts at remediation and reclamation by state agencies, most notably the Iron Range Resources and Rehabilitation Board (IRRRB). The IRRRB aimed to reshape and reimagine the Mesabi Range from a post-mining landscape into a recreational one (Felleson 1999).

Figure 6.5 Overview of the Trout Lake Concentrator, 1940s

Source: Courtesy of Todd Monroe: Personal collection from the Iron Range Research Center

The process of reclamation and remediation involved cleaning up the extensive environmental legacies left over from a century of mining, including the widespread removal of abandoned or derelict mine buildings, the revegetation of mine waste piles, and the stocking of abandoned and flooded mine pits with fish favored by anglers (Manuel 2015; Baeten 2017). In doing so, the IRRRB hoped to attract a new economic driver to the Mesabi Range, in the form of tourist dollars, while at the same time preserving specific elements of the Mesabi's mining heritage, such as iconic head frames and active mine viewing areas. These elements highlight the enormous technologies deployed on the range but 'blur' their environmental costs. Although the IRRRB's focus on post-industrial reclamation was widely successful in its mission, it also contributed to making invisible many of the environmental consequences of mining. Today, an abundance of mine waste extends at geographies greater than the Mesabi Range itself, much of which exists in isolation from the industrial facility that created it (Baeten, Langston, and Lafreniere 2016). Recontoured, capped with topsoil, and planted with grasses and trees, these historic wastescapes appear today as both foreign and natural – too uniform to not be manmade but too living to be waste (Felleson 1999).

These efforts to revitalize the Mesabi's post-industrial economy have not only obscured many of the environmental impacts from mining, but they have also promoted many of the area's resources as being either pristine or pure, in an attempt to attract recreationists seeking to vacation in the Northwoods. When environmental legacies from mining are removed from the landscape and erased from memory, the process of forgetting can begin. These post-mining patterns are not unique to the Mesabi Range, rather they affect all post-mining landscapes, where ore and profits were exported out of extractive landscapes, while waste has been left for contemporary and future publics to contend with. Today, historic waste streams continue to manifest from a vast global network of post-mining landscapes, a pressing problem that land managers and mining communities have been left to negotiate. These post-industrial wastescapes represent a new heritage of the Anthropocene and have been treated as environmental problems by governments, environmental scientists, and heritage organizations, a practice that both obfuscates the cultural value of the wastescapes, along with the significant historical lessons that contamination and pollution might hold for future generations to reflect on.

Illuminating the wastescape

In the following sections, I detail a theoretical perspective, that of *contamination as artifact*, along with a geospatial methodology for reconstructing a post-mining landscape. This demonstrates ways in which we might try to understand, analyze, and interpret these post-industrial spaces. The methodological approach can help researchers elucidate many spatiotemporal questions about a post-industrial landscape, such as a) when, where, and how an industrial landscape developed and declined; b) when, where, and how a wastescape developed and who was responsible for its creation; and c) how these historical processes are retained on the landscape and within community memory. The theoretical approach considers post-mining wastescapes as culturally significant artifacts that have physically, socially, and chemically connected distant and disparate populations across both space and time. Contextualizing contamination as material recognizes the environmental legacies of industrialization, such as polluted soils or contaminated water, as byproducts of human labor and extends the sociocultural lens to encompass the wastescape. Furthermore, this approach expands the spatiotemporal framework in which post-mining sites are often situated, generally positioned spatially as local occurrences and temporally with a defined beginning and end. This theoretical perspective can affect not only how we interpret a post-mining landscape but also how we designate its spatial and temporal bounds. In doing so, we can begin to ask more complex epistemological questions about our post-industrial heritage such as, where do wastescapes begin, and when do they end?

Contamination as artifact: a critical industrial heritage approach

Post-mining landscapes are messy, busy, and confusing. They represent a continuum of changing values, technologies, and environmental feedbacks to these historical technologies. From an environmental viewpoint, post-mining landscapes can be seen as dangerous and toxic, hazardous blights representative of a capitalist ethos. On the other hand, post-mining landscapes read through the lens of industrial heritage or cultural geography might reveal a surreal or sublime landscape that contains value-laden reminders of the past, representative of a community's identity. However, the focus of industrial heritage has been directed at either the preservation of the built environment (generally that of worker's housing, machines, or large industrial facilities) or the promotion and development of a heritage tourism industry rooted in either technological or economic nostalgia (Ebert 2012). Although these approaches have shaped our understanding of post-industrial heritage and have paved the way for the preservation of countless sites and structures, they have also promoted a particular practice of studying and understanding our industrial past. This process has simplified the complex nature in which these landscapes developed and avoided speaking to their lasting environmental costs. While many industrial heritage organizations have drawn on labor history and recognize the conflicted relationship between workers and management, the recognition of the equally conflicted relationship between industry and environment has been universally under-represented.[1] This underrepresentation is concerning, as the environmental legacies of industrialization are arguably the most ubiquitous cultural features found within a post-industrial site, both hidden in the subterranean and exposed on the surface. Furthermore, post-industrial wastescapes reflect contemporary concerns regarding human–environment interactions and offer the ability to reflect on our past uses and abuses of the environment.

Thankfully, contemporary scholarship related to the industrial heritage of post-mining sites has argued that, if preserved in situ, waste features have significant value, because they articulate with the broader cultural landscape and provide a historical context to the technological systems utilized within that given landscape (Francaviglia 1991; Goin and Raymond 1999, 2003; Hardesty 2001; Quivik 2007). These studies recognize the cultural value of wastescapes as it relates to preservation, such as in the retention of slag heap piles or tailings basins. Likewise, cultural geographers have also studied how the decay of industrial sites, including wastes and ruins, convey certain meanings about past people, places, and events and hold significant heritage value for contemporary and future populations (Edensor 2005; DeSilvey 2017). However, the less visible (or less obvious) environmental legacies of industrialization, such as soil contamination, polluted waters, and deformed fish, also contain significant heritage value, whether they remain visible within the landscape or not. Recognizing and interpreting these less-obviously industrial, often invisible, legacies of industrialization can help illuminate the complexity, intensity, and extensivity of how historical industrial processes shaped a landscape, as well as the ongoing relationships between technology and the environment that still occur at these sites today.

How we understand a post-industrial site is owed heavily to both historical narratives and collective memory, processes that shape each other reciprocally. For example, analyzing the historical narrative of the Mesabi Range reveals a comprehensive story of iron mining, including a detailed account of the development of direct shipping ores, the ethnic make-up of mining communities, labor unrest within the mining industry, and the technological transition to taconite mining. However, this narrative has notable omissions, including the history of washable ore mining and processing, the landscape-scale transformations from open-pit excavations, and the long history of community concerns over the environmental impacts from mining. Furthermore, within Mesabi Range industrial heritage sites we see a concerted effort to promote the region's past through the lens of tourism-driven nostalgia while glossing over the historical processes that shaped the regional landscape, as well as the environmental consequences these processes have left for current communities to negotiate.

Heritage organizations in the Mesabi Range have promoted the region's industrial heritage through a discourse that reflects historical policy directives, technological and economic nostalgia, and an emphasis on the enduring strength of mining in the region – as both an active industry as well as a pillar of the Mesabi's identity. This discourse represents an aspect of what anthropologist Laurajane Smith refers to as "authorized heritage discourse," a management tool used to legitimize official institutions to promote a specific narrative of the past, defining which aspects of heritage they wish to promote and who should be able to speak for it (Smith 2006, 4). In the Mesabi Range, the authorized heritage discourse has been deployed primarily by the IRRRB as a tool to revitalize the local economy, but in doing so it has obfuscated much of the region's more conflicted past, including the environmental legacies and consequences of more than a century of intensive iron ore mining.

In addition to being influenced by both historical narratives and authorized heritage discourse, the collective memory of a post-mining landscape is shaped by the region's built environment, specifically what is visible on the landscape. The built environment of the Mesabi Range has undergone dramatic changes over the past 50 years – more than half of the region's open-pit mines now exist as lakes and are managed as recreational areas rather than cultural resources, while the majority of the historical processing plants, such as the Trout Lake concentrator, were removed from the landscape decades ago. Although the processing plants are no longer materially present and the historic mines no longer conceptually present, their legacies remain embedded on the landscape and continue to influence the ways that humans interact with the environment. This process is referred to as the 'presence of absence' by anthropologists, a rhetorical tool that argues that "something can be there even when it is not there" (Bille, Hastrup, and Flohr 2010, 11; Meskell 2010).

The sites that we, as a society, recognize as being meaningful and assign heritage significance to, often promote a one-sided vision of a landscape's complex history, evident in the memorials, monuments, and interpretive signage deployed by heritage organizations (Waterton and Watson 2015). Industrial heritage organizations imprint a specific identity onto a specific place through recognizing and memorializing particular elements of the post-industrial landscape, such as in the preservation of head frames or the erection of interpretive signage at mine-viewing areas. While industrial-heritage organizations have certainly memorialized landscapes that have experienced hurtful, contested, or painful pasts, these have been limited to conflicts between workers and management or the loss of life due to some technological failure (Foote 2003). However, notably absent from this authorized heritage discourse is the memorialization of sites where industrial activities damaged the environment, such as at contaminated lakes, even though these wastescapes occupy the largest extent of the post-industrial landscape. Heritage organizations aim to articulate the past, including all of its messiness, to present populations, yet the stories told through industrial heritage channels have primarily focused on economic or technological nostalgia, producing a historical narrative that fails to recognize the environmental legacies of industrialization (Price 2006; Harrison 2013).

While heritage organizations have obfuscated the environmental consequences of industrialization through their authorized heritage discourse, other factors, such as the technologically intensive process of active and post-mining reclamation, have also worked to conceal the post-industrial wastescape. For example, the Mesabi Range's mining landscape has experienced more than a century of mining, much of which occurred in overlapping technological phases, where older mine sites were re-mined with new technologies, and historic waste piles were reprocessed to recover finite values of iron ore originally discarded as waste. Coupled together, historic mining and post-mining reclamation have created a landscape in the Mesabi Range that reflects a palimpsest, where much of its historic development appears blurred and buried amongst more modern activity (Storm 2014). Historian Elizabeth Raymond describes how the ongoing articulations of industrial mining with post-mining reclamation have produced a Mesabi landscape that "incorporates a number of disparate visions of what a mining landscape is and means. Technology works simultaneously to create this landscape and to obliterate it in the interests of a more natural version" (Goin and Raymond 2003, 275).

Due to funding constraints, mine land reclamation initiatives have often targeted only immediate physical risks, while the more enduring environmental hazards, such as soil contamination and tailings, have remained embedded in the landscape and ultimately forgotten by land management agencies (Baeten 2018). Further, these reclamation efforts often put post-mining communities in a bind, where they are faced with having to sacrifice elements of their community heritage for the promise of environmental safety (Keeling and Sandlos 2015). Post-mining reclamation and industrial heritage are often framed in conflict with one another, because during reclamation physical elements of the mining landscape, such as derelict buildings, are removed. Yet, industrial heritage and reclamation may also work in concert, shaping a mining landscape that conceals the widespread environmental legacies of mining. Likewise, the coupling of reclamation efforts aimed at cleaning up a post-mining landscape along with heritage organizations concerned with attracting visitors for tourism further draws attention away from the significance and lasting presence of the wastescape itself.

Revealing the post-industrial palimpsest – a methodology

Although government agencies, such as the U.S. Bureau of Mines and the U.S. Geological Survey (USGS), have tracked the locations where many historic mines were located in the U.S., far less attention has been paid to the broader mining landscape.[2] Previous research has shown that these government datasets have accurately accounted for the location and name of individual mines, but no government dataset exists that captures features of the broader mining landscape, such as the location of ore processing facilities, transportation networks, or wastescapes (Baeten, Langston, and Lafreniere 2016). A mine is much more than a hole in the ground, yet these government datasets fail to capture this reality. To address this gap and to understand a) how historic mining activity was retained within the Mesabi's post-mining landscape; b) the extent of industrial loss; and c) what environmental legacies remain on the landscape; archival data, historical aerial imagery, LiDAR data, and findings from contemporary landscape reconnaissance surveys were integrated and mapped into Historical GIS (HGIS). The use of an HGIS has shown the utility of mapping archival data to better understand landscape evolution over long periods, including the comparison of historical environments and landscapes to contemporary ones (Cunfer 2008; Hatvany 2011; Knowles 2013).

The construction of the HGIS began with a spatial inventory of the Mesabi Range's mining landscape. This process was aided by the previously mentioned datasets managed by the USGS, which included the names and spatial coordinates for mines but failed to capture any quantifiable metric to understand how mine X compared to mine Y in terms of their environmental demands. To address this gap, we mined production statistics from historical trade journals and added annual ore shipments for each mine in the Mesabi Range from 1897–2012.[3] This HGIS then contained a comprehensive dataset revealing the development of mining on the Range, but the landscape of ore processing remained absent.

To address this gap, we developed an inventory of iron ore beneficiation plants. Unlike the USGS dataset of mine locations, no government agency has tracked the development of ore processing facilities, making this process much more complicated and time-consuming. To produce a historic inventory of beneficiation plants, we conducted an extensive archival survey of company reports, historic maps, and historic aerial imagery, as well as examined modern aerial imagery and LiDAR data to pinpoint where the facilities were historically located. Once the landscape of beneficiation was complete, these plants were then tied to the mines from which they were receiving ore, such as connecting the Trout Lake concentrator to the Canisteo mine. We additionally looked to archival sources, such as company flow sheets and engineering handbooks, to ascertain how each of these plants compared in terms of their waste production and water consumption. These data were added to the HGIS and provided a metric to gauge the environmental demands of individual plants based on the quantity of ore they handled (Baeten, Langston, and Lafreniere 2016).

Coupled together and mapped, this HGIS consists of over 14,000 lines of data, demonstrating how the mining landscape of the Mesabi Range developed from 1898–2012 across both space and time (see Figure 6.6). Once digitized and mapped, these historical data can be utilized to both generate visualizations, such as time series animations – which provide opportunities to demonstrate how flows of material moved across landscapes – and to reveal the expansion, concentration, and decline of mining across space and time. Additionally, these data can be interrogated against modern environmental datasets, to compare how past mining activity compares with current environmental concerns (Baeten, Langston, and Lafreniere 2018). The HGIS showed that historical data can provide new insights into the evolution of a mining landscape that archival data alone would not reveal.

Building an HGIS to reconstruct the historical development of a post-mining landscape also offers opportunities for public outreach and post-industrial interpretive strategies useful for the digital age. Integrating these datasets into interactive web platforms, such as ESRI's online story maps, allows users to explore these data as either interactive or static databases. Story maps make complex geospatial data available either to audiences not familiar with GIS or to those who do not have a license for GIS software. By combining geospatial data with maps, narrative text, images, and videos, story maps offer a platform to articulate the story behind the GIS data and the landscape to which it is anchored. For example, the story map created for this project, *The Lake Superior Iron District: Changing Landscapes of Water and Waste*, demonstrates the utility of this approach. Through

Table

Mines

FID	Year	Range	Mine_name	Tons_ship	source	Ore	Owner	Mining_Co
560	1913	Gogebic	Atlantic	119770	The Iron Trade Review Vol. 54 (191	Soft, red, non-bessemer	Oglebay, Norton & Co.	Montreal Mining Co
569	1913	Marquette	Austin	107366	The Iron Trade Review Vol. 54 (191	Soft, red, bessemer and non-besse	Cleveland-Cliffs Iron Company	
584	1913	Mesabi	Bangor	119705	The Iron Trade Review Vol. 54 (191	Non-bessemer	Pickands Mather & Co	Bangor Mining Co
638	1913	Mesabi	Bennett	88931	The Iron Trade Review Vol. 54 (191	Non-bessemer. Part treated by was	Pickands Mather & Co	Bennett Mining Co.
736	1913	Mesabi	Biwabik	300924	The Iron Trade Review Vol. 54 (191	Bessemer and Non-bessemer	Pickands Mather & Co	The Biwabik Mining Co
842	1913	Mesabi	Bray	102439	The Iron Trade Review Vol. 54 (191	Non-bessemer. Crushed and scree	The M.A. Hanna Co	Hanna Ore Mining Co
871	1913	Marquette	Breitung	104757	The Iron Trade Review Vol. 54 (191	Soft, bessemer, non-bessemer and	Jones & Laughlin Steel Co	
899	1913	Mesabi	Brunt	202969	The Iron Trade Review Vol. 54 (191	Non-bessemer	The M.A. Hanna Co.	Hanna Ore Mining Co
953	1913	Mesabi	Burt	622951	The Iron Trade Review Vol. 54 (191	Bessemer and Non-bessemer	Oliver Iron Mining Co	
996	1913	Marquette	Cambria	169473	The Iron Trade Review Vol. 54 (191	Soft, brown, non-bessemer	Cleveland-Cliffs Iron Company	
105	1913	Mesabi	Canisteo	1099727	The Iron Trade Review Vol. 54 (191	Bessemer and Non-bessemer. Wa	Cleveland-Cliffs Iron Company	
119	1913	Gogebic	Cary	217349	The Iron Trade Review Vol. 54 (191	Hard, blue-red, non-bessemer.	Pickands Mather & Co.	Odanah Iron Co
125	1913	Gogebic	Castile	57595	The Iron Trade Review Vol. 54 (191	Soft, red, bessemer and non-besse	Oglebay, Norton & Co.	Castile Mining Co
126	1913	Mesabi	Cavour	118404	The Iron Trade Review Vol. 54 (191	Non-bessemer	Cavour Mining Co	
132	1913	Vermilion	Chandler	51403	The Iron Trade Review Vol. 54 (191	Hard, red, bessemer. Part of it treat	Harper Sibley et al	Chandler Mining Co
134	1913	Marquette	Chase	52930	The Iron Trade Review Vol. 54 (191	Hard, non-bessemer and high phos	Cleveland-Cliffs Iron Company	
138	1913	Mesabi	Chisholm	641788	The Iron Trade Review Vol. 54 (191	Bessemer and Non-bessemer	Oliver Iron Mining Co	
142	1913	Mesabi	Clark	402893	The Iron Trade Review Vol. 54 (191	Bessemer and Non-bessemer	Oliver Iron Mining Co.	American Mining Co
145	1913	Marquette	Cleveland Cliffs	997520	The Iron Trade Review Vol. 54 (191	Hard, red, non-bessemer. Crushed	Cleveland-Cliffs Iron Company	
154	1913	Gogebic	Colby	305744	The Iron Trade Review Vol. 54 (191	Soft, reddish-brown, bessemer and	Corrigan McKinney Steel Co	
160	1913	Mesabi	Commodore	484188	The Iron Trade Review Vol. 54 (191	Bessemer. Part washed	E.W. Coons Co	
166	1913	Mesabi	Corsica	225140	The Iron Trade Review Vol. 54 (191	Bessemer and Non-bessemer. Cru	Pickands Mather & Co	Corsica Iron Co
169	1913	Mesabi	Crosby	219065	The Iron Trade Review Vol. 54 (191	Bessemer and Non-bessemer. Wa	The M.A. Hanna Co	Butler Brothers
172	1913	Mesabi	Croxton	50033	The Iron Trade Review Vol. 54 (191	Non-bessemer. Part direct shippin	The Hedman Mining Co	
173	1913	Mesabi	Cyprus	82121	The Iron Trade Review Vol. 54 (191	Non-bessemer. Screened and was	Pacific Isle Mining Co.	
175	1913	Mesabi	Dale	621415	The Iron Trade Review Vol. 54 (191	Bessemer and non-bessemer. Lat	Pacific Isle Mining Co	
203	1913	Mesabi	Eaton	3548	The Iron Trade Review Vol. 54 (191		Pickands Mather & Co	Ontario Iron Co
205	1913	Mesabi	Elba	126236	The Iron Trade Review Vol. 54 (191	Bessemer	Pickands Mather & Co	Hobart Iron Co.
208	1913	Mesabi	Elizabeth	17105	The Iron Trade Review Vol. 54 (191	Non-bessemer	Clare Iron Co	Clare Iron Co

Figure 6.6 Overview of HGIS

Source: John Baeten

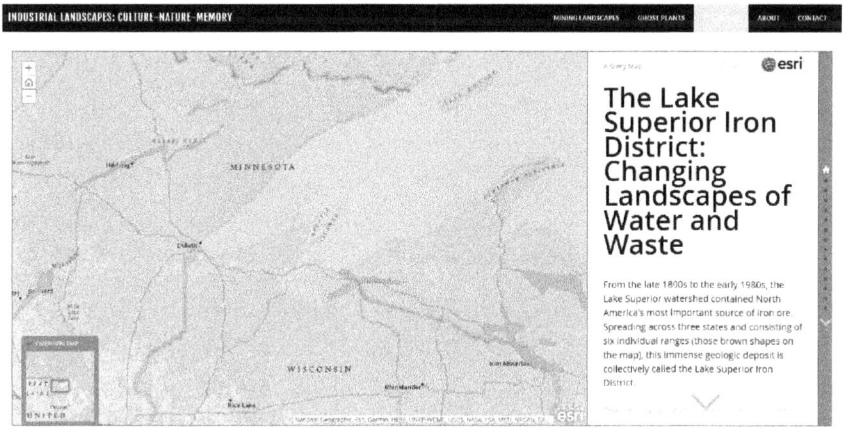

Figure 6.7 Story map used to communicate findings to the public

Source: John Baeten

the incorporation of our geospatial database with results gleaned from academic publications, we designed a public-facing and accessible resource that tracks the development, expansion, and abandonment of iron mining across the Lake Superior district (see Figure 6.7).[4]

The modern landscape of the Trout Lake concentrator

Using the data within this HGIS to analyze the landscape of the Trout Lake concentrator today reveals insights about how the landscape developed. Figure 6.8 compares the current landscape of the Trout Lake concentrator with that of 1947. The historical image clearly shows the linear transportation system used to haul ore to the plant and to ship iron ore concentrates from the facility, as well as the evolving tailings disposal systems that were employed at the plant; features that have become obscured on the contemporary image. On the historical image, it is possible to see the dark gray mass leading up to the bank of Trout Lake directly to the southwest of the plant. This is the remains of the Trout Lake concentrator's first tailings dump, which was used from 1910 to the early 1940s. To the east of the plant the more recently constructed tailings basin is apparent.

From comparing the historical image to the modern image of the landscape, we see that much of the detail that is clear in 1947 is either absent today or has blended in with the natural environment, such as the historic tailings dump that today appears as a grassy wetland. The concerted effort to remove beneficiation plants has made it difficult to articulate where much of the waste on the modern landscape originated. Furthermore, this process of reclamation and removal has made the broader mining landscape appear disparate and unconnected, where

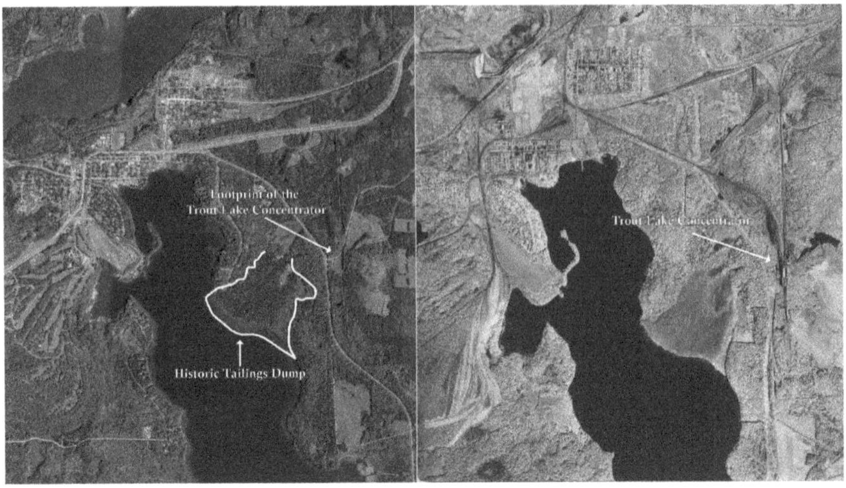

Figure 6.8 Comparison of the modern Trout Lake concentrator landscape with an aerial image from 1947

Source: John Baeten

mining features, such as tailings basins, seemingly exist as islands as the visible technological system that created them have been removed from the landscape altogether. Furthermore, when we look at the modern landscape using LiDAR imagery, a method that uses satellite imagery to allow us to see the surface of the earth, some of these historic features become clearer, such as the linear transportation routes and the footprint of the historic waste dump seen in the following image (see Figure 6.9).

Conclusions

Active and post-mining landscapes embody ongoing societal and environmental transformations, evident in the economic booms and busts that accompany industries of extraction, along with the widespread environmental impacts produced during and after the removal of ore from the ground. Mine waste and legacy contamination residing within active and post-mining landscapes are a growing international concern, as evidenced in the recent tailings disasters in Brazil (Carneiro 2019) and massive bird kills from stopovers in the polluted waters of Montana's Berkeley Pit (Leech 2018). The latent pollution that resides within post-mining landscapes enacts a form of slow violence against post-mining communities and their environments and extends the impacts of historic mining across both space and time (Nixon 2013). Often framed solely as an environmental problem requiring clean-up and remediation, the potential historical and cultural value embedded within these post-industrial wastescapes are routinely ignored by both land

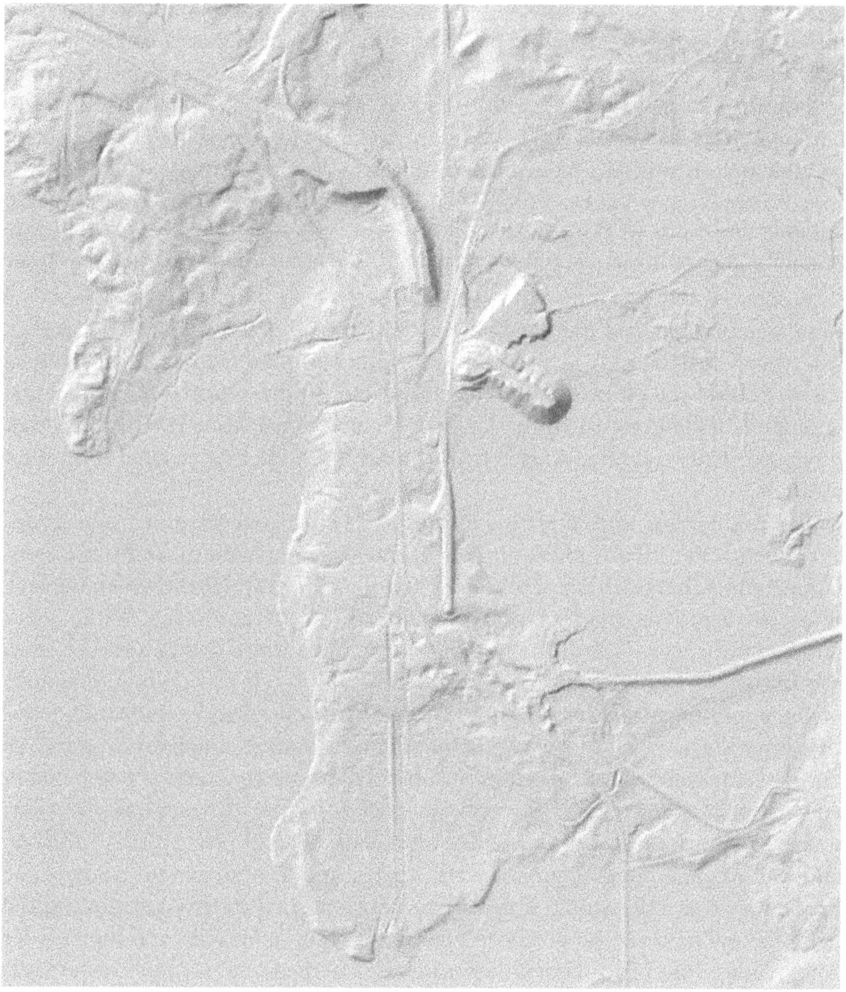

Figure 6.9 LiDAR Imagery showing the footprint of the Trout Lake concentrator and the details lost in contemporary aerial imagery (MNDNR)

Source: John Baeten

management agencies and heritage organizations. Likewise, the focus of industrial heritage organizations has seemingly been placed on celebrating the accumulation of wealth, striving to preserve and promote monuments of – and to – capital, while avoiding many of their hurtful environmental costs. However, by utilizing a theoretical approach that values waste and contamination as culturally significant artifacts, heritage managers can use wastescapes as examples to address contemporary concerns related to human uses and abuses of the environment.

The integration of archival datasets into an HGIS provides researchers with a tool to analyze the evolution of the post-industrial landscape over long periods, including the identification of where and when an industrial landscape was in production, as well as how a particular technology impacted the environment and the wastescapes that technology created. This approach can also be of use to land managers seeking to either develop strategies for managing post-industrial wastescapes or targeting their reclamation, as it provides a spatially explicit historical context at a landscape scale. Furthermore, through making these spatial datasets accessible to the public via story maps, the complex and messy history of post-industrial landscapes can become clearer, and perhaps sites like the Trout Lake concentrator will return to the discourse of local communities, and historical wastescapes might find the heritage recognition they deserve. Coupled together, this type of analysis adds an empirical and materialist perspective to the rhetorical theory behind the *presence of absence* and demonstrates that the environmental legacies of mining persist in the landscape much longer than the facilities that produced them and often longer than the corporations who profited from their creation.

The dismantling and scrapping of the Trout Lake concentrator in the 1980s effectively removed any physical trace of the former behemoth, and subsequent mining efforts have further obscured its historic footprint. Furthermore, the lack of any interpretive signage obfuscates the history of this landscape. Within post-mining landscapes, such as the Mesabi Range, mine waste and tailings are often the last remaining artifacts within the landscape, serving as telltale reminders of the environmental consequences that decades of intensive industrial activity can produce. The process of post-mining reclamation coupled with a lack of heritage interpretation jeopardizes the ability of future generations to remember and appreciate how these landscapes developed. To stay relevant, industrial heritage organizations and professionals must look beyond preservation, tourism, and rhetoric and begin to embrace the wastescapes that dominate many of the landscapes that they study. This can be accomplished by first recognizing the material and cultural significance of contamination, pollution, and the broader wastescapes and, next, through interpreting the meaning of these wastescapes to broader publics.

Notes

1 Industrial heritage sites that account for conflicts between labor and management in the U.S. include the American Textile History Museum, the Boott Cotton Mills Museum Lowell National Historic Park, and Rivers of Steel National Heritage Area. In terms of accounting for the environmental legacies of industrialization, the Zeche Zollverein museum in Germany's North-Rhine Westphalia region provides an excellent overview.
2 Data available at: https://mrdata.usgs.gov/
3 These included the Engineering and Mining Journal, The Iron Trade Review, and Skillings' Mining Review, all of which were accessed at Michigan Technological University's library.
4 Available at: www.industriallandscapes.org/story-map.html

References

Baeten, J. 2017. "Contested Landscapes of Displacement: Oliver Iron and Minnesota's Hibbing District." *Change Over Time: An International Journal of Conservation and the Built Environment* 7 (1).

———. 2018. "A Century of Red Water: Mine Waste, Legacy Contamination, and Institutional Amnesia in Minnesota's Mesabi Iron Range." *Water History* 10 (4): 245–66.

Baeten, J., N. Langston, and D. Lafreniere. 2016. "A Geospatial Approach to Uncovering the Hidden Waste Footprint of Lake Superior's Mesabi Iron Range." *The Extractive Industries and Society* 3 (4): 1031–45.

———. 2018. "A Spatial Evaluation of Historic Iron Mining Impacts on Current Impaired Waters in Lake Superior's Mesabi Range." *Ambio: A Journal of the Human Environment* 47 (2): 231–44.

Bille, M., F. Hastrup, and T. Flohr, eds. 2010. *An Anthropology of Absence: Materializations of Transcendence and Loss*. New York: Springer.

Carneiro, J. 2019. "Brazil Dam Disaster: Inside the Village Destroyed by Surging Sludge." *BBC News Brazil*. www.bbc.com/news/world-latin-america-47069784.

Cunfer, G. 2008. "Scaling the Dust Bowl." In *Placing History: How Maps, Spatial Data, and GIS are Changing Historical Scholarship*, edited by Anne Kelly Knowles, 95–122. Redlands, CA: ESRI Press.

DeSilvey, C. 2017. *Curated Decay: Heritage Beyond Saving*. Minneapolis, MN: University of Minnesota Press.

Ebert, W. 2012. "Industrial Heritage Tourism." In *Industrial Heritage Retooled: The TICCIH Guide to Industrial Heritage Conservation*, edited by J. Douet. Lancaster: TICCIH.

Edensor, T. 2005. *Industrial Ruins: Space, Aesthetics and Materiality*. Oxford: Berg Publishers.

Felleson, D.A. 1999. *Iron Ore And Taconite Mine Reclamation And Revegetation Practices On The Mesabi Range In Northeastern Minnesota*. University of Minnesota: Department of Horticultural Science.

Foote, K.E. 2003. *Shadowed Ground: America's Landscapes of Violence and Tragedy*. Revised and Updated. Austin: University of Texas Press.

Francaviglia, R. 1991. *Hard Places: Reading the Landscape of America's Historic Mining Districts*. Iowa City, IA: University of Iowa Press.

Goin, P., and E. Raymond. 1999. "Recycled Landscapes: Mining's Legacies in the Mesabi Iron Range." In *Technologies of Landscape: From Reaping to Recycling*, 267–84. Amherst, MA: University of Massachusetts Press.

———. 2003. *Changing Mines in America*. Santa Fe: The Center for American Places.

Hardesty, D. 2001. "Issues in Preserving Toxic Wastes as Heritage Sites." *The Public Historian* 23 (2): 19–28.

Harrison, R. 2013. *Heritage: Critical Approaches*. London: Routledge.

Hatvany, M.G. 2011. "Wedded to the Marshes: Salt Marshes and Socio-Economic Differentiation in Early Prince Edward Island." *Acadiensis: Journal of the History of the Atlantic Region* 30 (2): 15.

Keeling, A., and J. Sandlos. 2015. *Mining and Communities in Northern Canada: History, Politics, and Memory*. University of Calgary Press. Accessed February 20, 2017. http://dspace.ucalgary.ca/handle/1880/51021.

Knowles, A.K. 2013. *Mastering Iron: The Struggle to Modernize an American Industry, 1800–1868*. Chicago and London: University of Chicago Press.

Landis, P.H. 1934. "Community and Neighborhood: The Life Cycle of the Iron Mining Town." *Social Forces* 13 (2): 245–46.

Leech, B. 2018. *The City That Ate Itself: Butte, Montana and its Expanding Berkeley Pit*. Reno: University of Nevada Press.
Manuel, J.T. 2015. *Taconite Dreams: The Struggle to Sustain Mining on Minnesota's Iron Range, 1915–2000*. Minneapolis, MN: University of Minnesota Press.
Melosi, M. 1973. " 'Out of Sight, Out of Mind' The Environment and Disposal of Municipal Refuse, 1860–1920." *The Historian* 35 (4): 621–40.
Meskell, L. 2010. "An Anthropology of Absence: Commentary." In *Anthropology of Absence: Materializations of Transcendence and Loss*, edited by M. Bille, F. Hastrup, and T. Flohr. New York: Springer.
Nixon, R. 2013. *Slow Violence and the Environmentalism of the Poor*. Cambridge, MA: Harvard University Press.
Price, J. 2006. "Interpreting Industrial Heritage." In *Heritage Interpretation*, edited by A. Hems and M. Blockley. London and New York: Routledge.
Quivik, F. 2007. "The Historical Significance of Tailings and Slag: Industrial Waste as Cultural Resource." *IA: The Journal of the Society for Industrial Archaeology* 33 (2): 35–52.
Smith, L. 2006. *Uses of Heritage*. London: Routledge.
Soper, E.K. 1910. "New Plant for Washing Iron Ore, Mesabi Range." *The Engineering and Mining Journal* 90 (15): 712–13.
———. 1911. "Washing the Sandy Ores of the Western Mesabi." *The Iron Trade Review* 49.
Storm, A. 2014. *Post-Industrial Landscape Scars*. New York: Palgrave Macmillan.
Tarr, J. 1996. *The Search for the Ultimate Sink: Urban Pollution in Historical Perspective*. Akron: University of Akron Press.
Trout Lake Ore Washer Improvements. 1940. *Skillings' Mining Review* 28 (48): 9.
U.S. Steel to Dismantle Three Mesabi Facilities. 1981. *Skillings' Mining Review* 70 (26): 6.
Waterton, E., and S. Watson. 2015. "Heritage as a Focus of Research: Past, Present and New Directions." In *The Palgrave Handbook of Contemporary Heritage Research*, edited by E. Waterton and S. Watson. London: Palgrave Macmillan.

7 Geocreativity

Place rooted social engagement in industrial ruins – the case of Konvent, Spain

Rosa Cerarols and Antonio Luna

Introduction: geocreativity, questioning the limits of knowledge, ruins and belief

In the summer of 2018, a group of artists gathered together for an art residency project called Creença/Belief at an abandoned convent in the foothills of the Catalan Pyrenees. Creença/Belief was an international initiative promoted and curated by the Miami-based painter and muralist Axel Void (Void Projects/Creença 2018). It was hosted and organized by the local Konvent Cultural Association, the organization that has been taking care of this space for twenty-five years (see Kovent Puntzero 2018). The project was a two-month residency hosting over fifty local, national and international multidisciplinary artists to create site-specific installations and original works in a 19th-century convent and its vicinity.

The convent building is surrounded by the ruins of the Cal Rosal textile factory and the apartment buildings of the former workers. The whole industrial complex is scattered on both sides of the narrow valley of the Llobregat River and girdled by high mountains, forest and the viaducts of the road that connects Barcelona with the ski resorts of the Pyrenees (see Figure 7.1). The silence of the abandoned buildings contrasts with the buzzing of traffic crossing a few meters over our heads. Entering that space through the narrow alley creates a strange feeling of confinement and isolation from the road and the sound of the cars on the horizon. The viaduct does not connect but bypasses these old and decaying industrial infrastructures, a sort of physical metaphor stressing dualities such as new and old, connected and disconnected, abandoned and recovered, industrial and rural. Today, in this former convent we find a thriving cultural center and art residency called Konvent.

For Axel Void, this remote industrial complex became an ideal space to create a temporary independent art community. The Creença/Belief project appeared in art publications around the world and had a significant impact on both the local community and the national and international art scene (BSA 2018). For two months, nearly fifty international artists traveled to this remote location and created freely, transforming the old nunnery hallways, chapel, rooms, nursery and the surrounding areas into spaces of artistic creation and collaboration. At the end of the two months, some of the work was revealed in a three-day exhibit that

Figure 7.1 Konvent location map in Cal Rosal (Berga)

Source: Authors' own elaboration using Instamaps [ICGC]

attracted a combination of local public artists, dealers from Barcelona, and some international visitors.

Most of the artwork created by Creença/Belief was exhibited for only a few days during open-door events and then removed for exhibition in more conventional art galleries elsewhere. Yet, some of the most striking pieces of the exhibit stayed and are still found in some of the old and abandoned industrial premises. A few of them are just unfinished artistic exercises that the artists left in different parts of the buildings. However, others are finished and left there as a tribute to the space that allowed them to create freely in an inspiring environment.

Overall, one piece stands out: a large black and white mural by Reginald O'neal, Ivan Floro, Mohammed Lhagham, Alberto Montes and Axel Void that reproduces an old picture of the school run by the nuns of the convent for the children of the factory workers (see Figure 7.2 and 7.3). The painting, set in the empty space of one of the old industrial warehouses, shows a classroom with two nuns standing in the back and all the children seated turning their faces toward the camera, with all their eyes looking in the same direction. The effect of the painting in the emptiness of the industrial warehouse is both poignant and spine-tingling. Its distressing impact shows the emptiness and symbolizes ruin.

Now that the exhibit is over and the mural is out of context, the effect is even more striking, and the mural, like the old picture, is also becoming part of the history of the place, part of its heritage. It is another "layer" in the 150 years of

Figure 7.2 Archive picture of Convent's School

Source: Konvent Archive

Figure 7.3 Reginald O'neal (L.E.O), Ivan Floro, Mohammed Lhagham, Alberto Montes and Axel Void mural. Picture taken summer 2018

Source: Authors

the Cal Rosal factory that connects ruins with creative meanings of place. Thus, as DeSilvey and Edensor point out (2012, 479): "[r]uins merrily transgress and collapse a whole set of binaries: transience/persistence, nature/culture, attraction/repulsion; power/vulnerability; potential/purposelessness, abandonment/appropriation, presence/absence, aestheticization/abjection". In this sense, we believe that ruins can also trouble and transform the traditional conceptualization of legal/illegal and subversion activities.

Cal Rosal is now the site of new activities with changed and renewed social agency; for the last decade, it has become a space of creation linked to its past and its people through Konvent, the organization that hosted Belief/Creença. The mural shows the uniqueness of Konvent: it is a space of social engagement, a space of innovation, a cultural center of artists from different backgrounds and nationalities, but it is also a space of memory that honors the people and the history of an old factory that used to be the economic and social nucleus of the region. Konvent challenges the concept of ruins and place production (Lefebvre 2013; Massey 2011) by incorporating creativity into the equation (Cresswell 2010;

Crouch 2010; Hawkins 2012, 2014; Mould 2017), questioning our relationship with our past and our present through the use and management of industrial ruins in a non-conventional manner (Douet 2011; Edensor 2005).

In this chapter, we analyze Konvent, a distinctive place that confronts traditional preserving of industrial ruins by using creativity "in" place and creativity "of" place as a space of creation and interaction between locals and visitors and also between the past and the present heritage and community. It has also faced the inability of local and national administrations to accept new uses of industrial ruins beyond musealization or demolition (Douet 2016; Edelblutte 2009; Ganyet 2008; Kirkwood 2001; Trinder 1982). Konvent is a place, but it is also a way of life that is challenging the edges of history and geography by engaging with geocreativity (Bonnet 1992; Dear 2011; Kaye 2000; Loftus 2009; Mould 2017; Pollock and Sharp 2007). Creativity has become the power behind the transformation of this space. We understand geocreativity as a way to reinterpret the geographic experience with an artistic approach. Konvent is not only a space that shelters these creative activities but is also committed with the geography and the history of that place and tries to use the activities taking place at Konvent as a tool to reinterpret and reframe a new sense of place (see also Arboleda and Lorimer (2021), this collection).

The Konvent experience is an evolution of place-based locations of creation and innovation by bridging local and global knowledge through arts. As Bennet (2010) points out, emergent sensual, material and aesthetic qualities reveal the inherent vitalism of all matter, its "liveliness", meaning that Konvent is a unique example of "living heritage" (Poulios 2010), understood as an alternative to dominant heritage models, which privilege the preservation of original fabric and function by establishing a discontinuity between the past and the present. Living heritage instead privileges "change in the context of continuity and makes space for a much broader range of material practices, which might include replacement, renewal, and attrition" (DeSilvey 2017, 185).

The following pages refer to the research project on Geohumanities titled "Dialogues between art, landscape and territory in non-urban environments".[1] We see geohumanities as a resource for expanding epistemological frameworks that intertwine geography with other disciplines in the humanities and in different expressions of art (Cresswell et al. 2015) incorporating methodological innovations in research (Bolland 2015; Dear 2015). For this specific case, we propose a contribution that questions the limits of the production of academic knowledge in the sense that the contents that appear are the result of the negotiation of the profiles of the two people who sign them. As Fontdevila (2018) suggests, in the writing of this text there has been an "art of mediation" between Rosa Cerarols' activist practices – directly linked to the Konvent – and Toni Luna's geographical academic reflection. This exercise of mediation and cooperation within the analysis of the case study involves approaches to daily practice and interdisciplinarity approaches (Buller 2009; Dewsbury and Naylor 2003) with the intention of "expanding the field" (Hawkins 2012).

Before the ruins: Cal Rosal and its convent, the first textile colony at Llobregat's river basin

Industrial colonies were the most characteristic phenomena of the industrialization process in Catalonia,[2] inspired by ideas of Robert Owen's cooperative movement and following similar examples of industrial communities in the UK, France and Italy (Balcells 1974; Enrech 2009). However, the Catalan example along the Llobregat and Ter rivers were much denser than other European locations and meant a radical transformation of the region during the second half of the 19th century (Balcells and Serra 2019). Despite the diversity, each industrial colony commonly included a factory, a house for the owner or the chief manager, a residential area for workers and community buildings such as a church or a nun's convent, school, theatre, shops, nursery or bar (Busquets 2008). Rooted in the Berguedà region, the Rosal family founded the first textile factory in the Llobregat River in 1858. Initially it was granted the official and legal status of "industrial colony"; some years later they gave their family name to the colony, known today as Cal Rosal (Serra 2008, 2011). This location had two purposes: to use the hydropower energy of the river and to find a peaceful rural setting where workers would not be "influenced" by the political unrest of big industrial points of convergence like Barcelona (Català and Molas 2005; Enrech 2009; Marin 2009).

Cal Rosal (see Figure 7.4 and 7.5) grew to become one the biggest of all these factory towns, created as a closed social system in which the factory, workers

Figure 7.4 One of the first existing pictures of Cal Rosal

Source: Konvent Archive

Figure 7.5 Contemporary overview of Cal Rosal

Source: Konvent Archive

apartments, schools, markets and theater, all overlooking the church and the owner's house, constituted a clear social and economic hierarchical enclosure (Balcells and Serra 2019; Busquets 2008; Marin 2009). These factories also developed an area of the territory that in the nineteenth century was still relatively poor and economically isolated, depending mostly on subsistence agriculture. Cal Rosal, as well as other factory settlements, were the biggest transformation of the region in centuries and facilitated reverse migration flows creating jobs for locals and increasing its population with workers coming from other parts of the country (Marin 2009). The Llobregat River basin – and other Catalan rivers like the Ter – experienced a major social transformation at the turn of the 20th century with the creation of over fifty industrial colonies (Balcells 1974; Balcells and Serra 2019).

The convent – or nunnery – was created at the same time as the factory and acted as an infirmary, a primary school and a kindergarten and also as a residence for young single peasant women that started to work at the factory before getting married and who could not commute from their remote farm homes (Balcells 2015; Borderías 2012; Català and Molas 2005; González 2009; Vilardaga 2009). Following a strict protocol, as soon as the young women got married, they moved to the workers' apartments building for families (now in ruins). A second group of apartments separated by the river was also created for single male workers. Eventually, the families would bring their children to the school run by the same nuns who once were their hostesses (Balcells 2015; Borderías 2012); these very same nuns who appear in the mural described earlier.

The relationship between economic and religious power in the industrial development of the colonies is a distinctive feature of early industrialization in Catalonia (Marin 2009). The owners of Cal Rosal could get the support of the bishopric to get a church and a nunnery from the order of the Jesus Sacred Coeur (Serra 2008). Social order, therefore, was both organized by capitalistic rules and reinforced by a strict catholic morality (Balcells and Serra 2019; Ferrer Alòs 1994; Llonch 2004). Workers and their families worked and lived in the same complex and contact with nearby towns or cities was limited (Busquets 2008). The church acted as a cultural center and as a means of social control with all workers attending Sunday services seated in the chairs according to their status in the factory. During the weekdays, the nuns maintained the moral order of the single girl workers and also educated the future workers (Balcells 2015; Borderías 2012; Vilardaga 2009).

The Cal Rosal factory survived difficult political moments, with the uprising of collectivization during the second Spanish Republic (1931–1936) and during the Spanish Civil War (1936–1939). The dictatorship favored these kinds of industrial complexes and reinforced the link between religion and capitalist bourgeoisie (Casas and Grané 2014; Marin 2009). The factory reached its highest number of workers during the 1950s and 1960s with over 1,200 workers, most of them living in the same colony with their families (Serra 2011). The international economic crisis of the 1970s and 1980s, together with the end of the dictatorship, catalyzed a critical moment for the colony factories model, and in a few years, most of them started to close and move their production elsewhere (Casas and Grané 2014). Most of the factories and the rest of the buildings attached to the productive life of the industrial colonies, were rapidly abandoned, while some workers refused to leave their houses and remained in the same apartments. There is clearly an emotional link with those places by many people that once used to work and live in these factories (Ferrer Alòs 1994).

Cal Rosal factory closed down in 1992, and the last nuns still living in the convent also left. From then on, the colony slipped gradually into ruination, and the whole area transformed into "slow ruins". This "leaving-behind process" in the industrialized Llobregat basin has led to significant degradation of its industrial heritage and its socio-cultural community dynamics. Since then, the entire colony also was classified and perceived as a residual and unproductive place. It became, as Guilles Clément named (2004), an example of a "Tiers paysage" site, an obsolete leftover but equally open to appropriation and recuperation.

Before leaving the convent in 1992, the last nuns asked the neighbors to maintain the convent gardens. Despite the area being quickly vandalized, some locals did get involved. Some neighbors, mostly older women, kept gardening the convent's surrounding area, while young people started using the basement of the building to gather in a section of the old nunnery to rehearse and play music. Later on, an engaged group of activists led by Pep Espelt, born at Cal Rosal (and son of one of the ladies taking care of the garden), expanded their actions incrementally to other parts of the building and the surrounding areas to transform the former convent. In 2004, he created a Cultural Association to invigorate the place through artistic practices and cultural activities. It was the beginning of Konvent, and since then they have organized a regular calendar of activities and have caught the interests of national and international artists, creators and cultural managers, emerging as a cultural center for the whole region.

C to K: from a Convent of nuns to a Konvent of artists

Konvent has become a unique example of practicing geocreativity "in" place as a source of social engagement against dereliction (of place) and as a cultural developer agency in the local-regional geography of Central Catalonia (see KonventZero 2020; Konvent Agenda 2020). Over twenty years, the Konvent project has transformed the old nunnery into a self-managed site-specific Contemporary Art Center (see Figure 7.6). Its trajectory has been a work-in-progress initiative, a kind of organic social structure challenging uphill struggles such as legislation procedures, political and economic lethargy.

Konvent's walls show what could not be found in most museums or conventional galleries. It is a space for art, but unlike others, it is also a way of remembering and honoring the layered past via the personal attachment of some of its members to the history of the old textile colony. By using this space, the cultural association bridges the past with the present – much like the children's mural of the Belief/Creença exhibit – and simultaneously acts as a cultural catalyst connecting local residents with national and international artists and visitors. The whole area should be understood as a geographic palimpsest, with different layers, purposes and meanings for different audiences (Crang 1996; Cresswell 2014, 2019; Marvell and Simm 2016; Smith et al. 2009). Konvent's main function is, thus, cultural mediation through site-specific art dissemination activities. It seeks

Figure 7.6 The Konvent building surrounded by Cal Rosal textile factory abandoned warehouses

Source: Konvent Archive

authenticity by promoting freedom, combining different sensibilities, while also moving away from the institutionalized forms of art exhibition.

The basis of the project is rooted in local agency and self-managed volunteer bottom-up effort aimed at preserving locally sourced heritage after industrial abandonment. Despite a quite disorganized and improvised beginning, the official constitution of a non-profit cultural association in 2004 made a big difference in the targeted achievements. In this sense, Konvent Cultural Association internal principles deal with three main interrelated concepts: art, culture and territory. Annually, the members of the association in a general assembly set short- and long-term goals to dignify the abandoned settlement and make the project economically sustainable. Since 2004, Konvent has changed from an uninhabited space abandoned, vandalized and mostly in ruins to a cozy inhabited residency for artists. The physical transformation of the space was slow but constant, starting with limited actions in the convent building during the first years to include large sections of the factory and beyond; expanding their actions to a larger area and developing projects related to the territory.

For a decade (2006–2016), Konvent organized an annual contemporary art festival in June called KonventZero, where Zero emphasizes the idea of a new path for ruin, a rebirth, the will to set the ruins in motion. Each year the festival call was more ambitious, and the exhibition spaces grew, recuperating abandoned rooms of the building. In 2016, some members of the organization and a few artists decided to establish and live in the former convent building, enlarge the idea of the festival to all-year-round cultural and artistic activities and open a restaurant in the building basement as a source of income.

The existing urban legislative framework regulates the type of activity that can be carried out depending on the classification of the land. Most of the buildings in the Cal Rosal colony are still industrial urban land, where only activities related to industrial production and storage can be developed. For this reason, a cultural association settled in an industrial ruin cannot obtain a legal activity license according to local legislation on health and safety protocols. Therefore, a few months after its opening the restaurant was forced to close. However, the legal and administrative denial to obtain an activity license at Konvent building was understood as an opportunity to expand Konvent's philosophy and activism beyond the old factory buildings, opening two new business in nearby locations: the Corpus restaurant in Berga's old town and Victoria winery in Gironella, which could be operated without restrictions as they obtained the restaurant and bar operation licenses.

Thus, the cultural association continues operating at Konvent as a socially engaged community for artistic and cultural dynamization and also as a long-term strategy to preserve and raise awareness of local industrial heritage. Over the years, Konvent association has been working to enhance the environment, a unique mutant landscape of abandoned buildings in different stages of decadence and rampant vegetation that is taking over the old factory spaces on the riverbank. In contrast to other postindustrial sites in urban settings, the transformation of the natural landscape around Konvent is becoming a sort of rural imbricated space (Loughran 2016) in which the old industrial buildings are gradually becoming integrated with the forest and the riverside vegetation, bringing an emerging postindustrial ecology (Millington 2013; Langhorst 2014; Pikner 2014; Chelcea 2015). A new form of cultural landscape is developing that also serves as a source of inspiration for artists working in different disciplines. Konvent eventually arranged and hosted numerous ateliers for local residents, and some abandoned spaces of the former factory buildings were adapted to enable interdisciplinary artistic residences.

Apart from the reclaiming of the abandoned spaces, Konvent has also worked to position itself as a platform for cultural innovation, the practice of contemporary art and local activism for human rights and sustainable development. In the fall of 2016, for example, Konvent organized the first cyborg art meeting from a posthuman perspective, mixing art and technology with the participation of Neil Harbinson and Moon Ribas (see Cyborgarts 2020; Creators 2017). During 2018, Konvent was the filming setting of the short film *Suc de síndria* (2019) [Watermelon juice] and the film *7 raons per fugir* [7 reasons to run away](Catalan Films and TV 2019), both recently awarded by the Catalan and Spanish film academy. From a global perspective, in cooperation with the international organization *Artists at risk*, Konvent offered three months residence to the Kenyan LGTBI activist Grammo Suspect, endangered in her country (see Artists at Risk 2019). From a more localized perspective and dealing with climate change and sustainable development, in October 2019 Konvent hosted the Ruralism and Climate Emergency Days to discuss resilient alternatives of local food economies organized by Central Catalonia Athenaeum of Cooperatives (see L'Ateneu Cooperatiu 2020).

There are no pre-established or limiting requirements for artistic production at Konvent since it is not bound to any official budget requirement and is placed in a ruin, a kind of *terrain vague* that allows multiple creations. Most of the collectives' choices respond to different forms of social and cultural resilience. Konvent offers a unique space that offers facilities for all types of activity, whether individual or collective, as well as common spaces to allow all kinds of cultural exchanges and social interactions. In return, they seek proposals that bring a renewed look to the world of cultural creation. They are open to projects that enrich, discourage, deconstruct or add authenticity to artistic discourse. However, they are responsive to any proposal that wants to work with the environment and the common and everyday territory. Since the beginning of Konvent cultural association till now, the project evolved. The assessment of each activity experience allows Konvent to redirect their practices toward achieving a more "organic" project that could grow in membership, internationalized artistic projects and trans-disciplinary cultural agenda.

Committed landscapes, hyperconnected geographies: strategies of social and cultural dynamization in non-urban ruins through artistic and creative activities

Post-industrial ruins emerged mainly as a symbol of both failures (of local industry) and of growth (elsewhere). Capitalist logic favors the mobility of capital, constantly searching to maximize benefits (Harvey 1989, 1996; Smith 2010). As we moved into more interconnected and globalized capitalism, the mobility of capital became faster and more ubiquitous. Factories in traditional industrialized countries became rapidly abandoned as the production moved to other parts of the planet, where the production factors (labor, energy resources, raw materials) were more favorable. With the oil crisis of the 1970s, many factories in Western Europe and in North America moved to "developing" countries, creating a landscape of industrial decay and ruins in many well-developed regions, as in, for example, Detroit in the US (Doucet 2017) or the Ruhr region in Germany (Dahlbeck and Gärtner 2019).

The use of old industrial spaces for creation and innovation or as a shelter for art communities is not new, and it may be found in different parts of the industrialized world. In Spain the examples we find are mostly are urban, top-down enterprises and financed with public money. Notable examples are *El Matadero* in Madrid (Matadero Madrid 2020; Rey, González, and Carmona 2018; González Juárez 2020), an old slaughterhouse that provided meat to the capital and today is a center of contemporary creation; *La Laboral* in Gijón, constructed as a mining orphanage that was transformed to a Labour College during the dictatorship and finally was recognized as a "city of culture" (Laboral Ciudad de la Cultura 2020; Martín Rodríguez et al. 2014); *La Alhóndiga* in Bilbao, a modernist wine and oil cellar and now the Center of Society and Contemporary Culture (Alhóndiga Bilbao 2020; Rementeria 2007); or *Fabra & Coats* in Barcelona, a former Catalan-British textile industry and now converted into a municipal "creation factory" (Barcelona 2020; Bacardit and Ruisanchez 2013; Garcia, Eizaguirre, and Pradel 2015). Changes in the ruins of economic production also challenge dominant ways of relating to the past and may force a reconsideration of conventional strategies for practically and ontologically ordering space.

Beyond those examples of urban industrial reconversion into cultural and artistic venues, Spain also faces the effects of industrial economic restructuring from agricultural traditional society and economy, to industrial and post-industrial economic transformation in rural areas. These areas have been named "the empty Spain" (Del Molino 2016) due to the significant depopulation dynamics. In that context, in the Aragon region, there is *Pueblos en arte* [Villages in Art] (Pueblos en arte 2020; García 2018; Valeroa and López 2019; Ramon and Ferrero 2019), an initiative that claims "to bet on art and culture as tools to reactivate territories affected by depopulation, connecting the art of cities with rural areas and the people with the artist". Similar conceptions can be found at CAN (Center for Art and Nature) in Farrera at the Catalan Pyrenees (see CAN Farrera de Pallars 2020) or at CACIS (Center of Contemporary Art and Sustainability) in Calders, an old lime oven traditional in the Catalan proto-industrial landscape (see CACIS 2020). These examples illustrate some isolated geographical responses to actual rural tensions but, like Konvent, they are closely connected to territory, art and culture.

Beyond these tensions, industrial ruins may also symbolize failure and abandonment. They are the material evidence of administration indifference and social stagnation. There are numerous examples of this process around the world, both in urban settings and also in non-urban spaces, in which the contrast between the past and the present is even more evident. What we would like to point out in this chapter is how art, culture and territory – or geocreativity – can be understood as a source of social engagement against dereliction and as an empowered agency of local and regional development in one of those nonurban industrial ruin's locations. Indeed, the so-called third landscape (Clément 2004), *terrain vague* (De Solà Morales 1995) or wastelands (Lynch 1990) emerged as a latent space in which the absence of formal use can create a sense of possibility and freedom, a committed landscape of hyperconnected geographies. In the lives and landscapes left behind by industries, some memory traces, in the form of ruined factories and abandoned infrastructure, contain the potential for contestation of the passive acceptance of economic decline. Therefore, ruins can be understood as painful reminders of loss but also can activate forces for mobilizing and materializing collective anger and resistance. This is the case of Konvent.

One of Konvent's latest actions was the installation of large-scale photos on the abandoned facilities of the industrial colony. This project aimed to beautify the outer public space (see Figure 7.7) while recovering local memory following previous research carried out by Gerard Vilardaga (2009), who published a book of the oral memories of the young girls living at the nunnery at the beginning of the 20th century. Enlarged old photographs are exposed in order to commemorate the past, to dignify social memories in place and to create an open-air heritage interpretation center with an evident female protagonist, since women comprised the majority of the labor force in textile factories like Cal Rosal (Balcells 2015; Ferrer Alòs 1994; González 2009; Llonch 2004). This action is integrated with AviArt and Bat Photojournalism Festival created by Konvent in Avià, a nearby municipality. AviArt combines pictures of the recent Mediterranean migration crisis by local photographer Samuel Aranda, winner of the World Press Photo

Figure 7.7 The historical large-scale photos installation on the abandoned facilities of Cal Rosal

Source: Konvent Archive

Award in 2012 (see Ferrer 2012) with pictures of everyday life at Avià and Cal Rosal to reflect on issues of forced migration, displacement, abandonment and national and international humanitarianism and human rights (see also Canturri 2019; Plana Pey 2019).

Konvent, therefore, works at a *glocal* scale and has a multidisciplinary dimension (Massey, Swyngedouw 1997; Brenner 1998; Massey 1991, 2005). This means that apart from programming with a continuous agenda of state-of-the-art artistic events, it also disseminates cultural proposals in the neighboring communities. The maintenance of the building and the dignity of the site are part of the tasks oriented to the dialogue with the local community. The relations between innovative proposals, the different meanings of place and the diverse interests of the local community force them to maintain a permanent discussion to consider place and action, translating into even more subversive activists' proposals. It is, in summary, a place with political statements based on a cultural revulsive movement. Embedded in this context, they reshape the territorial geometries, to redo the supposed peripheries. In fact, its scale of action is mainly local but often with a global reach, breaking the urban–rural dialectics.

Conclusions: ruins as land for creative futures

Over the last century, the romantic conception of ruins has been challenged by the speed and the scope of destruction of industrial infrastructures. Despite an increasing academic interest in ruins and post-industrial geographies, there is still very little consideration from a political and legislative perspective (Manero Miguel and García Cuesta 2017). In most cases, maintaining the ruins' industrial land use category paralyzes any legal change for new productive activities. In some instances, the historical heritage statutes of many of those factories limits both the use of the space and types of ownership. However, in large complexes, as in the case of industrial colonies like Cal Rosal, new land-use plans should find new solutions to the needs of post-industrial communities. As DeSilvey and Edensor pointed out (2012, 474):

> In an era when heritage has been a key ingredient in the regeneration of places and the consolidation of place identity, ruins present striking opportunities to cast a critical light on the glorification of some historical sites and the neglect of others.

Still prevalent is a critical relationship between ruins and political and economic orders, especially on those spaces that are still considered "leftovers". In that context, it is important to point out that examples of geocreativity including artists' sensibility, combined with place-rooted social activism, could challenge administrative and legal changes, especially in economically depressed regions. Examples like Konvent could, therefore, demonstrate the contradictions and inconsistencies of traditional property rights and land use regulations in contemporary spatial planning management.

Despite all these obstacles, Konvent has succeeded in presenting an alternative to traditional uses of industrial ruins. These alternative geographies of post-industrial ruins create the conditions for the emergence of new forms of imaginative appropriations in highly regulated spaces. In parallel, ruins could disrupt normative divisions of public and private space suggesting hybrid understandings of the entanglements of nature and culture (DeSilvey 2017) and also could become a powerful critique of normative ideas about productive-unproductive space. The use of artistic actions in some ruins could create new meanings to place resilience, space production and living memory.

In summary, Konvent is an exercise of critical geocreativity and place-rooted social engagement. It uses and the "re-invents" the nun's convent of the industrial complex of Cal Rosa while it takes care of its history and preserves its built heritage. It also unsettles the pervading conservative social structure, with bottom-up organizational principles and with its own presence and the activities, far away from religious principles that once ruled the whole factory. From a geographical perspective, it is important to underline the three main concepts defining a broader sense of their ideology rooted in specific-site place practices. The first one is art, understanding ruins not as "bad" land but as an opportunity to create alternative ways of getting involved in community everyday lives from creative engaged practices. Similarly, culture is conceptualized as a place-rooted project and self-organization that allows them to be free of institutional norms and restrictions while offering diverse possibilities for artists and local/nonlocal audience. Finally, the idea and values of territory itself are considered. The artists that makeup Konvent are aware of particularities of the region, especially its economically depressed background and its rural context. It works for a better social landscape, strengthening a new sense of place that could overcome the inherited sense of abandonment and isolation from the urban dynamics of the Barcelona demarcation. "Practicing place" in Konvent includes a number of resilience practices as a way to overcome the limitations of the norms of the administration to maintain their everyday life activities. It also necessitates a non-hierarchical organization of the many individuals that over the years have joined the project, living or working in that space and engaging themselves in the uses and values of this community of artists.

Notes

1 Funded Research Project by Ministerio de Economía, Industria y Competividad, Gobierno de España. Proyectos I+D [Excelencia] SCO2017–86136-P.

2 For further information in relation to Catalan industrial heritage, see mNACTEC's (2020) interactive map. To learn more about industrial colonies, see Parals (2020).

References

Alhóndiga Bilbao. 2020. "Azkuna Zentroa – Home." Accessed May 26, 2020. www.azkunazentroa.eus/az/ingl/home.

Arboleda, P., and H. Lorimer. 2021. "Notes from a shrinking market 'Anticipatory nostalgia' and place-making in the midst of change." In *Geographies of Post-Industrial Place, Memory, and Heritage*, edited by M. Rhodes, W. Price, and A. Walker. Abingdon: Routledge.

Artists at Risk. 2019. "AR Resident – Grace Munene aka Grammo Suspect." [online] Accessed May 26, 2020. https://artistsatrisk.org/2019/10/04/ar-resident-grace-munene-aka-grammo-suspect/?lang=en.

L'Ateneu Cooperatiu. 2020. "L'Ateneu Cooperatiu organitza la jornada 'Ruralisme i emergència climàtica' al Konvent de Cal Rosa." [online] Accessed May 26, 2020. www.coopcatcentral.cat/2019/09/24/lateneu-cooperatiu-organitza-la-jornada-ruralisme-i-emergencia-climatica-al-konvent-de-cal-rosal/.

Bacardit Segués, Francisco, and Manuel Ruisánchez Capelastegui. 2013. "Fabra i Coats, Fábrica de creació." *D'UR* 04/2013: 102–7.

Balcells, A. 1974. *Trabajo industrial y organización obrera en la Cataluña contemporánea*. Barcelona: Laia.

———. 2015. "Working Women in the Factories and Home Workshops of Catalonia in the 19th and First Third of the 20th Centuries." *Catalan Historial Review* (8). IEC.

Balcells, Albert, and Rosa Serra. 2019. *Les colònies industrials de la conca del Llobregat, 150 anys d'història*. Barcelona: Diputació de Barcelona.

Barcelona. 2020. "Fabra i Coats: Centre d'Art Contemporani de Barcelona i Fàbrica de Creació." Accessed May 26, 2020. www.barcelona.cat/fabraicoats/.

Bennet, J. 2010. *Vibrant Matter: A Political Ecology of Things*. Durham, NC: Duke University Press.

Bolland, E. 2015. "Every Place a Palimpsest: Creative Practice, Emotional Archaeology, and the Post-Traumatic Landscape." *Geohumanities* 1 (1).

Bonnett, A. 1992. "Art, Ideology and Everyday Space: Subversive Tendencies from Dada to Postmodernism." *Environment and Planning D: Society and Space* 10: 69–86.

Borderías, C. 2012. "La reconstrucción de la actividad femenina en Cataluña circa 1902." *Historia Contemporánea* (44).

Brenner, Neil. 1998. "Global Cities, Glocal States: Global City Formation and State Territorial Restructuring in Contemporary Europe." *Review of International Political Economy* 5 (1): 1–37.

BSA Brooklyn Street Art. 2018. "Spanish 'el Konvent' Welcomes Street Artists and Nurtures Collective Culture." Accessed April 10, 2020. www.brooklynstreetart.com/2019/09/30/spanish-el-konvent-welcomes-to-street-artists-and-nurtures-collective-culture/?fbclid=IwAR2uELJA53Get55EbkS2XV5AK4OpAFY4tuie04xMbGJ3wbKKC_wv-OhzDco.

Buller, H. 2009. "The Lively Process of Interdisciplinarity." *Area* 41: 395–403.

Busquets, J. 2008. "habitatges singulars de la colònia Rosal (Berguedà)." *Habitatge obrer i colònies industrials a la peninsula Ibèrica*. Terrassa: Museu de la Ciència i de la Tècnica de Catalunya.

CACIS. 2020. "CACiS | CACiS – Centre d'Art Contemporani i Sostenibilitat El forn de la calç, Cacis.elforndelacalc.cat." [online] Accessed May 26, 2020. http://cacis.elforndelacalc.cat/.

CAN- Farrera de Pallars. 2020. "Enllaços d'interes – CAN." [online] Accessed May 26, 2020. https://farreracan.cat/enllacos-dinteres/.

Canturri, M. 2019. "Un dels millors fotògrafs del món aterra a Avià per omplir les parets del poble de fotoperiodisme, Aquí Berguedà." Accessed May 26, 2020. www.aquibergueda.cat/2019/07/23/un-dels-millors-fotografs-del-mon-aterra-a-avia-per-omplir-les-parets-del-poble-de-fotoperiodisme/.

Casas, P., and J. Grané. 2014. "Els jardins de la industrialització. Un exemple de la colonització simbòlica del territory." *Revista d'Etnologia de Catalunya* (39).

Català, R., and A. Molas. 2005. *Les colònies del LLobregat. Paisatge i vivència*. Barcelona: Publicacions de l'Abadia de Montserrat.

Catalan Films and TV. 2019. "7 raons per fugir." [online] Accessed May 26, 2020. http://catalanfilms.cat/en/productions/7-reasons-to-run-away-from-society.

Chelcea, Liviu. 2015. "Postindustrial Ecologies: Industrial Rubble, Nature and the Limits of Representation." *Parcours anthropologiques* 10: 186–201.

Clément, G. 2004. *Manifeste du Tiers paysage*. Paris: Éditions du Commun.

Crang, M. 1996. "Envisioning Urban Histories: Bristol as Palimpsest, Postcards, and Snapshots." *Environment and Planning A* 28 (3): 429–52.

Creators. 2017. "Cyborg Performance Art." [online] Accessed May 26, 2020. www.youtube.com/watch?v=-NJMkpSRG6s.

Cresswell, T. 2010. "New Cultural Geography – An Unfinished Project?" *Cultural Geographies* 17: 169–74.

———. 2014. *Place: An Introduction*. Hoboken, NJ: John Wiley & Sons.

———. 2019. *Maxwell Street: Writing and Thinking Place*. Chicago, IL: University of Chicago Press.

Cresswell, T., D. Dixon, P.K. Bol, and N. Entrikin. 2015. "Editorial." *Geohumanities* 1 (1).

Crouch, D. 2010. "Flirting with Space: Thinking Landscape Relationally." *Cultural Geographies* 17: 5–18.

Cyborgarts. 2020. "Cyborgarts.com." [online] Accessed May 26, 2020. www.cyborgarts.com/.

Dahlbeck, Elke, and Stefan Gärtner. 2019. *Just Transition for Regions and Generations. Experiences from Structural Change in the Ruhr Area*. Berlin: WWF Germany.

De Solà Morales, I. 1995. "Terrain Vague." In *AnyPlace*, edited by C. Davidson, 118–23. Cambridge, MA: MIT Press.

Dear, M. 2011. "Geocreativity. Creativity and Place." In *Geohumanities Art, History, Text at the Edge of Place*, edited by M. Dear, et al, 5–25. London: Routledge.

———. 2015. "Practicing Geohumanities." *Geohumanities* 1 (1).

Del Molino, S. 2016. *La España vacía. Viaje por un país que nunca fue*. Madrid: Turner Libros.

DeSilvey, C. 2017. *Curated Decay, Heritage Beyond Saving*. Minneapolis: University of Minessota Press.

DeSilvey, C., and T. Edensor. 2012. "Reckoning with Ruins." *Progress in Human Geography* 37 (4): 465–85.

Dewsbury, J.D., and S. Naylor. 2003. "Practising Geographical Knowledge: Fields, Bodies and Dissemination." *Area* 34: 253–60.

Doucet, B. ed., 2017. *Why Detroit Matters: Decline, Renewal and Hope in a Divided City*. Bristol: Policy Press.

Douet, James. 2011. "The 'art Factory', a Natural Re-Use Process." En Paper presented at VCPD Research Centre for Industrial Heritage conference, 15.

———. 2016. *Industrial Heritage Re-Tooled: The TICCIH Guide to Industrial Heritage Conservation*. Abington, UK: Routledge.

Edelblutte, S. 2009. *Paysages et territories de l'industrie en Europe. Héritages et renouveaux*. Paris: Édicions Ellipses.

Edensor, T. 2005. *Industrial Ruins. Space, Aesthetics and Materiality*. Oxford: Berg.

Enrech, C. 2009. "Orígens I formació de les colònies industrials a Catalunya (1868–1923)." In *Colònies industrials*. Barcelona: Museu d'Història de Catalunya.

Ferrer Alòs, Ll. 1994. "Notas sobre la familia y el trabajo de la mujer en la Cataluña Central (siglos XVIII-XX)." *Revista de Demografía Histórica* XII (2–3).
Ferrer, I. 2012. "El español Samuel Aranda gana el World Press Photo." *EL PAÍS*. February 10. Accessed May 26, 2020. https://elpais.com/cultura/2012/02/10/actualidad/1328869732_719096.html.
Fontdevila, O. 2018. *El arte de la mediación*. Barcelona: Consonni.
Gancedo, María Ramón, and Germán Ferrero Carrera. 2019. "DE BUENAS PRÁCTICAS."
Ganyet i Solé, Joan. 2008. "The Industrial Architecture of the Llobregat Valleys in Spain: A Valuable Cultural Landscape in the Process of Change." *Futuropa: For a New Vision of Landscape and Territory* (1): 8.
García, Marisol, Santiago Eizaguirre, and Marc Pradel. 2015. "Social Innovation and Creativity in Cities: A Socially Inclusive Governance Approach in Two Peripheral Spaces of Barcelona." *City, Culture and Society* 6 (4): 93–100.
García, Victoria Quirosa. 2018. "La gestión patrimonial desde la periferia: el arte contemporáneo como regenerador del espacio rural." *Sémata: Ciencias Sociais e Humanidades* 30.
González, R. 2009. "El treball de les dones a les colònies tèxtils catalanes durant l'últim terç del segle XIX I el primer del segle XX." In *Colònies industrials*. Barcelona: Museu d'Història de Catalunya.
González Juárez, Elva Araceli. 2020. "Matadero Madrid: ruina moderna, ciudad de las artes." *DOSSIER: TEATRE I cIuTAT. EScEnOGRAfIES PREExISTEnTS*: 93.
Harvey, D. 1989. *The Condition of Postmodernity*. Vol. 14. Oxford: Blackwell.
———. 1996. *Justice, Nature & the Geography of Difference*. Oxford: Blackwell.
Hawkins, H. 2012. "Geocreativity and Art. An Expanding Field: Site, the Body and Practice." *Progress in Human Geography* 37 (1): 52–71.
———. 2014. *For Creative Geographies. Geography, Visual Arts and the Making of Worlds*. London: Routledge.
Kaye, N. 2000. *Site-Specific Art: Performance, Place and Documentation*. London: Routledge.
Kirkwood, Niall, ed. 2001. *Manufactured Sites: Rethinking the Post-Industrial Landscape*. London: Spon Press.
Konvent Agenda. 2020. "Konvent Agenda." [online] Accessed May 26, 2020. https://konventzero.com/.
Konvent Puntzero. 2018. "Creença Exposició." [online] Accessed April 10, 2020. www.konvent.cat/creences/.
KonventZero. 2020. "Konvent." [online] Accessed May 26, 2020. https://konventzero.com/.
Laboral Ciudad de la Cultura. 2020. "Laboral Ciudad de la Cultura." Accessed May 26, 2020. www.laboralciudaddelacultura.com/.
Langhorst, Joern. 2014. "Re-presenting Transgressive Ecologies: Post-Industrial Sites as Contested Terrains." *Local Environment* 19 (10): 1110–33.
Lefebvre, H. 2013. *La producción del espacio*. Madrid: Capitán Swing.
Llonch, M. 2004. "La feminització del treball textile a Catalunya (1891–1959)." In *Treball tèxtil a la Catalunya Contemporània*. Lleida: Pagès Editors.
Loftus, A. 2009. "Intervening in the Environment of the Everyday." *Geoforum* 40: 326–34.
Loughran, Kevin. 2016. "Imbricated Spaces: The High Line, Urban Parks, and the Cultural Meaning of City and Nature." *Sociological Theory* 34 (4): 311–34.
Lynch, K. 1990. *Wasting Away*. San Francisco, CA: Sierra Club Books.
Manero Miguel, F., and J.L. García Cuesta, cords. 2017. *Territorial Heritage and Spatial Planning. A Geographical Perspective*. Pamplona: Aranzadi and Thomson Reuters Proview.

Marin, J. 2009. "Conflictivitat I pau social a les colònies industrials: l'oasi artificial." In *Colònies industrials*. Barcelona: Museu d'Història de Catalunya.
Martín Rodríguez, A., F. Suárez Domínguez, J. J. del Coz Díaz, A. Lozano Martínez-Luengas, and A. Cuartas Suárez. 2014. "Rehabilitación de los talleres de la Universidad Laboral de Gijón= Rehabilitation of the Workshops of the Labour University of Gijón." *Revista electrónica ReCoPar* 5: 63–75.
Marvell, Alan, and David Simm. 2016. "Unravelling the Geographical Palimpsest Through Fieldwork: Discovering a Sense of Place." *Geography* 101 (3): 125–36.
Massey, D. 1991. "A Global Sense of Place." *Marxism Today* (38): 24–29.
———. 2005. *For Space*. London: Sage.
———. 2011. "Landscape, Space, Politics: An Essay." http://thefutureoflandscape.wordpress.com/landscapespacepolitics-an-essay.
Matadero Madrid. 2020. "Matadero Madrid- Home." [online] Accessed May 26, 2020. www.mataderomadrid.org/.
Millington, Nate. 2013. "Post-Industrial Imaginaries: Nature, Representation and Ruin in Detroit, Michigan." *International Journal of Urban and Regional Research* 37 (1): 279–96.
mNACTEC. 2020. "Mapa del patrimoni industrial de Catalunya." [online] Accessed May 26, 2020. https://mnactec.cat/150elements/.
Mould, O. 2017. *Urban Subversion and the Creative City*. London: Routledge.
Parals, M. 2020. "[INTERACTIU] Mapa de les colònies industrials de Catalunya." *Sapiens*. April 26. [online] Accessed May 26, 2020. www.sapiens.cat/historia-casa/interactiu-mapa-de-les-colonies-industrials-de-catalunya_17860_102.html.
Pikner, Tarmo. 2014. "Enactments of Urban Nature: Considering Industrial Ruins." *Geografiska Annaler: Series B, Human Geography* 96 (1): 83–94.
Plana Pey, J. 2019. "Samuel Aranda: 'Vull que, amb les meves fotografies, la gent d'Avià empatitzi amb els països llunyans.'" Accessed May 26, 2020. www.aquibergueda.cat/2019/07/23/samuel-aranda-vull-que-amb-les-meves-fotografies-la-gent-davia-empatitzi-amb-els-paisos-llunyans/.
Pollock, V., and J. Sharp. 2007. "Constellations of Identity: Place-ma(r)king Beyond Heritage." *Environment and Planning D: Society and Space* 5: 1061–78.
Poulios, I. 2010. "Moving beyond a Values-Based Approach to Heritage Conservation." *Conservation and Management of Archaeological Sites* 12 (2): 175.
Pueblos en ARTE. 2020. "Pueblos en ARTE, Pueblosenarte.com." Accessed May 26, 2020. www.pueblosenarte.com/.
Rementeria, Iskandar. 2007. *Paisaje urbano y lugar del arte en la construcción del imaginario*. El caso del Centro Cultural Alhóndiga de Bilbao.
Rey, Juan Rey, Pablo Vegas González, and Jacinto Ruiz Carmona. 2018. "Estrategias de intervención estructural sobre edificios del patrimonio histórico industrial de Madrid: realizaciones recientes." *Hormigón y Acero* 69 (285): 91–99.
Serra, R. 2008. "*Els Rosal, industrials I politics*". *Cal Rosal 150 anys (1858–2008)*. La Pobla de Lillet: Ajuntament d'Olvan.
———. 2011. "Industrial Colonies in Catalonia." *Catalan Historical Review* 4: 101–20. Institut d'Estudis Catalans, Barcelona. doi:10.2436/20.1000.01.53, ISSN: 2013-407X.
Smith, M., J. Davidson, L. Cameron, and L. Bondi. 2009. *Emotion, Place and Culture*. Farnham: Ashgate.
Smith, Neil. 2010. *Uneven Development: Nature, Capital, and the Production of Space*. Athens: University of Georgia Press.
Suc de Síndria. 2019. "Suc de Síndria." Accessed May 26, 2020. http://sucdesindria.com/es/.

Swyngedouw, Erik. 1997. "Neither Global nor Local." *Spaces of Globalization: Reasserting the Power of the Local. Londres: Gulford*: 137–66.

Trinder, B. 1982. *The Making of the Industrial Landscape*. London: JM Dent & Sons Ltd.

Valeroa, Diana E., and Lucía López Marco. 2019. "Interdisciplinariedad en la innovación social frente a la despoblación rural." *Economia Agraria y Recursos Naturales* 19 (1380–2019–2989): 17–36.

Vilardaga, G. 2009. *El convent del tèxtil. Biografies mínimes*. Berga: L'Albí.

Void Projects 2018. "Creença, Spain." [online] Accessed April 10, 2020. www.voidprojects.org/#/creencaspain/.

8 Dramatising deindustrialisation

Experiential authority, temporality and embodiment in a play about nuclear decommissioning

Leila Dawney

Aleksandr: How does one close the Ignalina Nuclear Power Plant? Just like any other nuclear power plant. They halt its operation. They plan and stop the reactor, plan and inventory equipment, plan and carry out the characterisation of equipment, plan and dismantle. They also plan and conduct radiological characterisation, plan and sort, plan and pack, plan and characterise radioactive waste. They plan, plan, plan. A part of the waste can be considered non-radioactive and taken out for disposal or reuse. The rest is radioactive waste. This, after radiological characterisation and appropriate processing, will have to be packaged and buried in a repository.

By the year 2037, the INPP is to be replaced by a green meadow and three repositories of radioactive waste. A green meadow and three repositories of radioactive waste – that's what should be in the place of the INPP by 2038. Three repositories of radioactive waste. Waste containing radionuclides, short-lived and long-lived, highly hazardous and not so much.

Nuclides, the half-decay periods of which are from several years to millions of years. All this will be stacked in packages, surrounded by structures and geological materials and left here forever. Will our city remain here? Forever?

Script excerpt, *Green Meadow*

Introduction

Green Meadow is a documentary theatre production by the Lithuania National Drama Theatre. It uses participatory theatre techniques to explore the ongoing decommissioning of the Soviet-designed Ignalina Nuclear Power Plant in north-eastern Lithuania, and the effects of the decommissioning on the residents of Visaginas, a purpose-built satellite town that houses the workers of the plant.[1] The play was co-devised and performed by a group of people who live and work in Visaginas. It addresses how the decline of modernity's great projects are experienced by those whose lives were shaped by them: how they make sense of loss and change and how memory and embodied habit are folded into the everyday uncertainties of the present.

This chapter seeks to make visible the embodied subjectivities that emerge in communities centred on a single industry. It also seeks to consider the role of memory, habit and identity in making sense of shifting lives when these places undergo transition and decline. The theatre production – and my own ethnographic research in the town – challenge dominant ways of knowing and representing postindustrial spaces that are rooted in tropes of melancholic loss and spectacular decay, focusing instead on community transition and endurance and on how lives are made liveable in the present. By dramatising and personalising the politics of energy transition, the play foregrounds the experiential and community effects of wider economic and political processes. Playing with scale and temporality, it moves between singular events and *longue durée* histories, meshing the affective present with geological time.

The name *Green Meadow* describes the ultimate aim of decommissioning: to erase the huge architectural structure of both reactors as well as all auxiliary facilities and to replace everything with flora typical to the region. Yet this erasure is more than architectural: the plant, the town and its inhabitants are the materialisation of the Soviet nuclear dream. The process of decommissioning is part of a wider set of global changes: post Chernobyl, post-Soviet, post-Europeanisation, post-progress. These changes have, in bringing about the closure of the plant, marked the town and its inhabitants as relics of a past and have ended – according to some – a shameful era.

Interspersing excerpts from the script of *Green Meadow* with a discussion of performance, subjectivity and deindustrialisation, I highlight how drama – and documentary theatre in particular – mines the body as historical archive, offering an account of experience and subjectivity that moves beyond social science methods that focus on texts alone. The production process and the performance, foreground embodied practice, movement and affect. Here, the body-as-archive becomes a site of experiential authority, where non-professional actors, the origin of their own experience, interact with audiences. By foregrounding memory, habit, experience and feeling, the play reveals the deep and intimate ways in which town and plant were entwined and how Visaginas' inhabitants are coming to terms with the slow, ongoing dismantling of the fundamental telos of their town.

The chapter first discusses the dramatological process and methods used in *Green Meadow* to demonstrate how drama as social science reveals these embodied sensibilities. I then consider how the ethos of the production generates a form of "experiential authority" that gives weight to performers' experiences, focusing on how the everyday nuclearity of the town is made visible through these embodied testimonies. The final section of the chapter argues that the complex temporalities of the play situate everyday life, memory and habit within broader histories of energy and matter, opening up the event of the plant's closure and folding everyday life and experience into the nuclear Anthropocene.

Deindustrialisation, affect and subjectivity

Visaginas, formerly known as Sniečkus, was an *atomgrad*, one of a series of purpose-built towns constructed during the 1970s and 1980s to house the workers of nuclear facilities (Wendland 2015).[2] These towns both showcased the success of the Soviet planned economy and provided pleasant, egalitarian living spaces for the workers of the plant. Workers were posted to the Sniečkus from other, often closed, nuclear sites elsewhere in the Soviet Union and helped to build the town and the plant. With the fall of the Soviet Union, the decision to close the plant was announced, a trade-off condition of Lithuania's accession to the European Union. At the time, no alternative economic plan was put in place outside of the long and painstaking work of dismantling the plant. While a large number of the town's residents left Visaginas to explore the opportunities offered by the free movement of labour with the EU, many remained to work on the decommissioning or lived off redundancy money, pensions and the piecemeal alternative work available (Šliavaitė 2015; Dawney forthcoming).

Divorced from the Soviet planned economy, monoindustrial places like Visaginas are fragile. The first nuclear age promised near limitless power; now, what seemed like the future of fuel generation is increasingly uncertain. Indeed, in Visaginas, the closure of the plant is an indirect consequence of the breaking up of the Soviet Union and subsequent independence of Lithuania, the accession of Lithuania into the European Union, the aftermath of the Chernobyl disaster (Ignalina II used the same RBMK-500 reactors and indeed much of the HBO TV series *Chernobyl* was filmed at the plant) and ongoing uncertainty regarding nuclear power. A focus on deindustrialising communities reveals the lived experience of structural change – the affective, emotional and sensorial shifts that take place as the tectonics of livelihood, dwelling and belonging pull apart. It enables us to pay attention to the way that these connections are sedimented in memories, affects, bodily habits, expertise and subjectivities and to the processes of adapting to change.

There is a small but significant literature in the social sciences on the relationship between affect, community and deindustrialisation. Walkerdine and Jimenez' (2012, 72) sensitive discussion of affect and community after the closing of a steelworks in South Wales describes the closure as an existential threat, seen to rupture a community's "sense of continuity of being". They relate how the residents experienced collective trauma, using the metaphor of "skin" to describe the holding power of the steelworks and the "overwhelming anxiety and threat of annihilation" that were the effects of its removal (Walkerdine and Jimenez 2012, 56). Concern with the affective fallout of deindustrialisation is echoed by Stewart, discussing the embodied and traumatic effects of the closure of coal mines in West Virginia:

> The bodies wheezed. They reeled. They were hit by contagious outbreaks of "the nerves." People "fell out." They said it was like they were being pulled down by a hand that grabbed them in the middle of their back. The force of things amassed in floods of stories and in ruined objects that piled up on the landscape like an accrual of phantom limbs.
>
> (Stewart 2011, 447).

In these studies, a focus on affect and community brings to the fore the intensified connections between place, labour and community in deindustrialising places and the trauma that processes of economic, political and technological change can bring about.

Other scholars of deindustrialised places have attended to the relationship between landscape and affect and the visible traces of former industrial processes on the landscape. Storm (2014, 1) develops the concept of the landscape scar as "a reminder, the trace of a wound . . . marks of sorrow and betrayal, of the abuse of power and latent hazards . . . they bear tales of communities and dreams, of achievements and resistance". This attention to place and subjectivity is also stressed by Alice Mah (2012), whose concept of "industrial ruination" reveals landscapes of uncertainty, disruption and traumatic collective memory. In cultural geography, material traces of former industrial glory have been ripe grounds for melancholic ruminations on memory, loss and ruination that both highlight the significance of material remains and at the same time feed into "ruin-gazing" tropes (Edensor 2005; Strangleman 2013; Dawney 2020; DeSilvey and Edensor 2013; Millington 2013; Fraser 2018).

While this literature indeed offers sensitive and nuanced accounts of the capillary endings of deindustrialisation, foregrounding how macroeconomic and political changes play out at the community level, they rely largely on conventional social science methods – such as interviews – or on the researcher's own interactions with postindustrial landscapes. Using drama as a social science method can offer an increased focus on embodiment, movement and experience. This embodied approach reveals how day-to-day habits, cultures and ways of life are inscribed on and through bodies, foregrounding these bodies as spaces through which material, economic and affective transitions take place. Here, it is the bodies themselves, not only their recorded testimonies, that act as archives of the event.

Drama, experiential authority and the body as archive

While investigating these relationships between affect, deindustrialisation and community in Visaginas in 2016 with two photographers, I stayed by coincidence in the same guest house as the team from the Lithuanian National Drama Theatre, who were in the early stages of developing *Green Meadow*. This serendipitous meeting led to our collaboration. I subsequently conducted a workshop with the creative team to explore the conceptual themes of the play. These discussions drew together observations from my fieldwork during 2016 and 2017 and from the LDNT's early work with theatre participants, as well as discussions of academic texts including *Problems of Hope* (Dawney, Blencowe, and Bresnihan 2017) and Nixon's *Slow Violence* (Nixon 2011). On future visits, I attended a theatre workshop in Visaginas, watched three performances of *Green Meadow* and conducted interviews with the creative team and some of the performers.

Green Meadow's actors were recruited by setting up a stall in the middle of town, near to the (now removed) radiation monitor. Those who were interested took part in a series of weekly workshops to develop the play. The script was based on interview transcripts and drama workshops. Early versions of the production were staged within the town in 2017, offering opportunities for audiences to contribute to the production process. The play was then staged at the Lithuanian National Drama Theatre in Vilnius, then toured regional towns in Lithuania including Visaginas.

Drama can make embodied histories visible, expanding the forms of data available to researchers to include habit, movement, gesture and affect: registers that are less available in more traditional social science methods such as the interview. Recent geographical research has highlighted the use of drama as social science method, both to communicate and disseminate research and to allow marginalised voices to be heard, for example in Pratt and Johnston's important work with Filipina domestic labourers in Canada, Mike Richardson's exploration of Irishness and masculinity through theatre, and Ruth Raynor's collaborative theatre production with a women's group in Gateshead exploring everyday understandings of austerity (Pratt and Johnston 2013; Richardson 2015; Raynor 2017a, 2017b; see also Rogers 2018). In each of these examples, drama is used as a powerful tool for understanding complex economic, social and psychosocial phenomena, both giving a voice to the powerless and facilitating participants in making sense of their own experiences. In addition, drama can also facilitate collective-sense making through the construction of stories (Raynor 2017b). In this way, these practices follow a long tradition in Boalian theatre of the oppressed (Boal 2006) and the work of early feminist consciousness-raising practices that seek to externalise and make public – and therefore political – privately felt and unacknowledged experiences (e.g., Sarachild 1978). In the context of Visaginas, a town where people feel forgotten and abandoned by the institutions that inflicted change upon them, the collective production of a play about these changes helped to build community narratives and to communicate their stories to those from outside the town. My own interviewees had discussed with me the way they felt shame when discussing where they are from and how the town is treated as an object of ridicule or derision by those from other parts of Lithuania. The play enabled the performers to generate and tell their stories to a broader public, to speak about their hometown with pride and authority, offering a medium for exploring lived politics and the "voice of the street" (Stephens 2019).

There are parallels between *Green Meadow* and the work of the Berlin-based company Rimini Protokoll, whose theatricalisations of the everyday involve performers as "experts who play themselves" (McKechnie 2010, 76). Rimini Protokoll aims to construct everyday utopias, where the authority of these "experts of the everyday" is augmented to give equal voice to those who may not otherwise be heard (Dreysse 2008). Kristina Werner, one of the directors of the play, aims to create a space where individuals are being witnessed and "seen in totality rather than as a limited extract of whom they represent or how others imagine them to be" (Balevičiūtė 2019 n.p.).

Documentary theatre, as a realist form, promises to offer a more "true" account of events through its reliance on documentary evidence. This usually relies on the written archive – the performing of a script based on documentary records (of interviews and archival documents). Here, it is the actors' bodies themselves that are the living archives from which the performance is devised. Unlike other forms of documentary theatre, such as verbatim theatre, where professional actors adapt and perform the experience of others, in *Green Meadow*, the audience directly encounters those whose stories are being told. Using the same body as both archive and performer foregrounds the play's liveness, promising a direct engagement with experience. In *Green Meadow*, performers who had worked in the nuclear plant were asked to develop a repetitive movement that related to their work. In this "dance", the choreography of movement and gesture gives thickness to the representation of experience and to the testimonies of the performers.

Using living bodies as archives, rather than the static representation of an oral history interview, allows the scripting to become more fluid and responsive. Director Kristina Werner encouraged performers to actively engage with the script throughout the play's lifespan: for each iteration of the performance, the performers amend the script, asking whether this holds as truth in the present. As the actors' lives develop and change and as they view their pasts in different ways in relation to their present, so the performance adapts. As a result, the instability of memory and the changes to people's lives in the present are incorporated in the script at every new performance, meaning that the archive is in a constant process of remaking.

Previously, I have discussed the concept of "experiential authority", drawing on the testimonies of those who have undergone major and often traumatic life experiences (bereavement, war) to show how the affective power of their own embodied experience generates relations of authority in the public sphere (Dawney 2013,

Figure 8.1 The "dance"

Source: Courtesy of Lithuanian National Drama Theatre, photography by Dmitrij Matvejev

2019). Here, the audience encounters this authority through direct engagement with these "experts of the everyday". The abstractions of energy politics become personalised, amplifying voices that may otherwise not be heard and bringing authenticity and voice to their complex dynamics. The production plays with realism and fiction, truth and authenticity, involving genuine but staged testimonies of "experts by experience", blurring together dreams, memories and imagined realities and future. From the audience's perspective, the performance of the play by those who live in the town augments the sense of truth, authenticity and authority of experience, producing alternative, vernacular histories that undercut and slice through narratives from above.

Memory and nuclearity

While there are similarities between experiences of deindustrialisation, nuclear energy production is notably different from common case studies, such as the extractive or metals industries. It involves different expertise, skills and safety-focused modes of attention, meaning that nuclear communities operate in a world of everyday nuclearity (Hecht 2012). This everyday nuclearity is visible throughout the town, in the form of sirens on the sides of buildings, play structures shaped like subatomic particles, a radiation indicator (now removed) in the middle of town and street names like Energetikų (Dawney forthcoming).[3] Nuclear workers do not garner the same sympathetic and sentimental response as other workers affected by deindustrialisation – the heroic figure of the miner or steelworker that mobilises left-wing nostalgia does not hold in the context of nuclear work, which is, as many of the participants in my ethnographic research revealed, associated with contamination and fear. For these reasons, among others, the specific histories of nuclear decommissioning are rarely discussed in academic work on deindustrialisation. This project provides a welcome discussion of these histories, demonstrating how nuclearity – and its position within 20th-century imaginaries, shapes the lives of those who work in the nuclear industry and the way in which they experience its decline.

Green Meadow testifies to the deeply entwined worlds of nuclear sociotechnical assemblages in the lives of Visaginas' inhabitants through recalling memories, first of growing up near the plant, second of the Chernobyl disaster, and third of the night of the shutdown of the last reactor. The theatre process brings to the fore personal memories and embodied habits that constitute everyday life in the *Atomgrad*.

In the following extract, the playful, collective recitation of safety procedures taught in school reveals the shared histories of nuclearity held by the residents of the town, while at the same time drawing attention to the everyday affective modalities (fear, complacency) informed by the possibility of an accident.[4]

Gerdas: We had a class called Civil Safety. During that class we would play cards or eat sunflower seeds. Or skip it altogether.

Edita: One time, I remember we were in a forest, picking mushrooms or berries. And the sirens started howling.

Figure 8.2 Enacting everyday nuclearity

Source: Courtesy of Lithuanian National Drama Theatre, photography by Dmitrij Matvejev

Dima: Sirens were cool. Every time I heard them, I thought, maybe something finally happened? Nope, just a routine check.

Edita: I got so scared because it sounded like a giant vacuum cleaner.

Gerdas: I had a plan as a boy that if something happened to the plant, I'd hide underground until the wave passed.

Edita: As a child, I already knew about Chernobyl and that vacuum cleaner sound was a sign of disaster to me.

Maša: We were shown films about Chernobyl. I didn't really care about it. It seemed so long ago and far away, like on another planet.

Edita: And I imagined a nuclear disaster being like a gas stove explosion.

Aleksandr: I was six when Chernobyl happened.

Maša: I was sitting at my school desk, looking at the teacher writing something on the blackboard.

Aleksandr: I don't remember any news related to the tragedy.

Maša: Suddenly a siren blasted. "What if the plant exploded and my parents are there? What am I gonna do?"

Aleksandr: We were visiting friends, and Dad and his colleague read about it in a newspaper . . .

Maša: I thought, if there's evacuation and I'm allowed to take only three things, what would they be?

Aleksandr: Certain mushrooms couldn't be eaten from then on because they accumulate heavy metals and radionuclides.

Maša: I decided to take my beloved doll, my chinchilla, and some chinchilla food.

Gerdas: One night there was a big blast outside my window.
Dima: They taught us at school what to do in case of a nuclear disaster.
Gerdas: I jumped into my bed: what happened? Did the plant explode?
Dima: They gave us a ton of instructions.
Gerdas: But it was just thunder.
Edita: If you're driving, pull over, turn the ventilation off and roll up the windows.
Dima: Turn on the radio or TV.
Maša: Don't drive any further and don't get out.
Olia: If you're outside, get in.
Aleksandr: Look for an evacuation plan – it shows where the buses will come.
Gerdas: Don't touch any injured people – they may be radioactive.
Edita: Cover your mouth with a wet cheesecloth.
Maša: Having returned from the outside, put your clothes and shoes into a plastic bag and remove it from the premises.
Dima: Don't drink, eat, or smoke in a contaminated area.
Gerdas: Seal all air vents.
Maša: Wash yourself thoroughly with soap.
Edita: Wash your dog or cat if they've been outside.
Aleksandr: Shut the windows.
Olia: Wash your hair.
Maša: Take a few iodine pills.
Gerdas: Cover any water wells.
Edita: Warn your neighbours.
Maša: Do not panic.

Here, the experiences of growing up in a space of everyday nuclearity and the intertwining of bodies and the plant is made visible through childhood memory. Safety procedures are reeled off like mantras, as the shared histories of risk mitigation are related with humour and levity. Earlier in the play, the ritualised and habitual practices of daily work in a nuclear plant offer a repetitive, cyclical temporality that Lisa Baraitser describes as the "time of maintenance" (Baraitser 2017): ongoing, banal work of keeping things going, performing safety checks in the context of foreclosed futures. The performance rests on both the instability of memory and the complex and unstable relation between past and present. Two events, in particular, feature prominently: the night when the final reactor stopped and the Chernobyl disaster.

Maša: December 31, 2009. The power plant's last day of operations. I offered to my friends to go there, listen to its sounds one last time, and say goodbye to it. We bought tickets for the bus that used to bring the employers in and out of the plant every day.

On the way there, I tried to imagine what I was going to see. I expected to hear all kinds of noises, like in factories. Smoking chimneys, people shouting "Bring in the uranium!" or something along those lines. And so, we arrived at the plant. The bus door opened and . . . nothing. Silence. There was nobody outside.

You could almost see the tumbleweed rolling around. We decided to walk around the territory.

We reached a printing house. It's in a separate building, where my mother once worked. I recalled one New Year's Eve when Santa brought me a doll. I took it to mother's work, where I fed it, gave it a drink, and put it to sleep. Mother's colleagues would say, "Oh, what a cute girl. Here's a candy for you." It would make me so happy. We walked around a little longer, then we left.

Back home, sitting at the festive table on New Year's Day, I imagined that as I was eating Russian salad, out there in the plant, a man in a white uniform was sitting and waiting for midnight to arrive so he could shut the plant down. There he goes to an "ON/OFF" switch, pulls it, and shuts the power plant down. And then the lights go out, the city is dark, and lightbulbs explode in every home. There I was, a few minutes past midnight, waiting for this to happen. And nothing. Just silence. Not even a spark in a socket or a flicker in a lightbulb. Nothing.

If it had been a movie, after shutting down the plant, the man would leave the plant, put a huge lock on its door and go home. He would be sad as he walked the streets and everybody would yell at him, "What have you done? Why did you turn the plant off? What were you thinking?" And they'd throw tomatoes at him. Then he would go home and tell his wife, "That's it. Turned it off." "God, you're an idiot." She'd collect her stuff and leave him. Then he'd pick up a gun and shoot himself.

But that would be like in the movies.

In reality, my mom and I sat at the table and ate salad.

Aleksandr: 2010.

It was only five days that later I realized that something had changed. It took me while to understand what it was.

I went to the turbine room and listened. The silence . . .

Not as quiet as it is nowadays, before or after the work day, when no workers are dismantling things. But way quieter than it used to be when the turbines were running. Like standing next to an ascending airplane. Plus the turbine room got colder. The working machines used to generate a lot of heat. There was no point in heating a huge hall, especially when they started cutting heating costs.

All of that is memory games. It comes and goes. Images emerge and dissolve in the air. A kaleidoscope.

As usual, the monitoring schedule was set one year in advance. A few weeks later, we realized we could do away with some of the measurements the following year. We were given new tasks and new duties. Together with the new Head of Division we started working on a bulky waste characterisation methodology.

It was a very intense time. Everyone needed the methodology to be able to begin the dismantling works. The work began. Running around the controlled zone with a huge gamma-ray spectrometer. The management was anxious to receive the methodology and begin the dismantling. The workers avoided it like the plague.

I guess they couldn't understand that it was all over. They were hoping for a re-launch of the plant. I couldn't understand it myself, despite being part of the impulse that started the dismantling.

That winter and spring in Europe were very cold. Plus, natural gas prices skyrocketed.

In Slovakia, for example, their plant was shut down and then restarted for six months, in order to bring the country's power production costs down.

Here people hoped for the same. It's a psychological thing. If you don't want something to happen, you keep pushing it away as much as you can. Serious changes take time.

With time, the staff learned the instructions better than I did. They can even correct me now if I misquote something. Everybody got used to the new order. Things settled down.

Yet knowing that everything changed forever is very sad.

Vova: On the night of the shutdown, my parents and I were looking at a website that showed the levels of energy produced by the plant. We saw the indicators gradually descending. In the morning, they were down to zero.

Aukse: I don't remember what I did on that night. I just noticed that lightbulbs got dimmer after the shutdown. They really used to be brighter.

The closing of something is unspectacular. There is no ceremony, no rite of passage, just the slight dimming of lightbulbs as the town's electricity supply gets switched to the main grid. The production draws attention to the difficulty of dramatising these slow processes of change – in attempting to focus on the event, it is revealed as a let-down. Maša's memories of granting significance to the event by imagining the closure cinematically are juxtaposed with (safety worker) Alexandr's practical account of the changes in the working day at the plant. During the dramaturgical process, fragments of memory rise to the surface: of a childhood inflected by nuclearity, of eating salad as the lights dim during the closing of the plant, of building a town now left to fend for itself. These fragments show how the plant is inscribed onto bodies – through the repetitive processes of the working day, for example – or through memories of the chocolate eclairs from the plant bakery, of the plentiful heat and hot water that maintained bodily comfort in sub-zero temperatures.

Complex temporalities

Deindustrialisation is a long, slow process. The decommissioning of the plant itself will take 30 years. At the community level, coming to terms with change is slow and incremental. As Sherry Linkon points out, using an apposite metaphor for this case, deindustrialisation has a "half-life", and spectacular events such as the closure of a factory or plant have extended, ongoing reverberations through communities (Linkon 2018). In our conceptual workshop, we drew on recent discussions of "slow violence" (Nixon 2011) to situate the event in the context of memories of quotidian life, ongoing sense-making in the present, histories of industrialisation and the afterlives of nuclear matter to reveal the longer, more complex temporalities of industrial processes. The play deals with the difficulty of making sense of these overlapping temporalities by juxtaposing specific events with the ongoing, mundane everydayness of life in the plant and *longue durée* histories of radioactive matter. The lived and felt events of the closure of the plant and the learning about the Chernobyl disaster are woven into speculative histories and futures that span hundreds of thousands of years. The experiences of the performers of *Green Meadow*, as first-hand witnesses to the building and closure of the Ignalina power plant, personalise and dramatize these broader temporalities of industrialisation, deindustrialisation and the Anthropocene. Their bodies are thus positioned as shifting, material repositories for histories of energy, hubris, progress, power and endurance.

Figure 8.3 The timeline

Source: Courtesy of Lithuanian National Drama Theatre, photography by Dmitrij Matvejev

Avoiding the for and against arguments so beloved of those discussing nuclear power or inviting the audience to engage with "issues", *Green Meadow* dramatizes a site of the nuclear Anthropocene as it plays out through bodies haunted by memories, histories and lost futures (Carpenter 2016). The play opens with a timeline: a collective narration of the personal, the political and the planetary.

Beginning with the first appearance of *homo sapiens* – via the discovery of uranium, the occupation of Lithuania by the Soviet Union, the personal histories of the actors' relatives who built the town, the Chernobyl disaster, individual achievements and memorable events of the cast – and ending in the year 800362, the timeline accelerates toward its speculative conclusion:

Olia: 2012. Working and living in London, I learn that I'm pregnant and decide to go back to Visaginas. Here, on May 14, my son Robert is born.

Gerdas: 2013. My dog Harley wins the explosive detection championship.

Dima: September 2015. I return from my travels to Visaginas and decide to put down roots here.

Vova: October 2016. I join the Green Meadow project.

Violeta: 2038. The power plant is closed. In its place there is now a brown field instead of a green meadow.

Edita: 2068. A long-term waste storage facility 750 metres underground starts operating

Gerdas: Year 200030. A 60-tonne chondrite meteorite falls on Kalviškiai village, 5 kilometres from the deep storage facility.

Auksė: Year 300101. The threat arises that aliens might land on Earth and use the nuclear fuel for military purposes.

Aleksandr: Approximately 500014. The nuclear fuel now used is comparable to natural uranium in terms of its radiotoxicity.

Maša: Year 800362. . .

Conclusion

Drama can reveal the affective and embodied effects of postindustrial change. Weaving together memory, habit, movement and experience, theatre offers a method for teasing out the intimacies of nuclearity and the effects that the closure of the plant has on the symbolic and affective life of the community living alongside it. By using theatre methods such as movement to activate memory and reflection, *Green Meadow* generates creative ways of representing lived experience, drawing out performers' affective relations to historical events. Drama as social science method is a powerful form of collective theorising, bringing together embodied experience, memory, philosophy, affective attachments and material engagements to produce multiple, entangled and differently scaled stories and provide counter narratives to official histories.

In this chapter, I have discussed how *Green Meadow* generates a form of experiential authority, augmenting vernacular experiences and bringing new voices into public discussions around deindustrialisation and energy politics. The production offers powerful alternative narratives that contest dominant deindustrialisation stories of loss and decline. While memory is central to the stories told, the ongoingness of *Green Meadow* refuses closure, inviting audiences to consider the ways that performers move on, make new paths and get by. It thus avoids stock characterisations and formulaic modes of storytelling mired in melancholy and loss, instead drawing out moments of humour and levity. It pays attention to the cultures that persist in deindustrialising places and the social glue that these cultures offer as a means to endure the present. Performers are seen in all their complexity, rather than figures that stand for a moment in history or as archetypal victims of processes beyond their control.

Participatory theatre can elicit these stories and experiences, revealing personal and collective memories and communicating them to wider audiences. *Green Meadow* creates a platform and means for the experiential authority of those directly involved in the closure of the Ignalina II plant to enter broader issues of energy politics, deindustrialisation and radioactive waste management. In giving voice to those who live in Visaginas, it makes visible the cultural and community aspects of everyday nuclearity, showing how peoples' lives are shaped by the nuclear promise of the 20th century and perhaps allowing more informed discussions of the community implications of nuclear decommissioning. In this way, the work of the LDNT augments the authority of these "everyday experts". As art, research method and public engagement, the play offers multiple, complex and fragmented histories, presents and futures, making explicit the participation of quotidian practices in planetary histories and processes.

Acknowledgments

Thanks to the creative team of *Green Meadow:* Rimantas Ribačiauskas, Kristina Savickienė, Jonas Tertelis, Kristina Werner, all the performers, Jonty Tacon, Laurie Griffiths and the many others I met during fieldwork in Visaginas.

Notes

1 Verbatim theatre is a form of documentary theatre that uses the words of real people, rather than fictional characters. The process usually involves interviewing participants and then producing a script based on the interview transcripts.

2 Other *Atomgrads* include Sosnovyi Bor, Kurchatov, Desnogors in Russia and Energodar and Prypiat/Slavutych in Ukraine.

3 Elsewhere, I highlight the spatial articulations of this everyday nuclearity in Visaginas, drawing attention to its role in providing community identity.

4 Visaginas is primarily Russian speaking, while the play was performed in Lithuanian venues such as the National Drama Theatre. Its performers' first languages were Russian, Lithuanian and English. All performers spoke in their mother tongue, while surtitles in each of the other two languages were displayed during the performance. The extracts form the script here are taken from the English surtitle translations, where necessary.

References

Balevičiūtė, R. 2019. Interview with Kristina Werner. In *Teatro žurnalas*.

Baraitser, L. 2017. *Enduring Time*. London: Bloomsbury Publishing.

Boal, A. 2006. *The Aesthetics of the Oppressed*. Abingdon: Routledge.

Carpenter, E. 2016. *The Nuclear Culture Source Book*. London: Black Dog Publishing.

Dawney, L. 2013. "The Figure of Authority: The Affective Biopolitics of the Mother and the Dying Man." *Journal of Political Power* 6: 29–47.

———. 2019. "Affective War: Wounded Bodies as Political Technologies." *Body & Society* 25: 49–72.

———. 2020. "Decommissioned Places: Ruins, Endurance and Care at the End of the First Nuclear Age." *Transactions of the Institute of British Geographers* 45: 33–49.

———. forthcoming. "Atomic Cities, Analogue Dreams: Infrastructural Ontologies and the Memories of Lost Futures." *Environment and Planning D: Society and Space*.

Dawney, L., C. Blencowe, and P. Bresnihan. 2017. *Problems of Hope*. Lewes: ARN Press.

DeSilvey, C., and T. Edensor. 2013. "Reckoning with Ruins." *Progress in Human Geography* 37: 465–85.

Dreysse, M. 2008. *Experts of the Everyday: The Theatre of Rimini Protokoll*. Berlin: Alexander-Verlag.

Edensor, T. 2005. *Industrial Ruins: Spaces, Aesthetics and Materiality*. Oxford and New York: Berg.

Fraser, E. 2018. "Unbecoming Place: Urban Imaginaries in Transition in Detroit." *Cultural Geographies* 25: 441–58.

Hecht, G. 2012. *Being Nuclear: Africans and the Global Uranium Trade*. Cambridge, MA: MIT Press.

Linkon, S.L. 2018. *The Half-Life of Deindustrialization: Working-Class Writing about Economic Restructuring*. Ann Arbor, MI: University of Michigan Press.

Mah, A. 2012. *Industrial Ruination, Community, and Place: Landscapes and Legacies of Urban Decline*. Toronto: University of Toronto Press.

McKechnie, K. 2010. "Instance: Rimini Protokoll, Mnemopark (2005)." In *Mapping Intermediality in Performance*, edited by C.K. Sarah Bay-Cheng, Andy Lavender, and Robin Nelson, 75–81. Amsterdam: Amsterdam University Press.

Millington, N. 2013. "Post-Industrial Imaginaries: Nature, Representation and Ruin in Detroit, Michigan." *International Journal of Urban and Regional Research* 37: 279–96.

Nixon, R. 2011. *Slow Violence and the Environmentalism of the Poor*. Cambridge, MA: Harvard University Press.

Pratt, G., and C. Johnston. 2013. "Staging Testimony in Nanay." *Geographical Review* 103: 288–3.

Raynor, R. 2017a. "(De) composing Habit in Theatre-as-Method." *GeoHumanities* 3: 108–21.

———. 2017b. "Dramatising Austerity: Holding a Story Together (and why it falls apart . . .)." *Cultural Geographies* 24: 193–212.

Richardson, M.J. 2015. "Theatre as Safe Space? Performing Intergenerational Narratives with Men of Irish Descent." *Social & Cultural Geography* 16: 615–33.

Rogers, A. 2018. "Advancing the Geographies of the Performing Arts: Intercultural Aesthetics, Migratory Mobility and Geopolitics." *Progress in Human Geography* 42: 549–68.

Sarachild, K. 1978. "Consciousness-Raising: A Radical Weapon." In *Feminist Revolution*, edited by K. Sarachild, 144–50. New York: Random House.

Šliavaitė, K. 2015. "'Homeland is Where Everything is for the People': The Rationale of Belonging and Citizenship in the Context of Social Uncertainty." In *Ethnographies of Grey Zones in Eastern Europe: Relations, Borders and Invisibilities*, edited by I.H. Knudsen and M.D. Frederiksen, 107–22. New York: Anthem Press.
Stephens, S. 2019. *Rage*. London: Bloomsbury Publishing.
Stewart, K. 2011. "Atmospheric Attunements." *Environment and Planning D: Society and Space* 29: 445–53.
Storm, A. 2014. *Post-Industrial Landscape Scars*. Basingstoke: Palgrave Macmillan.
Strangleman, T. 2013. "'Smokestack Nostalgia,' 'Ruin Porn' or Working-Class Obituary: The Role and Meaning of Deindustrial Representation 1." *International Labor and Working-Class History* 84: 23–37.
Walkerdine, V., and L. Jimenez. 2012. *Gender, Work and Community after De-Industrialisation: A Psychosocial Approach to Affect*. Basingstoke: Palgrave Macmillan.
Wendland, A.V. 2015. "Inventing the Atomograd. Nuclear Urbanism as a Way of Life in Eastern Europe, 1970–2011." In *The Impact of Disaster: Social and Cultural Approaches to Fukushima and Chernobyl*, edited by T.F.L.G. Thomas Bohn and Arndt Graf, 261–87. Berlin: EB Publishers.

Part 3

De-romanticizing industrial heritage

9 Agrarian ruins of the Khmer Rouge

The post-industrial landscapes of a rural economy

James A. Tyner and Stian Rice

Introduction

You are standing before a colonnade of hulking concrete pillars. Each one supports a hefty block of bridgework, pockmarked by the elements and discolored by black mold. An unruly tangle of climbing plants has turned the pillars and crosspieces into a giant trellis. Not far away, other concrete structures come into view. The angular remains of buildings open to the sky, their wooden roofs long-lost to time and termites. Concrete buttresses supporting rusted steelworks. Midden heaps of long-forgotten building materials, rocks, and fill. You might be forgiven for thinking you were staring at the ruins of an enormous factory or industrial complex; in fact, you are standing in a Cambodian rice field. Lime-green seedlings carpet the earth around you. Water buffalo graze at the forest margin. The mosaic of bunded fields is as flat as a chessboard. And yet, this seemingly common agrarian landscape is dotted with odd concrete monuments – some long and narrow, others short and squat – like the bones of a colossal beast that got its heavy feet stuck in Cambodia's sticky clay and died. As the sun sets, the hulking concrete skeletons throw long shadows across the freshly seeded fields.

Those pillars are the remains of Cha-Roek Dam (Figure 9.1), part of an irrigation network in Pursat Province intended to supply water to rice fields near the city of Battambang, dozens of kilometers away (Figure 9.2). Built between 1976 and 1977 by the Communist Party of Kampuchea (CPK, also known as the Khmer Rouge), the Cha-Roek dam was part of a national program to increase agricultural production throughout Cambodia. The expansion of agriculture – especially rice cultivation – was the cornerstone of the CPK's socialist revolution and economic plan. To achieve their goals, Party leaders sought to triple rice production through large-scale intensification: targets that could only be reached through the large-scale management of water. During its four-year rule, the Party embarked on an extraordinary program of hydrologic development – a program predicated on forced labor, food rationing, and the threat of execution. By 1979, one in four Cambodians had died, making the CPK one of bloodiest regimes in modern history (Slocomb 2010). And like the ruins of Cha-Roek, the colossal remains of the CPK still cast a long shadow over Cambodia.

Figure 9.1 Remnants of Cha-Roek Dam, Pursat Province, Cambodia

Source: James A. Tyner

In this chapter, we reflect on the diverse remnants and ruins of Democratic Kampuchea's (DK) irrigation infrastructure as a form of post-industrial landscape. To do this, we begin by challenging conventional distinctions between 'industrial' and 'agrarian' (cf. Arrow 1988). We argue that these concepts do not denote distinct spatial domains or mutually exclusive sets of processes. Rather, industrialization and agrarianism operate as a dialectic – a relationship clearly expressed in Democratic Kampuchea. For the Khmer Rouge, industrialization was inextricably connected to agricultural growth: on the one hand, agricultural exports were expected to provide the revenue necessary to jumpstart industry; on the other, industry was to provide the advanced mechanical and chemical inputs needed to improve agriculture. Inasmuch as industrial and agrarian processes were linked so too are the landscapes that now contain their ruins. For these reasons, we argue that a more complete account of post-industrial landscapes must bring 'traditional' industrial ruins (e.g., factories, mines, derelict structures) into conversation with their agrarian counterparts.

Furthermore, we follow Philpotts' (2014, 47) observation that the study of post-industrial landscapes is a question of the "relationship between ruins and the social systems that produce and receive them." This observation draws attention

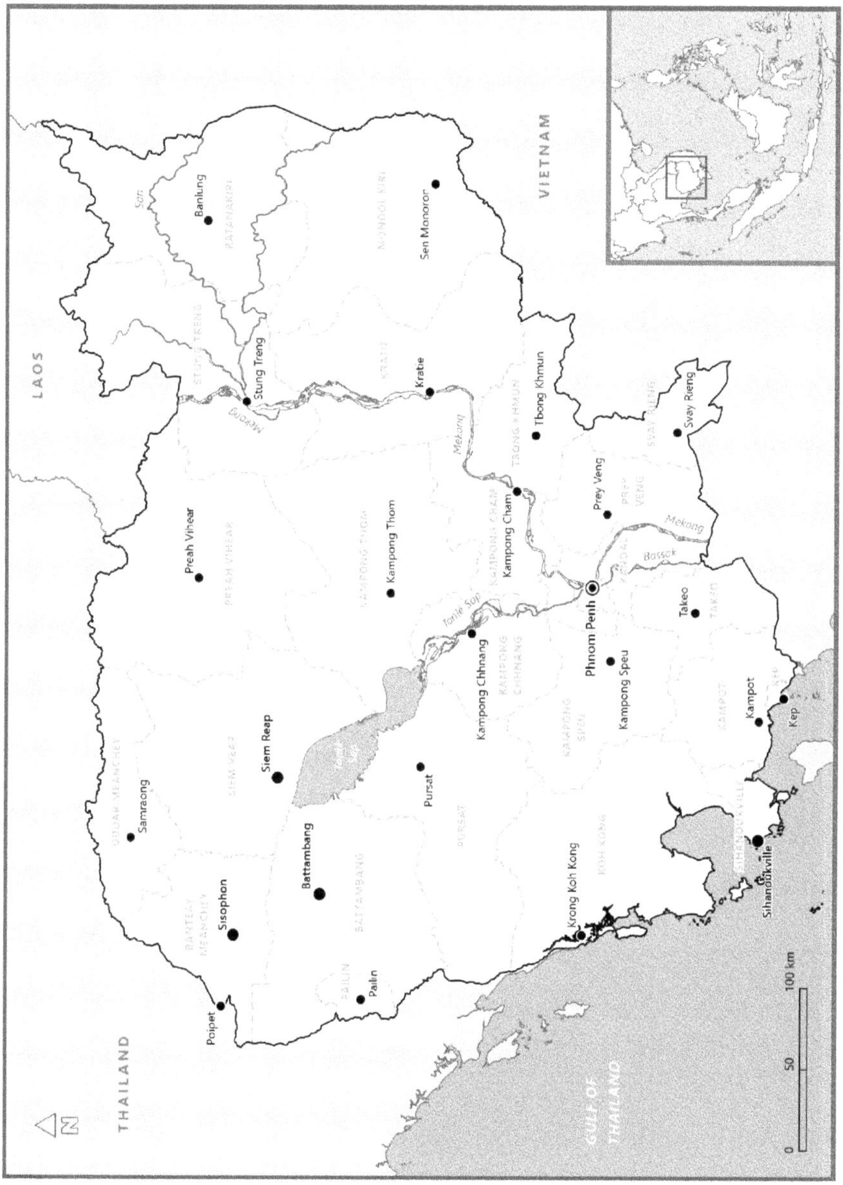

Figure 9.2 Overview map of Cambodia showing contemporary provinces, major cities, and waterways

Source: Stian Rice

to how "the derelict reality of the ruined present" is connected to the "grandiose ideological visions" of the regimes that built these structures (Philpotts 2014, 48). The concrete, earthen, and metal ruins that dot Cambodia's countryside are remnants of the CPK's failed attempt to build industrial agriculture. However, they are more than spectral traces (Edensor 2005) of a genocidal past; indeed, many of these structures continue to participate in the same project for which they were built: the movement of water to grow rice. In this vein, we recommend further engagement with agrarian ruins within post-communist landscapes (cf. Pusca 2010; Philpotts 2014) and encourage an openness to how these landscapes are being reused or repurposed today. Our chapter thus draws upon in-depth field work, remote sensing, and archival research (see especially Tyner et al. 2018; Coakley et al. 2019). Furthermore, without engaging in epistemological debates, considerable analytical work – through field visits, interviews, and data analysis of satellite imagery – is presented in descriptive form, i.e., a description of key findings, such as a typology of irrigation systems. Our intention is to demonstrate how the Khmer Rouge's modernization program – a vital component of which was to rapidly increase industrial capacity – was predicated on an expansion of agriculture. Hence, many of the industrial ruins appear in the rural areas of the country, as evidence of the metabolic relation of agriculture and industry.

This chapter is organized into the following sections. Sections one and two build a conceptual link between spaces and processes of industrialization and agriculture, setting the stage to include agrarian ruins within the study of post-industrial landscapes. Section three outlines the agricultural transformations undertaken by the CPK as part of the Party's overarching Four Year Plan. In section four, we detail the hydrologic projects undertaken to achieve these objectives and how parts of this infrastructure are being used today. Finally, section five returns to the discussion on post-industrial agrarian landscapes within the context of Cambodia, its past life under the CPK, and its future as a rice-oriented economy.

Industry and agriculture

A growing body of scholarship on post-industrial landscapes has explored industrial ruins in a wide range of contexts, including the spatio-temporal legacies of abandoned steelworks (Braae 2015), auto manufacturing (Kinney 2016), mining (Pardo Abad 2017), coalfields (Kitchen, Marsden, and Milbourne 2006; Stiles et al. 2017), and brownfields (Loures and Panagopoulos 2007; Hoefer, Wolfram, and Vera Vicenzotti 2013) among others, including within this collection (see Cerarols and Luna; Hollis et al.). In some contexts, 'post-industrial' is subdivided into more-or-less distinct "landscapes of industrial production and landscapes of waste and refuse" (Langhorst 2004, 65). Despite its expansive scope, the invocation of 'post-industrial' within landscape studies has come to denote spaces and processes that are (1) broadly urban or resulting from urban forms of metabolism and (2) direct legacies of the Industrial Revolution as expressed in the built environment (cf. Kolejka et al. 2013). Within this literature, agricultural landscapes are rarely addressed. 'Post-industrial agriculture' has been deployed in primarily two contexts: in reference to forms of farming or agroecology that follow from – or contravene – *industrial agriculture* (cf. Tweeten and Zulauf 1998; Innis 1983) and forms of agriculture, like urban farming, which emerge in de-industrializing contexts (cf. Millington 2013; Lawson and Miller 2012). In the former, 'industrial' is used to identify a distinct and historically specified form of agricultural production; in the latter, industry is an activity being replaced *by* agriculture.

Both usages reinforce an implicit distinction between industry and agriculture within work on post-industrial landscapes, further illustrating the strength of the term 'industrial' as an organizing concept. This distinction between industry and agriculture emerges from a long tradition within economics and European history of seeing these as separate sectors that are organized in different ways, employ distinct groups, occupy distinct spaces, and produce different landscapes. From these roots, it makes sense that theorization around processes of landscape change would begin by segregating farms from factories.

Following work on methodological cityism (Angelo and Wachsmuth 2015; Connolly 2019; Rice and Tyner 2017), we argue that such segregation may unintentionally limit research in post-industrial landscapes to a set of 'preferred' contexts. To the extent that post-industrial processes are associated with a particular kind of landscape – and a particular kind of landscape is associated with industrial legacies – the scope of analysis becomes self-limiting. That is, we come to identify post-industrial processes by looking at what is taking place within certain landscapes (e.g.,: abandoned factories, tailings, and brownfields) and simultaneously declare such landscapes to be 'post-industrial' because of the processes taking place there. Such self-validation may analytically privilege certain actors and processes while muting others. Critically, it limits the set of actors and processes seen to participate in post-industrialization, as well as the landscapes considered to be post-industrial.

That said, once these implicit limitations are relaxed, new types of 'industrial' participants, processes, and landscapes may emerge; notably, agricultural ones. Of course, these relationships are not new: scholarship on the so-called agrarian question has been weaving together processes of industrial and agricultural transformation for over a century (cf. Kautsky 1902; Polanyi 2001; De Janvry 1981). From farm subsidies to food welfare programs, industrial transitions throughout history have been built on the back of agriculture. Growth in agricultural production has enabled the accretion of workers and capital within cities since the 1700s through increases in food and industrial materials like cotton and wool. Later, these concentrations of industrial capital drove agricultural transition through the loss of farm labor and the corporate aggregation of farms. Recently, alienation and disenfranchisement with the wage labor system have led to a resurgence in smallholder farming in some locales, accompanied by discourses that idealize localized production and consumption, food sovereignty (Alkon and Mares 2012), and 21st-century yeomanry (Longman 2008). All play a role in industrialization and deindustrialization. For these reasons, we argue that agriculture and industry are best seen in dialectical relation, wherein the processes that animate one necessarily influence the other.

How, then, should we understand agricultural landscapes as industrial (or post-industrial) ones? More to the point, what constitutes industrialization (or de-industrialization) in an agricultural context? Two contrasting approaches offer a starting point. First, agricultural industrialization is synonymous with the increased use of industrial inputs like tractors, chemical fertilizers, pesticides, and improved seeds – in other words, agriculture is seen to become more industrial the more it uses the products of industry (for example, see Sachs et al. 2007). This *industrialization-as-input* approach frames industrial agriculture as a variation on traditional agriculture – one in which some traditional materials and practices have been replaced by others.

Another approach sees industrial agriculture as the consequence of a cluster of processes – collectively called 'industrialization' – on farming (Silbergeld 2016; Albritton 2009). These processes are commonly associated with the economic transformation of Britain in the 18th and 19th centuries. Using this approach, the industrialization of agriculture exhibits five characteristics. First, productive activities shift from subsistence to commodity production. Second, ownership of the means of production begins to shift from a large base of owners to a small group of powerful individuals or companies. In the case of state capitalism, the means of production is captured and controlled by the state. Third, as capital becomes concentrated, wealthy actors reinvest in technological inputs to increase productivity and push out competitors. Fourth, the labor force is transformed. Labor may be aggregated by cannibalizing workers from other economic sectors or made redundant through technological advancements. Either way, the effect is to suppress the wage rate and improve capital's ability to extract surplus value. Finally, capital is increasingly fixed in the landscape in ways that increase local productivity, attract additional capital investment, and leave a lasting, visible trace. This *industrialization-as-process* approach sees industrial agriculture as a distinct form of agricultural production, one in which traditional relations of production have been vastly altered.

As described later, the transition undertaken by the CPK constitutes a clear case of agricultural industrialization regardless of which approach is applied. That said, here we adopt the industrialization-as-process approach for two reasons. First, attention to process helps expand the scope of analysis to include the dialectical relationship between agriculture and industry. Indeed, the CPK had interlocking and complementary agendas for both sectors. Second, by highlighting the industrial nature of certain processes, the emphasis shifts from industrial revolutions to revolutions *that are industrial in nature*. The dramatic economic transformation orchestrated by the CPK between 1975 and 1979 was such a revolution, even though it took place in rural rice fields.

Agrarian 'ruins'

Industrialization-as-process lays the groundwork for a discussion of industrial ruins beyond the city, the factory complex, the mine, and the landfill. This approach expands the scope of existing theorization from traditional post-industrial landscapes into agrarian ones. For example, Pusca (2010, 240) notes the temporal impermanence of industrial ruins when she writes:

> Industrial ruins in Eastern Europe are seen to represent, perhaps more so than anything else, the hard shell of communism: the last remains of a now past era that are littered around the postcommunist landscapes, often empty and abandoned, stripped of any recyclable material to a point where their previous role becomes unrecognizable even to those who used to work there.

The hydrologic infrastructure of Democratic Kampuchea endured a similar fate. In the years following the ouster of the Khmer Rouge, survivors dismantled many of the structures as scavengers reused building materials or sold them for scrap. But not everything has suffered from erasure: sections of canal – no longer functional as a network – have been repurposed as local reservoirs for nearby fields. Elsewhere, the reanimation of these water-bearing bodies has been accomplished with sizeable infusions of Western capital (Saing et al. 2012). As noted in non-agrarian contexts, the historical intentions and functions behind a structure may be lost for a time, only to re-emerge under more promising economic and political contexts. As we discuss in later sections, many of Democratic Kampuchea's reservoirs, dams, canals, waterways, and pumping stations have been granted a purposeful life after the Khmer Rouge, one that encourages reflection on the utopian ideologies that motivated their construction in the first place.

Agrarian transformations during the Cambodian Genocide

Between 1975 and 1979, the CPK sought to establish a new society governed by a Marxist–Leninist inspired vision of collective ownership. In the process, upwards of two million people perished through disease, famine, torture, murder, and execution (Kiernan 1996; Hinton 2005). A widely held – and erroneous – presumption is that senior leaders of the CPK sought to turn back the wheels of time to recreate an agrarian utopia, one modeled after the Angkoran Empire that lasted from the 9th through the 14th centuries (see Vickery 2000; Chandler 2018). Far from an anachronistic project, however, the CPK's objective is best characterized as one of modernization. This social and economic revolution entailed the wholesale uprooting and conversion of traditional farming practices into an agrarian system that would feed the growth of industry. In so doing, the CPK followed in the footsteps of their Soviet and Chinese predecessors.

On the eve of the Khmer Rouge coming to power, two contradictory trends characterized Cambodia's rural landscape. On the one hand, the area of land under cultivation had increased appreciably throughout the 20th century. On the other, this expansion of farmland coincided with both the material fragmentation and social concentration of land (Willmott 1981; Kiernan 1982; Rice and Tyner 2017; Tyner 2017; Galway 2019). Overall, the agrarian sector comprised mostly small- and medium-sized family farms. Indeed, most farmers were small landowners, owning up to five hectares. Most pressing for these farmers, however, was the fragmentation of land: a problem predating – but exacerbated by – French colonialism. A typical farmer, for example, might hold five hectares of rice paddy, own agricultural tools and draught animals, but lack operating capital. Poor harvests, consequently, could portend financial ruin. Vulnerability to hunger followed from indebtedness and usury, not landlessness. Tenants and sharecroppers found themselves stuck in cycles of seasonal indebtedness, having to borrow money, repay interest, and borrow again the next season (Vickery 2000). Even small landholders, especially in the wake of poor harvests, found themselves having to borrow money or purchase necessary supplies on credit (Diepart 2015; Diepart and Sem 2018).

In April 1975, Khmer Rouge rebels captured the capital, Phnom Penh, ending a protracted civil war. Over the next few years, two objectives figured prominently in state economic planning: the necessity to raise the standard of living quickly and to increase capital from agriculture in order to modernize industry.[1] Both were to be achieved through the promotion of an economic strategy of import substitution industrialization (ISI) (cf. Gerber 2007; Tyner 2017). Such an approach is readily evident in surviving CPK documents. Minutes from a meeting held on May 8, 1976, for example, indicate, "We will decrease importing items next year, including cotton and jute, because we are working hard to produce ours. We will import only some important items such as chemical fertilizer, plastic, acid, iron factory, and other raw materials."[2]

To effectively promote a program of ISI, Party leaders determined what they could produce locally and what they had to import. CPK officials saw Democratic Kampuchea brimming with "such things as land, livestock, natural resource, water sources such as lakes, river and ponds," resources that afforded them "great advantages compared with China, Vietnam, or Africa."[3] However, senior CPK planners focused on agriculture as their primary comparative advantage. As indicated in the Four-Year Plan, "We stand on agriculture as the basis, so as to collect agricultural capital with which to strengthen and expand industry."[4] Officials postulated they could "export and sell many products such as kapok, shrimp, squid, elephant fish, and turtles" to "earn foreign exchange."[5] Indeed, so optimistic were Party leaders, they expounded, "There are great possibilities for exporting peanuts, wheat, corn, sesame, and beans. The objective would be to save up these products for export."[6] Ominously, the report cautions, "Almost anything can be exported, *so long as we don't consume it ourselves*, but set it aside."[7]

In their attempt to rapidly transform the country's traditional farming sector, Party members focused on those agricultural commodities that would ensure the best return for their investments. It was essential, the CPK explained, "to promote all kinds of variety in planting by every means and method" to solve the needs of the people but especially to "concentrate on crops which can give yields for export and sale abroad . . . in order to be able to find the maximum capital annually."[8] To this end, rice reigned supreme. For Party leaders, the decision was profit-oriented: "For 100,000 tons of milled rice, we would get US$20 million; if we had 500,000 tons, we'd get $100 million. . . . We must increase rice production in order to obtain capital. Other products, which are only complimentary, will be increased in the future."[9] To this end, government officials directed the peasantry to "Plant corn, plant potatoes, plant vegetables, plant gourds, plant pumpkins. Plant everything. Plant a lot."[10] Yet, above all, rice remained "the fundamental matter, the key related to the life and death of our revolution, our people, and our country."[11] Revenue derived from the international exchange of rice would, in turn, fund the modernization of Democratic Kampuchea's industrial sector.

To modernize industry through the mass production of textiles, machinery, and other durable goods, senior leaders of the CPK decreed that they would "only have to earn [foreign] capital from agriculture."[12] In practice, the CPK sought to expand production through deforestation and large-scale irrigation schemes. These efforts were coupled with the construction of an extensive network of dams and canals with the objective of bringing much-needed water into historically arid regions and convert once-unproductive lands into agricultural bounties (Tyner and Will 2015; Tyner and Rice 2016; Rice and Tyner 2017; Tyner 2017). In less than four years, forced laborers constructed approximately 7,000 kilometers of canals and dikes and over 350 reservoirs as part of an unprecedented hydro-infrastructure (Tyner et al. 2018; Coakley et al. 2019).

Khmer Rouge hydro-infrastructure

Rice cultivation requires abundant water. In traditional wet-field systems, newly sprouted seedlings are transplanted into rain-soaked fields. As the seedlings grow, farmers adjust the quantity of water in the field – enough to keep the roots covered but not so much as to swamp the plants. Rice plants receive nutrients primarily from the water in which they are partially submerged; as such, maintaining an appropriate water level within flooded fields is critical for the health of the plant and the viability of the seeds it produces. Flooded fields also prevent the growth of weeds, reducing the amount of labor required to maintain the field (Nesbitt and Phaloeun 1997). In monsoonal Cambodia, the timing and quantity of rainfall determines how many harvests can be achieved per year. Without irrigation, the best locations could achieve two harvests a year, but most were limited to one. Fields were fallowed during the dry months (January to April). The CPK's Four-Year Plan stipulated that total rice production was to be increased through both agricultural extensification and intensification; the latter accomplished by increasing the number of annual harvests in marginal areas from one to two and in productive areas from two to three. To achieve these goals, the CPK needed to alter the spatial and temporal distribution of water across the country's rice-growing regions – a task that required an unprecedented irrigation system.

In the broadest sense, irrigation schemes are constructed for one of two purposes: to contain and deliver transient water locally or to deliver water over longer distances. The hydro-infrastructure projects initiated and built under the guidance of the CPK may be classified into six categories based on the nature of storage and delivery of water, as well as the relationship of the structure to existing hydrology and geomorphology: external storage, internal storage, linked storage, segregated storage, large-scale canal systems, and topographically controlled systems (Tyner et al. 2018).

- *External storage systems* involve dams, dikes, and canals and are designed to store water upstream of the area being irrigated. External reservoirs are typically large; for example, the two interconnected reservoirs of the Stung Chinit irrigation scheme have a combined surface area of 34 km^2 connected by a 70 km-long canal.
- *Internal storage systems* are common throughout Democratic Kampuchea and range from very small (one km^2) to very large and are designed to slowly fill an area upstream from the retaining dykes, allowing rice production in the flooded areas. Some include one or more large canals to deliver water to areas tens of kilometers away.
- *Linked storage* schemes refer to situations wherein multiple, small dams are built along a single river or stream. The resultant reservoirs are ultimately connected to each other via the original stream.
- *Segregated storage* refers to the damming of multiple tributaries of a single river. These storage systems are commonly found in flat-bottomed valley settings, such as those north of the Tonle Sap in Kampong Thom Province.
- *Large-scale canal systems* are common throughout the flatlands of Democratic Kampuchea. In many places, long-distance canals crossed watershed and sub-watershed boundaries. Such large-scale systems were intended to carry water for tens of kilometers, providing access to water across a wide area, before adjoining another river. The longest canal built by the Khmer Rouge was the April 17th canal, measuring 97 km in length.
- Last, *topographically controlled systems* consist of dams and reservoirs where major topographic features on the landscape have been utilized as natural barriers to water flows. These systems may range in size – depending on local geomorphology – but tend toward the massive.

An essential material component – arguably *the* essential component – in all storage and canal systems was concrete. Concrete was necessary for sluicegates and spillways, pump houses, dam foundations, and wherever moving water threatened the premature erosion of earthen structures. As such, the CPK ensured that cement production was one of the first domestic industries restarted upon assuming power (cf. Twining 1989). In 1976, the CPK imported industrial equipment to support the construction of a cement factory at Châkrei Ting, with Chinese technicians assisting Cambodians in the construction and operation of the factory.[13] Similar demands were placed on steel production for rebar, gates, valves, pumps, and bridges. Beyond the need for concrete to manage water, the CPK made plans to accelerate industrialization in other agricultural input sectors; for example, tractors, chemical fertilizers, pesticides, and improved varieties of seed (Dalrymple 1986). Agronomic research in rice breeding conducted at sites in Battambang Province – initiated in the 1950s and 60s with support from the U.S. – was continued by the CPK, this time with Chinese advisors (Dalrymple 1986).

It is here, in the connection between rice cultivation, infrastructure, and agricultural inputs, that the dialectical relationship between agricultural and industrial sectors becomes obvious. First, industrial activities emerged to support agricultural intensification through the production of material inputs – an example of the industrialization-as-input approach. Factories, sand and gravel quarries, research stations, and diverse transport infrastructure received substantial injections of labor and capital to help drive the lifeblood of Democratic Kampuchea's planned economy: rice. Furthermore, the irrigation schemes undertaken by the CPK are exemplary illustrations of industrialization-as-process. The coordination and cooperation required to survey, plan, and implement hydrologic projects at this scale necessitated new forms of centralized control. To provide integration across political units, plans for irrigation schemes were passed up the CPK's political hierarchy. To organize the labor force, mobile work units (*kong chhlat*) were assembled and moved about the country as needed to bolster local workers (Twining 1989). Of course, this reorganization of labor could not have been accomplished without cannibalizing workers from other sectors. Finally, at its core, the underlying purpose of farming had shifted from subsistence to commodity production for exchange.

As such, we find that the material legacies of the CPK's irrigation projects are not merely 'industrial' because of concrete, rebar, and other ossified *products* of industry. Rather, these agrarian landscapes of ruin are 'industrial' because of the industrial *processes* that enabled and animated their construction.

Post-industrial landscapes of an agrarian economy

Following the industrialization-as-process approach, we find two compelling reasons to consider Democratic Kampuchea's agrarian transformation as a distinctly industrial revolution. First, through a reliance on ISI, the Party's agendas for industry and agriculture were clearly intertwined. The foreign exchange of agricultural commodities was intended to jumpstart industry, just as subsequent industrial inputs were intended to drive increases in agricultural yields. As such, processes in one sector necessarily influenced the other. No fact illustrates this better than the CPKs intention to "stand on agriculture as the basis . . . with which to strengthen and expand industry."[14] Rice cultivation became the sine qua non of industrial growth. Through agriculture, the CPK wanted to sow the seeds of industry; the hulking ruins broadcast across Cambodia are merely the discarded husks.

Second, not only was this agrarian transformation imbricated with industry, the transformation *itself* exhibited all the characteristics of a transition to industrial agriculture. In short order, a wide base of smallholders was replaced by a small group of powerful actors who controlled the means of production. Whereas in other agricultural contexts (e.g., the United States) this transition spanned several decades, in Democratic Kampuchea, consolidation of ownership took place essentially all at once.[15] Simultaneously, the mandate for production shifted from subsistence to commodity production for export. Quotas were established for each region of production, specifying how much rice had to be grown to produce a satisfactory surplus (Rice 2020). Party leaders sought to increase the production and distribution of tractors, chemical inputs, and improved seeds to increase yields. According to planning documents, by 1980, the CPK hoped to have 1,600 irrigation pumps, 500 rice mills, 6,500 threshing machines, and 1,000 tractors in operation, most manufactured domestically.[16]

Labor was organized in dramatic and violent fashion. In Britain during the Industrial Revolution, light and heavy manufacturing cannibalized agriculture for cheap labor – in some instances, the resulting rural-to-urban migration led to shortfalls in food production. In Democratic Kampuchea, the CPK directed most of the workforce into hard labor, either in rice production or the construction of hydro-infrastructure. In other words, Party leaders 'cannibalized' labor from non-farming sectors to support agriculture. Finally, the keystone supporting surplus rice production for export was an extensive irrigation network: an extraordinary volume of capital, literally sunk into Cambodia's laterite soils. Intended to transform agrarian space into crucibles of production for the state, these structures were built to navigate the twin imperatives of hydrology and capital accumulation. Cha-Roek dam and countless other sites remain as traces of that effort.

Yet, the productive legacy of these ruins is far from over. Throughout Cambodia, former prisons, killing fields, and mass burials have been privatized and marketized, not to torture or detain but ostensibly to educate new generations on the horrors of the Khmer Rouge (Hughes 2008). But in the case of many hydrologic ruins, recent interventions have less to do with re-*purposing* than re-*using* (for contrast, see Xie 2015; Günçe and Mısırlısoy 2015). Canals that no longer transport water still function as rainwater reservoirs for neighboring farms. During the dry months, farmers use gas-fueled pumps to pull standing water from canals up and over earthen dykes to feed parched fields. Some parts of the network have been repaired or renovated using public funds, while others, including large-scale systems like Stung Chinit, have seen sizeable injections of foreign capital (Saing et al. 2012). Water still moves through parts of the CPK's hydro-infrastructure but in the service of different masters.

It is widely accepted that industrial ruins participate in the production of memory; indeed, scholars have noted that post-industrial landscapes offer potential opportunities as monuments or tourist sites (cf. Pardo Abad 2017, as well as Price, this collection). Beyond memory production, abandoned structures and landscapes may offer material advantages over existing fixed capital, making such ruins desirable as sites for luxury apartments and condos, playgrounds, bike trails, wildlife preserves, and demonstration sites for sustainable urban design. In this way, post-industrial ruins can scaffold economic growth and new waves of capital accumulation. As Pusca (2010, 240; see also DeSilvey 2017) explains: "Decay need thus not always symbolize the death of a particular utopia but also the breeding ground of new hopes and utopias."

The ruins of Democratic Kampuchea's agrarian industrialization reflect this spirit of rejuvenation – but with a twist: the utopian dreams that inspired these structures in the 1970s bear a strong resemblance to the utopian dreams that are reanimating them today. Indeed, the production and export of surplus rice is the through-line that connects today's development plans with Pol Pot's dream of Angkar and the fantasies of the French Protectorate. What does this mean for the memory-work in which these landscapes participate? On the one hand, reuse may lead to de facto preservation – after all, the basic architecture of dams, canals, and aqueducts has changed little over the last 50 years. To the extent that the CPK's hydro-infrastructure is reused and valued *as* hydro-infrastructure, its continued existence is more-or-less assured. On the other hand, reuse can be a form of erasure (Schindel and Colombo 2014; Jones and Shaw 2006; Tyner 2014). Today, many of these structures serve as reminders of the extraordinary brutality experienced under the Khmer Rouge. It is unclear whether these reminders will remain after canals are dredged and concrete is re-poured. Such erasure affects much more than memory. Under the CPK's forced labor regime, workers who died from exhaustion or were executed during construction were simply buried in the earthworks. Unlike derelict buildings in other post-industrial landscapes, these ruins are not exactly empty, abandoned shells. They are tombs.

Conclusions

Across Cambodia, the ruins of the CPK's failed attempt to rapidly modernize agriculture remain. The concrete skeletons scattered across this landscape speak to an extraordinary, violent past. Indeed, the CPK's utopian vision of a country modernized through surplus rice and import substitution led to the deaths of one in four Cambodians, many of whom succumbed to exhaustion or starvation during construction of these hydrologic systems. In a curious (but alarming) irony, many of these ruined structures are being reused today to support the same vision. The ghosts of Democratic Kampuchea's water infrastructure – and the dead labor that animated it – are being reenlisted into the service of Cambodia's unfinished modernist revolution.

In this chapter, we argued that this ostensibly agrarian and rural landscape may be understood as a post-industrial one. Not only did the construction of the CPK's irrigation projects consume the products of industry, but the transformation of agriculture from subsistence to large-scale commodity production – and the concomitant need for irrigation – was propelled by processes of industrialization. In this way, we encourage a perspective on landscape transformation that sees industrialization as a set of processes applicable to – and underlying – a diversity of landscapes and social forms. As such, we see potential in including the ruins of industrial agriculture within the scope of post-industrial landscapes; for example, in the constellation of derelict granaries scattered across the central U.S., in Brazilian coral reefs dying from coastal nutrification (Costa et al. 2008), in the irrigation-induced desiccation of the Aral Sea (Cai, McKinney, and Rosegrant 2003), and in Cambodia's landscapes of agrarian genocide, among others. To exclude such spaces is to entertain a kind of methodological self-validation, one that privileges traditionally 'industrial' landscapes and processes over others.

You are standing in a Cambodian rice field, facing a colonnade of hulking concrete pillars. Each one is purpose-built to help manage the timing and distribution of life-giving water. Each one supports a hefty block of bridgework, but taken together, they support a ghostly vision of an economy built on commodity production for export. Despite being surrounded by rice and water buffalos with no city in sight, your overwhelming sense is that you are standing among the ruins of industry. We think your instincts are right.

Notes

1 Communist Party of Kampuchea (CPK), "The Party's Four-Year Plan to Build Socialism in All Fields, 1977–1980," in *Pol Pot Plans the Future: Confidential Leadership Documents from Democratic Kampuchea, 1976–1977*, ed. David P. Chandler, Ben Kiernan, and Chanthou Boua (New Haven, CT: Yale Center for International and Area Studies, 1988), 51.
2 Document No. D00698, "Cooperation with the Ministry of Commerce," archived at the Documentation Center of Cambodia, Phnom Penh.
3 CPK, "Four-Year Plan," 46.
4 CPK, "Four-Year Plan," 46.
5 Communist Party of Kampuchea (CPK), "Report of Activities of the Party Center According to the General Political Tasks of 1976," in *Pol Pot Plans the Future: Confidential Leadership Documents from Democratic Kampuchea, 1976–1977*, ed. David P. Chandler, Ben Kiernan, and Chanthou Boua (New Haven, CT: Yale Center for International and Area Studies, 1988), 200.
6 CPK, "Report of Activities," 200.
7 CPK, "Report of Activities," 200. Emphasis added.
8 Document No. E3/4, "Revolutionary Flag Issue 7, July 1976," archived by the Extraordinary Chambers in the Courts of Cambodia (ECCC) at www.eccc.gov.kh/en.
9 CPK, "Four-Year Plan," 51.
10 Document No. E3/760, "Revolutionary Flag Issue 6, June 1976," archived by the Extraordinary Chambers in the Courts of Cambodia (ECCC) at www.eccc.gov.kh/en.
11 Document No. E3/139, "Revolutionary Flag Issue 11, November 1976," archived by the Extraordinary Chambers in the Courts of Cambodia (ECCC) at www.eccc.gov.kh/en.
12 CPK, "Four-Year Plan," 96.
13 See for example "Interview with Van Rith in Khpop commune, S'ang district, Kandal province," archived at the Documentation Center of Cambodia, Phnom Penh.
14 CPK, "Four-Year Plan," 46.
15 Consolidation of land in rural areas under rebel control had been taking place steadily since the start of the civil war in 1970. The last remaining areas under republican control were consolidated shortly after the Khmer Rouge captured Phnom Penh on April 17, 1975.
16 Party Center, 1976, "Excerpted Report on the Leading Views of the Comrade Representing the Party Organization at a Zone Assembly," in *Pol Pot Plans the Future: Confidential Leadership Documents from Democratic Kampuchea, 1976–1977*, ed. D. Chandler, B. Kiernan, and C. Boua (New Haven, CT: Yale University Press).

References

Albritton, R. 2009. *Let Them Eat Junk: How Capitalism Creates Hunger and Obesity*. London: Pluto Press.

Alkon, Alison Hope, and Teresa Marie Mares. 2012. "Food Sovereignty in US Food Movements: Radical Visions and Neoliberal Constraints." *Agriculture and Human Values* 29 (3): 347–59.

Angelo, Hillary, and David Wachsmuth. 2015. "Urbanizing Urban Political Ecology: A Critique of Methodological Cityism." *International Journal of Urban and Regional Research* 39 (1): 16–27.

Arrow, Kenneth J., ed. 1988. *The Balance between Industry and Agriculture in Economic Development*. New York: Palgrave Macmillan.

Braae, Ellen Marie. 2015. *Beauty Redeemed: Recycling Post-Industrial Landscapes*. Basel: Birkhäuser Verlag.

Cai, Ximing, Daene C. McKinney, and Mark W. Rosegrant. 2003. "Sustainability Analysis for Irrigation Water Management in the Aral Sea Region." *Agricultural Systems* 76 (3): 1043–66.

Chandler, D. 2018. *A History of Cambodia*. Abingdon: Routledge.

Coakley, Corrine, Mandy Munro-Stasiuk, James A. Tyner, Sokvisal Kimsroy, Chhunly Chhay, and Stian Rice. 2019. "Extracting Khmer Rouge Irrigation Networks from Pre-Landsat 4 Satellite Imagery Using Vegetation Indices." *Remote Sensing* 11 (20): 2397.

Connolly, C. 2019. "Urban Political Ecology Beyond Methodological Cityism." *International Journal of Urban and Regional Research* 43 (1): 63–75.

Costa Jr, Ozeas S., Malcolm Nimmo, and Martin J. Attrill. 2008. "Coastal Nutrification in Brazil: A Review of the Role of Nutrient Excess on Coral Reef Demise." *Journal of South American Earth Sciences* 25 (2): 257–70.

Dalrymple, D.G. 1986. *Development and Spread of High-Yielding Rice Varieties in Developing Countries*. Washington, DC: Agency for International Development.

De Janvry, Alain. 1981. *The Agrarian Question and Reformism in Latin America. No. HD1790. 5. Z8. D44 1981*. Baltimore: Johns Hopkins University Press.

DeSilvey, Caitlin. 2017. *Curated Decay: Heritage Beyond Saving*. Minneapolis: University of Minnesota Press.

Diepart, Jean-Christophe. 2015. *The Fragmentation of Land Tenure Systems in Cambodia: Peasants and the Formalization of Land Rights*. Paris: Technical Committee on Land Tenure and Development.

Diepart, Jean-Christophe, and Thol Sem. 2018. *Cambodian Peasantry and Formalization of Land Right: Historical Perspectives and Current Issues*. Paris: Technical Committee on Land Tenure and Development.

Edensor, Tim. 2005. "The Ghosts of Industrial Ruins: Ordering and Disordering Memory in Excessive Space." *Environment and Planning D: Society and Space* 23 (6): 829–49.

Galway, Matthew. 2019. "Specters of Dependency: Hou Yuon and the Origins of Cambodia's Marxist Vision (1955–1975)." *Cross-Currents: East Asian History and Culture Review* 8 (2): 589–633.

Gerber, J.B. 2007. "41 Import Substitution Industrialization." *Handbook on International Trade Policy*: 441.

Günçe, K., and D. Mısırlısoy. 2015. "Questioning the Adaptive Reuse of Industrial Heritage and Its Interventions in the Context of Sustainability." *Sociology* 5 (9): 718–27.

Hinton, Alexander. 2005. *Why Did They Kill? Cambodia in the Shadow of Genocide*. Berkeley: University of California Press.

Hoefer, Wolfram, and Vera Vicenzotti. 2013. "Post-Industrial Landscapes: Evolving Concepts." In *The Routledge Companion to Landscape Studies*, 423–34. Abingdon: Routledge.

Hughes, R. 2008. "Dutiful Tourism: Encountering the Cambodian Genocide." *Asia Pacific Viewpoint* 49 (3): 318–30.

Innis, D.Q. 1983. "Aspects of Jamaican Post-Industrial Agriculture." *Journal of Geography* 82 (5): 222–26.

Jones, R., and B.J. Shaw. 2006. "Palimpsests of Progress: Erasing the Past and Rewriting the Future in Developing Societies – Case Studies of Singapore and Jakarta." *International Journal of Heritage Studies* 12 (2): 122–38.

Kautsky, Karl. 1902. *Die agrarfrage*. Germany: J. H. W. Dietz nachf. (g. m. b. h.).

Kiernan, Ben. 1982. "Introduction." In *Peasants and Politics in Kampuchea, 1942–1981*, edited by Ben Kiernan and Chanthou Boua, 1–28. London: Zed Press.

———. 1996. *The Pol Pot Regime: Policies, Race and Genocide in Cambodia under the Khmer Rouge, 1975–1979*. New Haven, CT: Yale University Press.

Kinney, Rebecca J. 2016. *Beautiful Wasteland: The Rise of Detroit as America's Postindustrial Frontier*. University of Minnesota Press.

Kitchen, Lawrence, Terry Marsden, and Paul Milbourne. 2006. "Community Forests and Regeneration in Post-Industrial Landscapes." *Geoforum* 37 (5): 831–43.

Kolejka, Jaromír, Martin Klimánek, Stanislav Martinát, and Aleš Ruda. 2013. "Delineation of Post-Industrial Landscapes of the Upper Silesian Corridor in the Basin of Ostrava." *Environmental & Socio-economic Studies* 1 (3): 21–34.

Langhorst, Joern W. 2004. "Re-Covering Landscapes: Derelict and Abandoned Sites as Contest Terrain." *Icon*: 65–79.

Lawson, L., and A. Miller. 2012. "Community Gardens and Urban: Agriculture as Antithesis to Abandonment: Exploring a Citizenship-Land Model." In *The City After Abandonment*, 17–40. Philadelphia, PA: University of Pennsylvania Press.

Longman, Phillip. 2008. "Yeoman's Return: Small-Scale Ownership and the Next Progressive Era." In *The Next Social Contract*. Washington, DC: New American Foundation.

Loures, Luis, and Thomas Panagopoulos. 2007. "From Derelict Industrial Areas Towards Multifunctional Landscapes and Urban Renaissance." *WSEAS Transactions on Environment and Development* 3 (10): 181–88.

Millington, N. 2013. "Post-Industrial Imaginaries: Nature, Representation and Ruin in Detroit, Michigan." *International Journal of Urban and Regional Research* 37 (1): 279–96.

Nesbitt, Harry J., and Chan Phaloeun. 1997. "Rice-Based Farming Systems." In *Rice Production in Cambodia*, edited by Harry J. Nesbitt, 31–38. Los Baños, Philippines: International Rice Research Institute.

Pardo Abad, Carlos J. 2017. "The Post-Industrial Landscapes of Riotinto and Almadén, Spain: Scenic Value, Heritage and Sustainable Tourism." *Journal of Heritage Tourism* 12 (4): 331–46.

Philpotts, Matthew. 2014. "The Ruins of Dictatorship: Prora and Other Spaces." *Central Europe* 12 (1): 47–61.

Polanyi, Karl. 2001. *The Great Transformation: The Political and Economic Origins of Our Time*. Boston: Beacon Press.

Pusca, Anca. 2010. "Industrial and Human Ruins of Postcommunist Europe." *Space and Culture* 13 (3): 239–55.

Rice, Stian. 2020. *Famine in the Remaking: Food System Change and Mass Starvation in Hawaii, Madagascar, and Cambodia*. Morgantown: West Virginia University Press.

Rice, Stian, and James A. Tyner. 2017. "The Rice Cities of the Khmer Rouge: An Urban Political Ecology of Rural Mass Violence." *Transactions of the Institute of British Geographers* 42: 559–71.

Sachs, W., T. Santarius, S. Murphy, and D.D.L.T. Ugarte. 2007. "World Trade and the Regeneration of Agriculture." *EcoFair Trade Dialogue Discussion Paper* (9).

Saing, Chan Hang, Socheth Hem, Chandarany Ouch, Dalis Phann, and Dorina Pon. 2012. *Foreign Investment in Agriculture in Cambodia*. Phnom Penh: Cambodia Development Resource Institute Working Paper Series, No. 60.

Schindel, E., and P. Colombo. 2014. *Space and the Memories of Violence: Landscapes of Erasure, Disappearance and Exception*. Berlin: Springer.

Silbergeld, E.K. 2016. *Chickenizing Farms and Food: How Industrial Meat Production Endangers Workers, Animals, and Consumers*. Baltimore: Johns Hopkins University Press.

Slocomb, M. 2010. *An Economic History of Cambodia in the Twentieth Century*. Singapore: NUS Press.

Stiles, Rochelle M., Jonathan W. Swan, Jaimie L. Klemish, and Michael J. Lannoo. 2017. "Amphibian Habitat Creation on Postindustrial Landscapes: A Case Study in a Reclaimed Coal Strip-Mine Area." *Canadian Journal of Zoology* 95 (2): 67–73.

Tweeten, L., and C. Zulauf. 1998. "Post-Industrial Agriculture." *Choices* 13 (2): 30–33.

Twining, Charles. 1989. "The Economy." In *Cambodia 1975–1978, Rendezvous with Death*, edited by Karl Jackson. Princeton, NJ: Princeton University Press.

Tyner, James A. 2014. "Violent Erasures and Erasing Violence: Contesting Cambodia's Landscapes of Violence." In *Space and the Memories of Violence*, 21–33. London: Palgrave Macmillan.

———. 2017. *From Rice Fields to Killing Fields: Nature, Life, and Labor under the Khmer Rouge*. Syracuse, NY: Syracuse University Press.

Tyner, James A., Mandy Munro-Stasiuk, Corrine Coakley, Sokvisal Kimsroy, and Stian Rice. 2018. "Khmer Rouge Irrigation Schemes during the Cambodian Genocide." *Genocide Studies International* 12 (1): 103–19.

Tyner, James A., and Stian Rice. 2016. "Cambodia's Political Economy of Violence: Space, Time, and Genocide under the Khmer Rouge, 1975–79." *Genocide Studies International* 10 (1): 84–94.

Tyner, James A., and Rachel Will. 2015. "Nature and Post-Conflict Violence: Water Management Under the Communist Party of Kampuchea, 1975–1979." *Transactions of the Institute of British Geographers* 40 (3): 362–74.

Vickery, M. 2000. *Cambodia, 1975–1982*. Chiang Mai, Thailand: Silkworm Books.

Willmott, William W. 1981. "Analytical Errors of the Kampuchean Communist Party." *Pacific Affairs* 54: 209–27.

Xie, P.F. 2015. "A Life Cycle Model of Industrial Heritage Development." *Annals of Tourism Research* 55: 141–54.

10 The cultural necrotechnologies of capital and the production of (post) industrial capital punishment

Alex R. Colucci

Introduction

The contemporary execution chamber in the United States is a relatively unremarkable space in terms of aesthetics and design. Generally, it is a well-lit, modestly sized room with nondescript walls containing only a clock, with several windows having curtains that can be drawn. There is only a medical bed or gurney and occasionally a chair and small table for placing implements. If every doctor's examination room had blank white walls, given only a quick glance, every execution chamber could easily be mistaken for where you receive your yearly check-up.

This highly medicalized and secluded space inside state- and federal-level prisons has not developed in isolation, nor have the material processes, knowledges, and technologies that exist in and organize this space. This location of post-industrial killing has been developed in an attempt to perfect the "gentle way of punishment" (Foucault 1977, 128–29) out of the ruinous landscape of industrialized killing that modernized the necrotechnologies of capital punishment over the past one-hundred and thirty years.[1] What this means is that there is both an abstract and material industrial heritage to the cultural objects and technological processes used in contemporary executions. The necrotechnologies of capital punishment, therefore, change based on political economic developments and how evolving political economies allow for material resources to be geographically distributed.

Capital punishment in the United States is and has been actively produced at different times within a constantly evolving social formation centered around a dominant capitalist mode of production and the values of indifferent commodity exchange. This production of capital punishment is embedded within and reflects prevailing currents of commodity production and circulation in specific historical-geographical contexts. Capital punishment, therefore, evolves alongside changes in the political-economy (how production and circulation are organized, for example) of a social formation and carries on features from the past with each successive form it takes (Colucci 2019a).

To situate this transitional production of capital punishment, I turn to work on material violence and material culture. The focus here is on the materiality of these two concepts because a materialist conception of human/nature relations allows for a grounded understanding of humans and nature as relationally co-productive, as opposed to idealist conceptions of space and history (Kirsch 2020). This materialist understanding foregrounds discussions of human/nature relations relative to economic activities by suggesting that human consciousness develops from our material interactions with the world around us. Indeed, as this perspective suggests, the human/nature relation is one that "is not fixed but interacts continuously" in mediating human consciousness as humans engage production processes in service of their survival needs (Anderson 1980, 172).

This insight into how the human/nature relation operates carries significant ramifications for the production of geographic knowledge. Following Anderson (1980, 176), "social forces do not exist independently of time and space; their location in time – space is one of their inherent material aspects." A materialist conception of violence and culture relative to capital punishment not only demonstrates the uneven distributions and place-to-place variations of the practice's political-economies but also grounds our understanding of the present landscape of post-industrial capital punishment production in its changing historical-geographical context. In short, the social forces that materially produce capital punishment today – and did so in the past – change with respect to the geographically situated state of human/nature relations where capital punishment is occurring. As political economies transition from industrial to post-industrial, forms of punishment in carceral landscapes transition in kind. To understand how, in certain places, new methods of capital punishment were developed and adopted, we must connect carceral spaces, like the execution chamber, to the material – and industrial – landscapes that produce them.

The remainder of this chapter proceeds from the material to the abstract in order to produce a theoretically and empirically grounded understanding of how the industrial and post-industrial landscapes of capital punishment have developed. As a brief outline, in the next section, I lay out a conceptual foundation that can be used to better contextualize the remainder of the chapter. A third section outlines the production of and transition between industrial and post-industrial modes of capital punishment. It details the extraction of resources and resulting industrial energy sources that are mobilized in the production of electrocution and lethal gas as necrotechnologies of capital punishment and then engages the state of knowledge production and transference as a resource in the production of lethal injection. A concluding section addresses the alienation of production processes and the state of academic knowledge production relative to the violence of capitalist alienation.

Political economies, capital punishment, material culture, and material violence

Following Scott Kirsch (2013, 435), "materiality is not so much 'indifferent stuff' but things, living and dead, woven in complex ways into the fabric of human and social being." He views "materialism in cultural geography as an underlying philosophy of explanation and framework for engagement – that which accords ontological priority to the material conditions of existence, and rejects non-material prime causes." The consequence of employing this thinking here is to understand capital punishment not as something that exists and manifests only through abstract cultural ideologies but rather something that exists and changes as a result of and response to material social relations.

To focus on the materiality of cultures and forms of violence, we must pay close attention to how the material conditions of life and death are created in certain fluid spatial contexts. When considering capital punishment, this means focusing on both culture's materially productive dimensions and the work done by scientists and politicians to produce new objects of nature, culture, and the human body (Kirsch 2014). In this way, capital punishment is just one of many material processes that demonstrate the values of our capitalist social formation. The values a social formation maintains are embodied in the material objects it produces, and it is these objects, when set in motion through human activation, that mediate social relations. For example, James Tyner's (2014) work on the Cambodian Genocide demonstrates how the social relations involved in the production of mass graves were made possible through the differential access certain populations had to rice and tools used to build irrigation infrastructure (also see Tyner and Rice's 2021 chapter in this volume).

This notion of materiality as both embodying and mediating social relations is likewise the subject of attention in recent geographies of violence literature (Davies 2018; Tyner 2015, 2016; Tyner, Inwood, and Alderman 2014). For example, Tyner and Inwood (2014, 780) write, "it is necessary to move beyond treating violence as simply existing and instead to materially ground it within the mode of production of a particular society." This reconceptualization of violence serves to break down the false binary of so called structural and direct violence to instead focus on the 'structures of violence' in which direct violence or the threat of it is embedded (Tyner 2015). The supposed difference between structural and direct violence rests in a conceptualization that direct violence can be traced to concrete persons or actors intentionally using physical force, while structural violence manifests from inequities built into the structures of a society, where a direct actor is not identifiable. This thinking must change; as Tyner and Inwood (2014, 780) write, "it is incumbent therefore to conceive of 'structural' violence as just as 'direct' as other concrete actions."

What this means for the spatiality of social relations is that they "transform with, as well as transform, the mode of production, and if we acknowledge that 'violence' is relational, it follows that 'violence' will likewise transform over time and space" (Tyner and Inwood 2014, 781). If changing modes of production transform what 'violence' is, that means violent material processes and the objects used in them will likewise transform and carry with them changing political-economic and cultural values. To understand the structural values embedded within objects, then, we must focus our attention on the material production of these objects as they relate to the violent lives and deaths of living things.

I bring these two literatures together through a brief example of the initial relations between capital punishment and the emerging capitalist social formation. From the 16th to 18th centuries, criminal codes in England punished several hundred simple property crimes by hanging (Federici 2004, 152; Linebaugh 2006; Wennerlind 2004, 141). Additionally, in England and France, labor militancy from Luddites and others, who resisted the mechanization of work and resultant loss of jobs by breaking machines, attacking factories, and otherwise protesting, was met with action from the state in the form of trials and executions (Horn 2005). Similar laws and state logics prevailed throughout developing Western liberal democracies and diffused throughout their colonial possessions. Justifications for these legal codes and state responses suggested that such severe punishment was warranted in order to discipline waged laborers to emerging political-economic logics and values of personal responsibility so as to avoid idleness (Federici 2004, 64; Perelman 2000). The plate engravings of William Hogarth's series *Industry and Idleness*, for example, incorporates scenes of responsible work and petty indolence culminating in a plate depicting the idle apprentice's execution. As his art demonstrates, the values of a given social formation – and the consequences for running afoul of them – are often represented in objects of material culture. These examples indicate how the installation and reproduction of capitalist cultural values occurs through the changing production and exchange of material objects, and how the processes of production and exchange are often violent. Repetitive, material industrial work in factories, therefore, reproduce capitalist cultural values by emphasizing the replaceability of laborers and normalizing the everyday violence of modern work by juxtaposing it with the spectacular state violence of execution.

Both the material uses of – and threat of death by – capital punishment was fundamental to the disciplining of labor to the values of capitalist production and consumption. When we ground our understanding of structural problems, like violence or poverty, in their particular historical-geographical material contexts, the uses of particular technologies – like those used in capital punishment – in producing abstract values becomes evident. In this case, the structural values of indifferent exchange – the circulation process that values only abstract exchange to generate surplus value at the behest of the actual material things being exchanged – are manifest in the material objects used to produce direct violence. This means that for a sovereign to produce a material death through capital punishment, the sovereign manifests its right over life in social spaces designed for orchestrated killing and dissemination of the cultural value of that killing. In turn, the values imparted by an occasioned execution are an attempt by sovereigns to delineate social relations. Ultimately, culture and violence – and where they intersect – are both produced and made to be productive. This geography – the *where* of the production of material culture and violence – requires us to briefly explore two related concepts: landscape and base/superstructure relations within social formations.

The production of culture and violence manifests in the form landscapes take, and landscapes themselves are a result of changing modes of production (Mitchell 2008; Schein 2012). As Mitchell (2008, 45) writes, "the spatial form of the landscape is both the result of and evidence for, the kind of society we live in." As an example, consider a city that invests in design features for park benches that do not allow people to lay down on them but does not enact housing reform or other measures to end homelessness. The form landscapes take reflects geographies of social (in)justice because it is in the materiality of landscapes where social relations are marked out, indicated, and concretized.

Landscapes both constitute and reflect the social formation of which they are a part. This is analogous to Peet's conceptualization of social-spatial relations within social formations (1978). The concept of a social formation is used to establish an understanding of an internally related social totality (the social world in total) in which humans exist. Far from deterministic, this concept aids in the examination of the dynamic internal (dialectic) relations within a totality by understanding the different but contextually related and changing levels that make up social formations: those of the base and superstructure (Peet 1978, 150). Existing as a dialectic, the base – land, labor, tools, etc. – is the material means of producing the necessities of human life (food, water, shelter), while the superstructure – law, education, morality, philosophy – is the abstract values humans produce and use to understand phenomena (c.f. Horvath and Gibson 1984, 14–15). The proposition is that social consciousness follows from the production of and spatial access to the material needs of life, not the other way around.

How and where the superstructure is organized and exists emanates from how and where humans have established the production and distribution of our material needs, though, oftentimes, through ideologies popularized in the superstructure, conditions at the base can be co-opted, which can alter both how humans access their material needs and the condition of social relations within a given social formation. This problem of access is fundamentally geographic and connects us back to Mitchell's contention regarding the connections between justice and the material form of landscapes: where are the material things humans need to survive, what is their relational distribution, who has greater or lesser access to them, and how is this distribution organized (politically and socially)?

In social formations where capitalism is a dominant mode of production, access to human material needs is geographically variable; even when production of these needs is significant, their distribution to sites of consumption is often inequitable. This inequality, as Mitchell and others make clear, manifests in the material condition of landscapes and demonstrates an underlying violence in the values and ideologies that circulate through material objects and their place as mediators of social relations. Like any other phenomenon, capital punishment exists through material social relations embedded within landscapes of production. For example, for an electric chair to function, electricity must enter a prison. What resources and infrastructure are used to produce that electricity and distribute it to prisons and execution chambers? Lethal gas chambers require poisonous, nitrogen-based gasses; where are these gasses produced and then distributed to execution chambers? For electric chairs and gas chambers to function, living human bodies must also be distributed to execution chambers. What material infrastructure and resources produce this distribution of human bodies? As material objects of capital punishment, how do these resources, energy sources, and human bodily movements constitute the material base of the practice and embody the social relations of their production and consumption?

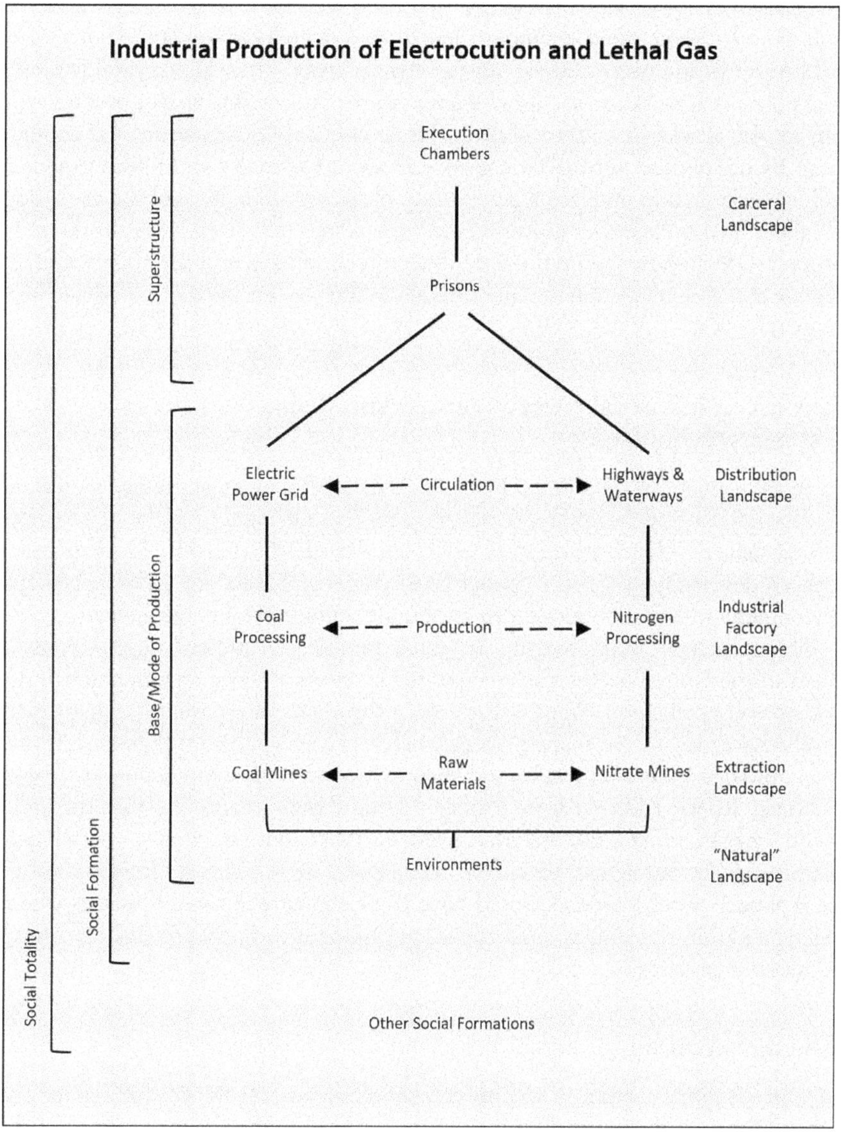

Figure 10.1 This figure demonstrates the organized material circulation of energy sources (electricity and nitrogen-based chemical compounds) in a capitalist social formation

Source: Alex R. Colucci

From this perspective, we can begin to see how the execution chamber is embedded within a wider landscape produced through the connected material cultures of violence and capitalism and therefore industrial work. That means we can see – and must understand more thoroughly – how the knowledges and technologies at work in execution chambers are connected to spaces beyond prisons as part of wider capitalist networks of production, consumption, and circulation. By tracing the networked energy sources of electricity and nitrates used to kill in electrocution and lethal gas execution, the embeddedness of the execution chamber in the American cultural landscape comes into stark relief. In the next section, I detail how the production of necrotechnologies and the energy sources they activate developed materially through indifferent exchange to produce dead human bodies.

Resources, industrial energy sources, knowledge, and necrotechnologies

In social formations dominated by capitalism, development or change is spurred by internal contradictions and resultant crises that emanate from the unevenness of that same development (Harvey 1982, 424; Peet 1978, 152–53). This process of uneven development (crisis – spatial fix – crisis – spatial fix etc.) is extant in any phenomena within such social formations, including capital punishment.

The movement from hanging to other methods of judicial capital punishment in the United States was precipitated by crises of 'over accumulation' in its widespread application. Simply, throughout the 1800s, there were too many high profile hangings, in too many places, which received significant popular scrutiny for both their gruesome results and their synonymy with extrajudicial lynchings (Colucci 2019a, 170). At issue for capital punishment states was that rope and wood for scaffolding – the materials needed to carry out hangings – were ubiquitous across the landscape: they were cheap and easy to access. If hanging was to be replaced, other materials would have to be similarly diffused in places where political authorities sought to fix capital punishment through a redevelopment of its material practice.

Industrial electricity

Significant advancement in electrical technology was developed throughout the United States in the late 1800s (Steinberg 2013, 113). The development of coal-fired power plants – and then direct and alternating current technology – was central in allowing for the relatively efficient widespread production and distribution of electricity. Such extensive production and distribution was made possible through the large-scale extraction and burning of coal from Appalachian coal mines and later mines in the Powder River Basin in Wyoming (Hudson 2002, 103, 300). The proliferation of rail lines made moving this coal to areas of high demand cost-effective, making electricity ubiquitous in areas with growing populations and industries. At the same time, states were in the process of constructing centralized, state-level prisons and phasing out less-secure county-level carceral facilities (Garland 2010, 123). Electrifying these large, centralized prisons became commonplace, especially in the eastern half of the United States – in areas roughly proximate to the centers of coal extraction and power plants. Simultaneously, access to electricity brought enhanced development to communities throughout the U.S., ostensibly improving quality of life at a population level.

This period of time also coincided with a crisis in the process of hanging as a method of execution (Colucci 2020, 11). In search of a fix that would maintain the practice of capital punishment in a way that conformed to legal statutes in the U.S. constitution that define cruel and unusual punishment, state officials in New York sought a 'more humane' way to kill. In 1888, the New York State Commission on Capital Punishment settled on electricity as a means of killing, citing its apparent painlessness in the seemingly instantaneous causation of death (New York Commission on Capital Punishment 1888). It was already widely in use for euthanizing stray dogs, New York State prisons were already connected to the developing power grid, and the abundance of electricity-adjacent industrial and domestic accidents had physicians of the time, when interviewed by the Commission, speaking glowingly of electricity's efficiency in causing death. Indeed, one physician interviewed by the Commission said of possible methods to replace hanging: "electricity is not only the least painful and repulsive, but, also, the quickest, most certain and most easily administered" (1888, 85).

As a result, New York state and eventually other states in the northeast, southeast, and Midwest throughout the late 1800s and early 1900s steadily developed and replicated their own electrical execution apparatuses connected to prison electrical systems. This squarely moved capital punishment into what we recognize today as the secluded prison death chamber. Yet, at the same time, capital punishment became increasingly and inextricably connected directly to the wider landscape of electrical infrastructure and thus political-economic systems of resource extraction and distribution.

To the coal mining companies and owners of electric power plants, it was and is irrelevant to whom and for what purpose their coal and electricity is purchased. They remain indifferent so long as it is exchanged to generate surplus value. Likewise, those who own electric power lines are indifferent to where those power lines distribute energy. Owners of rail lines are indifferent to where their coal cars diffuse coal and for what purpose it is burned.

Abstract surplus value takes the material form of money. The practical function of money is to act as the physical medium of circulation, while its value in exchange is abstract: in other words, not tied to the material qualities of the currency itself. In terms of capitalist exchange, money is merely the abstract equivalent measure of exchange relations, and increasing surplus value is the only relevant relational concern from the perspective of capitalists (Harvey 1982, 11). Whether used to run refrigerators to maintain the correct temperature for life-saving malaria vaccines or used in the five-minute cycle of an electric chair execution, the capitalist is indifferent to the use of the energy sources they produce or distribute so long as that energy is exchanged. Likewise, the workers involved in energy production (indeed within any industry) – who are forced to sell their labor power to the capitalist to survive – are largely indifferent to the materials upon which they work and the consequences of their production. In terms of capital punishment, this means that both capital and labor are indifferent to the reality that the production processes they activate result in killing human life.

Industrial gas

The development of industrial gas processing and technologies shares a similar story. Amid sporadic food shortages and soil fertility issues throughout Europe in the late 1800s, German chemist Fritz Haber was set on refining the process of efficiently producing synthetic nitrogen-based fertilizers. In 1909 his work resulted in what we know today as the Haber-Bosch Process (Topham 1985). It is a nitrogen fixation process that converts gaseous nitrogen in the atmosphere to ammonia by a reaction with hydrogen. This was a more efficient process for producing ammonia and solid-state ammonium nitrates, which allowed for the industrial mass production of nitrogen-based fertilizers and gasses (Appl 1982). The refinement of the Haber-Bosch process is considered arguably one of the most substantial technological advancements for humanity, leading to the development of intensive agriculture, generally less hunger worldwide, and subsequent population increase.

Synthetic nitrate production was also useful for munitions industries and militaries and served a central function in World War I in the development of stronger explosive ordinances and poisonous gasses (Travis 2015). In the 1920s nitrate production plants turned to solely producing fertilizers and pesticides. The eventual widespread availability of these products led to ten states adopting lethal gas as a method of execution and constructing gas chambers in state-level prisons between 1924 and 1955. Inspired by its effective use in World War I, Nevada legislators purchased twenty pounds of liquid hydrogen cyanide from the California Cyanide Company to carry out the first lethal gas execution in 1924 and future executions in the state (Christianson 2010). Hydrogen cyanide is a common nitrogen-based chemical compound, industrially manufactured for use as a pesticide and chemical precursor for the production of other compounds used to produce polymers and pharmaceuticals and in gold and silver mining. Other states, such as California, Missouri, North Carolina, Mississippi, and Maryland, also adopted lethal gas in this time period and are proximate to both major agricultural areas and centers of industrial chemical production.

As with industrial electricity, interest, from the perspective of capital, is to enter into exchange relations to generate surplus value. The producers of nitrates are indifferent to where, how, or why their chemical compound products are consumed, regardless of what that consumption does to living things.

Post-industrial lethal injection

Not dissimilarly from hanging, crises in the use of electrocution and lethal gas spurred the steady development and adoption of a different, dominant method of capital punishment (Colucci 2019a, 188). Any new method would, like those before it, reflect the changing material landscapes in which it was embedded, and its practice would be derived from certain ubiquitous materials and knowledges present in the organizing of the base-levels of this social formation. Likewise, the efficacy of any new method would be judged against romanticized understandings of how past necrotechnologies functioned in relation to the human body. Lethal injection developed as a fix in the 1970s, as court rulings defined prisoners' rights to healthcare in the United States (Rold 2008). With state corrections departments forced to comply in providing healthcare, the presence of medical equipment and knowledge became widespread in prisons, reflecting wider economic shifts in employment and industry in the United States from manufacturing to service sector employment.

The contemporary lethal injection procedure originated in the late 1970s in Oklahoma, and the Texas protocol for the process, developed in the early 1980s, has since become reproduced widely as standard practice in other killing states and at the federal level (Bohm 2011, 136). Rather than mechanical knowledge of the technological operations of switchboards and electric wiring or the physical reactions of chemical compounds, the process of lethal injection requires service-oriented technologic knowledge of human bodies.

Execution team members must be trained in the sanitary use of IV tubes, syringes, the administration of drugs intravenously, and the proper use of restraining gurneys (Colucci 2019a, 189). They receive this training, unchallenged, in standard emergency medical technician (EMT)/paramedic training and certification classes. Not dissimilarly, the intravenous drugs they use to kill in the process of capital punishment are, in other spatial contexts beyond the execution chamber, vital lifesaving substances used for the treatment of injuries and disease (Colucci 2019b). For example, midazolam – a sedative often used during lethal injections – is widely used as a general anesthetic and sedative in medical situations from basic dental procedures to treating seizures. The IV tubes and other medical equipment are not specially produced for prisons to carry out executions but rather are purchased alongside other supplies needed for prison hospitals from medical supply companies. The material training, drugs, and medical supplies are indifferently exchanged by their producers. It is largely irrelevant to pharmaceutical companies, medical suppliers, and producers of EMT training where, why, and how their products and training are materially used.

When detailing the materiality of these processes, the contradictions in the production of lethal injection executions are clear when examining the development of lethal injection in the context of providing prisoners with access to healthcare. The industrial legacy of reorienting otherwise life-giving energy sources, technologies, and knowledges remains in this post-industrial landscape of capital punishment through the production of a political practice of killing.

Circulating values through material capital punishment

This brief section details the geographies of a changing capital punishment. Far from enclosed or cut off from a wider society, this analysis demonstrates the direct connections between a particular carceral space and the related political-ecologic (the extraction of coal and nitrogen from environments) and political-economic (the industrial processing and distribution of coal and nitrogen to locations of consumption) landscapes of capitalist exchange and circulation that produce it (c.f. Gill et al. 2018). We have seen examples of the material objects circulated in the production of capital punishment, but, because the values of a social formation are embedded within the material objects produced therein, how are material cultures of violence reproduced? And, importantly, what abstract, cultural values are circulated and reproduced through the material objects used in the production process of capital punishment?

Energy sources and knowledges are made to flow between landscapes and levels in the social formation, from their base – as extracted raw materials – through to the material infrastructures of the legal system and execution chamber in the superstructure (see Figure 10.1). While in circulation as commodities, these energy sources and knowledges carry the capacity to set in motion both material and abstract production processes, like capital punishment. We also know that capital punishment is produced unevenly as a consequence of racist differentiation, and is therefore a capitalist production process that reinforces two abstract values: both the values of disciplined, indifferent labor and the differential valuation of human life based on race (Tyner and Colucci 2015; Kobayashi 2015). These abstract values that circulate within the execution chamber through commodities are those of an intertwined white supremacy and indifferent exchange. As a result, the spaces and places of capital punishment function not only to exhibit capitalist values but also to simultaneously influence social relations through a differential valuation of human life. The execution chamber, therefore, becomes a location of melding absolute social difference and indifference in space to produce material death.

Doing research after industrial capital punishment

To this point, we have seen how industrialized executions – operationalized through production processes that directed energy sources toward killing – laid the foundation for highly secluded, secretive post-industrial executions using technologies and knowledges that in other spatial contexts promote life by improving human well-being.

In doing so, this chapter has presented an inverted analysis of the geographic political economy of capitalist production, in that, typically, such analysis is directed at understanding how the necessities of human life are produced and distributed. This inversion of typical historical-geographical materialist analysis instead focused on a capitalist production process that does not produce access to any human needs through the use of energies and technologies that otherwise and emphatically do improve human material life. Capital punishment – as a production process with direct connections to specific industries and infrastructures that are deeply engrained in our everyday lives – is, instead, directed at producing a dead human body. Such an analysis, I argue, is potentially impactful when considering how to conduct research and teaching praxis in the future.

As scholars focused broadly on landscapes, industrial heritage, and material cultures, we must refocus our attention on objects through the lens of social and environmental justice, to confront the interrelated production of both violence and alienated human life. Recent discussion in geography has centered around acts of scholarly communication and knowledge production as they relate to the everyday politics of life and death for oppressed people and conscious positions of silent indifference (Alderman and Inwood 2018, 2019; Rose-Redwood et al. 2018). These debates offer an opportunity to reflect on the contradictory state of our knowledge production in a world where the production and reproduction of both material objects and knowledge is often exchanged indifferently amongst people for the purpose of ending human life. How we collectively (de)value life – and resultant processes of killing and letting die – must be at the forefront of our scholarly approaches (Tyner 2016).

There is no material necessity for humans to kill other humans. And, that we – the collective 'we' who are a complicit public for whom, in name, the state kills through capital punishment – continue to plan and precisely occasion the killing of humans out of no material necessity but rather only to demonstrate the values of disciplined labor and indifferent exchange, is an issue that deserves greater scrutiny. That this killing has persisted through the reorienting of otherwise life-giving and life-affirming material energy sources, technologies, and knowledges only serves to further place into stark relief our banal alienation from ourselves.

Note

1 For the purposes of this chapter I am restricting discussion of capital punishment to 'the West' in general, though primarily the United States as the practice has been banned in most Westernized states for several decades at least.

References

Alderman, Derek H., and Joshua F.J. Inwood. 2018. "While We Dialogue, Others Die: A Response to 'The Possibilities and Limits to Dialogue.'" *Dialogues in Human Geography* 8 (2): 152–55.

———. 2019. "The Need for Public Intellectuals in the Trump Era and Beyond: Strategies for Communication, Engagement, and Advocacy." *The Professional Geographer* 71 (1): 145–51.

Anderson, James. 1980. "Towards a Materialist Conception of Geography." *Geoforum* 11 (2): 171–78.

Appl, Max. 1982. "The Haber-Bosch Process and the Development of Chemical Engineering." In *A Century of Chemical Engineering*, edited by William F. Furter, 29–53. New York: Plenum.

Bohm, Robert M. 2011. *DeathQuest: An Introduction to the Theory and Practice of Capital Punishment in the United States*. 4th ed. Boston: Routledge.

Christianson, Scott. 2010. *The Last Gasp: The Rise and Fall of the American Gas Chamber*. Oakland, CA: University of California Press.

Colucci, Alex R. 2019a. "Knowledge Production, Capital Punishment, and Political Economy." M.A. diss., Kent State University, Kent, Ohio.
———. 2019b. "Making Killing Work: Capital Punishment and the Productive Circuits of the Death Chamber." Presented at the Annual Meetings of the American Association of Geographers, Washington DC, April 7.
———. 2020. "Capital Punishment." In *International Encyclopedia of Human Geography*, edited by Audrey Kobayashi. 2nd ed. Vol. 2, 9–14. Amsterdam: Elsevier.
Davies, Thom. 2018. "Toxic Space and Time: Slow Violence, Necropolitics, and Petrochemical Pollution." *Annals of the American Association of Geographers* 108 (6): 1537–53.
Federici, Silvia. 2004. *Caliban and the Witch: Women, the Body and Primitive Accumulation*. Brooklyn, NY: Autonomedia.
Foucault, Michel. 1977. *Discipline and Punish: The Birth of the Prison*. Translated by Alan Sheridan. New York: Vintage Books.
Garland, David. 2010. *Peculiar Institution: America's Death Penalty in an Age of Abolition*. Cambridge: Harvard University Press.
Gill, Nick, Deirdre Conlon, Dominique Moran, and Andrew Burridge. 2018. "Carceral Circuitry: New Directions in Carceral Geography." *Progress in Human Geography* 42 (2): 183–204.
Harvey, David. 1982. *The Limits to Capital*. Oxford: Basil Blackwell.
Horn, Jeff. 2005. "Machine-Breaking in England and France During the Age of Revolution." *Labour/Le Travail* 55: 143–66.
Horvath, Ronald J., and Katherine Gibson. 1984. "Abstraction in Marx's Method." *Antipode* 16 (1): 12–25.
Hudson, John C. 2002. *Across This Land: A Regional Geography of the United States and Canada*. Baltimore: Johns Hopkins University Press.
Kirsch, Scott. 2013. "Cultural Geography I: Materialist Turns." *Progress in Human Geography* 37 (3): 433–41.
———. 2014. "Cultural Geography II: Cultures of Nature (and Technology)." *Progress in Human Geography* 38 (5): 691–702.
———. 2020. "Historical-Geographical Materialism." In *International Encyclopedia of Human Geography*, edited by Audrey Kobayashi. 2nd ed. Vol. 7, 31–36. Amsterdam: Elsevier.
Kobayashi, Audrey. 2015. "Justice versus Justice: Geographies of the Death Penalty and Place-Based Activism in the Troy Davis Case." ACME: *An International Journal for Critical Geographies* 14 (4): 1118–31.
Linebaugh, Peter. 2006. *The London Hanged: Crime and Civil Society in the Eighteenth Century*. 2nd ed. New York: Verso.
Mitchell, Don. 2008. "New Axioms for Reading the Landscape: Paying Attention to Political Economy and Social Justice." In *Political Economies of Landscape Change*, edited by James L. Wescoat Jr. and Douglas M. Johnston, 29–50. New York: Springer.
New York Commission on Capital Punishment. 1888. *Report of the Commission to Investigate and Report the Most Humane and Practical Method of Carrying Into Effect the Sentence of Death in Capital Cases*. Ithaca, NY: Cornell University Library.
Peet, Richard. 1978. "Materialism, Social Formation and Socio-Spatial Relations: An Essay in Marxist Geography." *Cahiers de Géographie Du Québec* 22 (56): 147–57.
Perelman, Michael. 2000. *The Invention of Capitalism: Classical Political Economy and the Secret History of Primitive Accumulation*. Durham, NC: Duke University Press.
Rold, William J. 2008. "Thirty Years After Estelle v. Gamble: A Legal Retrospective." *Journal of Correctional Health Care* 14 (1): 11–20.

Rose-Redwood, Reuben, Rob Kitchin, Lauren Rickards, Ugo Rossi, Ayona Datta, and Jeremy Crampton. 2018. "The Possibilities and Limits to Dialogue." *Dialogues in Human Geography* 8 (2): 109–23.

Schein, Richard H. 2012. "Urban Form and Racial Order." *Urban Geography* 33 (7): 942–60.

Steinberg, Ted. 2013. *Down To Earth: Nature's Role in American History*. 3rd ed. Oxford: Oxford University Press.

Topham, Susan A. 1985. "The History of the Catalytic Synthesis of Ammonia." In *Catalysis: Science and Technology*, edited by John R. Anderson and Michel Boudart, 1–50. Catalysis. Berlin and Heidelberg: Springer.

Travis, Anthony S. 2015. *The Synthetic Nitrogen Industry in World War I: Its Emergence and Expansion*. New York: Springer.

Tyner, James A. 2014. "Dead Labor, Landscapes, and Mass Graves: Administrative Violence During the Cambodian Genocide." *Geoforum* 52 (1): 70–77.

———. 2015. "Violence." In *The Wiley Blackwell Companion to Political Geography*, edited by John Agnew, Virginie Mamadouh, Anna J. Secor, and Joanne Sharp, 114–26. Hoboken, NJ: Wiley & Sons.

———. 2016. *Violence in Capitalism: Devaluing Life in an Age of Responsibility*. Lincoln, Nebraska: University of Nebraska Press.

Tyner, James A., and Alex R. Colucci. 2015. "Bare Life, Dead Labor, and Capital(Ist) Punishment." *ACME: An International Journal for Critical Geographies* 14 (4): 1083–99.

Tyner, James A., and Joshua F.J. Inwood. 2014. "Violence as Fetish Geography, Marxism, and Dialectics." *Progress in Human Geography* 38 (6): 771–84.

Tyner, James A., Joshua F.J. Inwood, and Derek H. Alderman. 2014. "Theorizing Violence and the Dialectics of Landscape Memorialization: A Case Study of Greensboro, North Carolina." *Environment and Planning D: Society and Space* 32 (5): 902–14.

Tyner, James A., and Stian Rice. 2021. "Agrarian Ruins of the Khmer Rouge: The Post-industrial Landscapes of a Rural Economy." In *Geographies of Post-Industrial Place, Memory, and Heritage*, edited by M. Rhodes, W. Price, and A. Walker. Abingdon: Routledge.

Wennerlind, Carl. 2004. "The Death Penalty as Monetary Policy: The Practice and Punishment of Monetary Crime, 1690–1830." *History of Political Economy* 36 (1): 131–61.

11 Industrial heritage in an era of climate catastrophe

Contamination as heritage

Carolyn F. Thompson

Recent work across history, cultural studies, urban studies, geography and anthropology has increasingly grappled with the role of memory and heritage of industrial sites as cultural and economic phenomena (Frisch 1998; Graham, Ashworth, and Tunbridge 2000; Summerby-Murray 2002; Del Pozo and Gonzalez 2012; Hill 2013; Muehlebach 2017; Wallace and Wright 2017). This chapter explores the significance of the past in the industrial heritage of post-industrial cities in an era of environmental disaster and climate catastrophe. Emerging from a critical urban geography approach that sees the built environment as symbolic of our social, economic and political values and priorities (Goss 1988), I argue that particular sites communicate narratives about post-industrial place, memory and heritage that are contested and complex. While old mines, power stations, factories and other industrial sites are elements of the cityscape that evoke the productive power of the industrial economy, once facilitating the growth and development of industrial cities, these places today also represent the locally and globally felt environmental degradation and destruction characteristic of the Anthropocene. How do these sites represent contestation, contradiction and complexity as focal points of industrial memory and heritage in the 'restless' post-industrial urban landscape (Knox 1993)?

When dealing with the past, we are reminded that this is always a contested process. Any representation of the past is emerging from a particular understanding or perspective of that history, and moreover is filtered through the lens of the present. As Graham, Ashworth, and Tunbridge (2000, 2) wrote, anytime we "focus upon the ways in which we use the past now, or upon the attempts of a present to project aspects of itself into an imagined future, then we are engaged with heritage." As such, this chapter is concerned with industrial heritage and how it raises pertinent questions about the fraught relationship post-industrial cities have with their histories as viewed from the perspective of the present. Hill's (2013, 380) contribution to heritage research is particularly inspiring in this regard, in trailblazing work that aims to engage with "the manner in which the past influences and interrupts the present – those barely perceptible echoes from the past that have the power to move us in unexpected ways." Yet, we only make sense of the past from our current perspective, and in this way this chapter is concerned with how industrial sites are viewed in a post-industrial era; an era increasingly popularly recognized as the Anthropocene (Crutzen and Stoermer 2000; Crutzen 2002; see Castree 2014 for a synopsis), in which humans are the most powerful force shaping the globe. Presenting a case study of a disused electrical power plant in New Haven, Connecticut, this chapter demonstrates that industrial sites represent a contested and messy heritage in today's post-industrial cities, highlighting a tension between past and present, between industrial production and environmental decline.

In engaging with the past, memory and heritage, questions and contestations arise regarding what is remembered, how it is remembered and whose history is being told. In the context of industrial heritage, many sites of industry evoke histories of working class life and labor struggles, so remembering industrial sites is bound up in the contributions and work of a group of people often overlooked in history and monuments (Wallace and Wright 2017; see also Walker (2021), and Rhodes (2021), both this collection). These are places that represent the progress and development of many industrial cities, key infrastructure that allowed for the rise of the modern city, that is too often now overlooked and ignored (Kaika and Swyngedouw 2000; Dawney's 2021 chapter in this collection). Yet, these places, when viewed through the lens of the present, are also sites of environmental degradation, both immediately contaminating their surrounding neighborhoods as well as, in the case examined here, the site where countless tons of greenhouse gasses were emitted, perpetuating the present global climate crisis. Thus, the memory and heritage bound up in industrial sites very much hinges on the contentious ways the past is evoked and remembered. As Wallace and Wright point out, "reconstructing and remembering the industrial past often draws out unresolved antagonisms and contestations" (2017, 45). English Station, a 1920s power station in New Haven, Connecticut provides an insightful case study in exploring these issues.

In the economic reality of urban competition among post-industrial cities, many see ex-industrial brownfield sites like defunct factories, power stations and warehouses as eyesores or 'blank slates' in the urban landscape (Greenberg et al. 2000; Kaika and Swyngedouw 2000; Bjelland 2004; Susilawati and Thomas 2012; Frantál and Martinát 2013). In this way, the heritage of industrial places can be obscured for many people who live beside these sites and pass them daily. These brownfields are often seen as polluted 'problem' areas of the city that need to be remade and developed to be relevant in today's urban economies, and recognition of these sites as places of significant economic impact in prior eras is not necessarily prioritized. "Brownfields are . . . perceived as potential hazards to human health and the environment, burdens degrading the value of surrounding properties, barriers to local development and contributors to urban sprawl, grounds for neighborhood crime and other illegal activities" (Frantál and Martinát 2013, 2). As such, the heritage attached to industrial sites is often overlooked. These spaces are constructed as blank spaces in the urban landscape to be targeted for efficient 'infill' development. It is also in this way that these landscapes of out-of-commission industrial sites take on a 'spectral' (Edensor 2005; Hill 2013) or 'phantasmagoric' (Kaika and Swyngedouw 2000; Edensor 2008) element in urban geography, in that the postindustrial economy has rendered these places dead, yet the ghost of their forms, hulking and distinct on the landscape, haunt the cities where they were once the central economic driver.

Nevertheless, while concerns about the contamination and toxicity of post-industrial sites obscures the social and environmental complexities of their heritage and importance in the economic development of many cities, these concerns remain real and salient. Today, as the globe faces an era of climate catastrophe and environmental uncertainty, post-industrial cities harbor sites of considerable concern in terms of environmental contamination. The incredible economic growth propelled by industry was achieved through means that degraded local environments and embedded contaminants within the very fiber of the landscape of industrial cities. Of particular concern is the reality that many industrial cities are located on coastlines and waterways susceptible to flooding as sea levels rise with increasing global temperatures due to climate change (Duke et al. 2014; O'Connor et al. 2019). Therefore, not only are industrial cities locations of accumulations of contaminants and industrial toxins, but by nature of their location they are also often vulnerable to rising sea levels and flooding, risking unleashing these industrial 'nasties' into the wider environment via storm surge and flooding. So as the industrial heritage of these sites is composed in part by the built environment of disused industrial infrastructures, so too are these sites haunted by the legacies of contamination and environmental degradation.

English station in New Haven: powering the modern electrified city

English Station, a defunct electrical power plant in New Haven, Connecticut, serves as an example for demonstrating and considering the ways that industrial sites represent contested memories and narratives of the past. The station sits on Ball Island, an artificial island at the mouth of where the Mill River opens into New Haven Harbor (see Figure 11.1), originally constructed in the late 1800s to house a coal-burning power plant run by the New Haven Electric Company. Later, United Illuminating (UI) acquired the company and the power plant and between 1924–1929 constructed a new coal-burning power plant on Ball Island, named English Station. By the end of the 1950s, the station was transformed to an oil-burning plant after decades of coal-burning had significantly polluted the surrounding neighborhoods of Fair Haven and Wooster Square. The station, a massive 100,000 square feet structure rising ten stories high, with four smokestacks towering even higher, is a unique Janus-faced building with one end having been built in the early modern art deco style of red brick and the other end the more high modernist style precast concrete-clad addition when the plant was revamped in the 1950s. It remained in operation until 1992, by which time UI rose to be a major regional electricity supplier.

For the past three decades the station and the island on which it sits have remained disused, leaving a significant industrial 'absent-presence'[1] in New

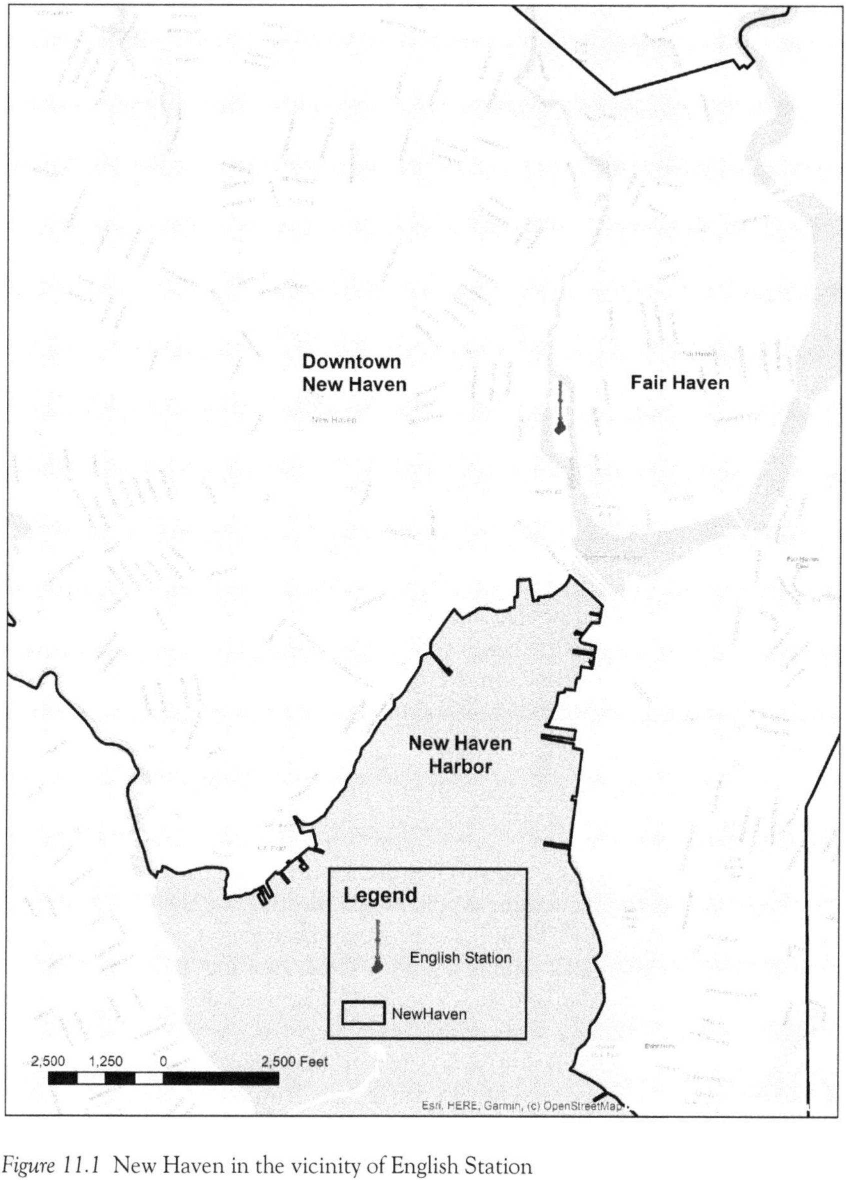

Figure 11.1 New Haven in the vicinity of English Station

Source: Carolyn F. Thompson

Haven's urban landscape – an enormous, empty, unlit structure haunting the cityscape and presenting a significant environmental challenge. Today, Ball Island remains significantly contaminated with polychlorinated biphenyls (PCBs), lead, asbestos, arsenic and other industrial contaminants. Amazingly in 2000, UI was able to offload the site to another local energy company, Quinnipiac Energies, by paying the company $4.15 million to assume ownership for the plant, including liabilities for contamination on the site (Turmelle 2014). However, in 2012 after numerous title transfers for the property – which became separated into two parcels – and after new site owners began to demolish parts of the station, the Connecticut Department of Energy and Environmental Protection (CT DEEP) issued a cease and desist order to halt demolition.

By 2015 CT DEEP and UI agreed to a Partial Consent Order holding UI responsible, as the original polluter, for remediating the site. This deal emerged out of decades of community activism around various environmental threats emanating from the site, as well as persistence on the part of municipal government and the state attorney general to hold UI responsible for the six decades of operations that contaminated the site (Gosselin 2015; Turmelle 2015b). Also important in this deal was the fact that Spanish multinational energy corporation Iberdrola SA wanted to purchase UI for $3 billion. However, this deal required approval by the state government's Public Utilities Regulatory Authority; the state regulators finally had incentive to convince UI to remediate the site and did not approve the acquisition of UI by Iberdrola until it agreed to the Partial Consent Order (Bass 2015). UI's compliance with this order means they are committed to spending an estimated $30 million (of electricity ratepayer funded money) to cleaning up the site, which began in 2018. Since this remediation has begun and likely indicates future reuse, the site has captured the attention, activism and imagination of New Haveners, who are invoking different notions of remembrance and heritage around English Station.

Note on methods

This chapter is informed by two years of archival research on English Station, as well as participant observation in community meetings on the remediation of English Station hosted by UI and in community management team meetings for the neighborhood where the site is situated. These meetings took place within one mile of English Station and were attended by between 30–50 people. I took detailed hand-written field notes during these meetings. As a longtime resident of New Haven, having grown up in a neighborhood adjacent to the case study neighborhood, I also have tacit knowledge of New Haven and its neighborhood and community dynamics. I use discourse analysis to interpret the media and documentary data that was gathered from June of 2017 to December of 2019, to identify the dominant narratives and ideologies represented by the community, local media and various actors engaged in the public discussion around English Station. I analyzed this data with attention to how members of the public saw English Station, what narratives they used to engage with the site, what their main concerns were with the site's remediation and how they envisioned the future of the site.

Remediation and potential redevelopment bring community concern to the fore

The ongoing remediation of English Station has invigorated community debate around this site. Within this debate there are two identifiable areas of community concern:

(1) over the quality and thoroughness of the cleanup process and possibilities for negative environmental impacts on the community and;
(2) around the preservation and adaptive reuse of the site as a building of architectural merit and historic significance.

These two areas of community concern represent the main avenues that New Haveners have taken in engaging with community debates on the site. Many New Haveners engaged with the issue, this author included, have concerns about both. At community meetings addressing the site's remediation, discussion and debate has been led by activists and local environmental organizations – like Environmental Justice Network and the Environmental Advisory Council – and local architectural preservation organizations, like New Haven's Urban Design League. A further group of 'regulars' who are concerned about the plans for English Station are those Fair Haven residents who are not involved with either of these aforementioned groups.

Concerns about contamination

English Station is a site in New Haven that has consistently generated debate, activism and community politics around the issue of contamination. This was the site of fossil fuel burning electricity generation for over 100 years, but this process generated much more than electricity for the region. It also generated immediate pollution to the local area in terms of elevated particulate matter in the air that contributed to higher asthma rates in the latter part of the twentieth century, as well as heavy metal and PCB contamination in the site and soil. It was community activism and agitation around the polluting effects of coal dust from the plant that pushed UI to switch from coal to oil fuel for the plant in the mid-twentieth century (Odermann 2016).

More recently, after Quinnipiac Energies assumed responsibility for the site in 2000, the company wanted to again generate power at the shuttered plant, but public pressure around the air pollution and elevated asthma rates in the Fair Haven neighborhood meant the Connecticut attorney general intervened to stop the plans to reopen the plant, disallowing further emissions from the Ball Island site (Turmelle 2001, 2015a). A decade later, after Quinnipiac Energies sold the site to a company called Asnat Realty, again the site became the center of a debate around contamination, this time because the new owners were haphazardly dismantling and selling parts of the plant for scrap, while by night illegal scrappers were pillaging the old facility. A major 'red flag' went up when Asnat tried to sell used oil from the plant's transformers for recycling and the transport and recycling operators rejected it because it was found to contain 99% concentration of PCBs (Leff 2011). Once DEEP was notified, community activists learned of the plans and began agitating for the city and state governments to regulate this deeply contaminated site more closely. They demanded that the piecemeal demolition of the plant by the new owners be stopped before any other pollutants could escape the site. Consistent public pressure and activism around environmental issues relating to English Station's contamination ultimately influenced municipal actors and the state DEEP and attorney general to broker the deal in 2015 that would require UI to remediate the site (Gosselin 2015; Turmelle 2015b).

Now that there is finally an agreement in order for UI to remediate the site, concerns around the quality of the remediation and the potential for contaminants to escape, either during the remediation process or in the future, have been central to community discussions about English Station. At two public meetings UI has held since beginning remediation of the site, on 11 March and 19 November 2019, local residents and environmental activists focused on the possibility of contamination escaping the site, particularly through the tidal waters of the Mill River. One resident who has been engaged in longtime community activism around the issue of water pollution in the neighborhood made it clear in no uncertain terms that he felt UI was "poisoning our waters where people are fishing, crabbing and boating" without any repercussions (author's field notes). Currently the order UI has agreed to in its deal to clean up the site only includes Ball Island, the structures and the bulkhead itself and does not require any testing or monitoring of waters surrounding the island. This has been a major source of contention among environmental activists and community members who feel this represents UI's approach to fulfilling only what they are minimally obligated to do in terms of remediation. Most recently, in December 2019, this issue again came to the fore when community and environmental activists made an announcement that they had uncovered documents that DEEP had cited UI with a number of violations of their remediation order in October of that year; one of these relating to runoff coming from drainage pipes that empty from Ball Island's bulkhead into Mill River, which DEEP testing had shown contained elevated levels of lead and arsenic. So, even though remediation of this site is ongoing, the threat of environmental contamination continues to be an issue that dominates the narratives around how this site is seen and interpreted. Issues of contamination and environmental threat are arguably the primary aspect of English Station that engages community interest and discussion.

Besides the environmental and community activism around English Station that has focused on local contamination, these actors have also voiced concerns about the global scale environmental problems to which this power plant has contributed. At the community update meetings UI held in 2019 on the remediation of the site, members of the public voiced their uncertainty and distrust of the thoroughness of the cleanup to protect against contaminants migrating from the site, considering the possibility of sea level rise and increased storm surge risk associated with global warming (author's field notes; Appel 2019). What will happen to all those contaminants should there be another Superstorm Sandy with major coastal flooding? UI admitted the bulkhead falls within the floodplain zone of the harbor. These sorts of questions suggest this site does not just represent local environmental degradation, but community members see this as connected and integrated within the wider global scale of environmental uncertainty in an era of climate catastrophe.

Concerns about preservation and heritage

While the concerns about contamination have a decades-long history around public engagement with English Station, for at least the last ten years, environmental activists have allied themselves with preservationists, who are interested in the architectural value and cultural heritage of this site (Leff 2011). Local organizations like the Urban Design League argue that the power plant is an iconic structure in New Haven's built environment and advocate for its preservation as an important part of the city's cultural fabric. The power plant's original 1920s art deco architectural details are highly regarded by preservationists. This architectural merit has attracted the attention of New Haven's Urban Design League and Preservation Trust, as well as students and faculty from the Yale School of Architecture, who have all advocated for these industrial structures of English Station to be preserved as notable features in New Haven's urban heritage. Besides the concerns of contamination, the main theme to arise in public meetings around English Station surrounded the need to preserve the structures on Ball Island as much as possible and to adaptively reuse them in a way that incorporates them into the wider city.

In meetings on the remediation of the site, the viability of preserving the structures on Ball Island has been one of the central topics of discussion, albeit pressed by a small but vocal group of about five to ten people advocating for preservation and creative reuse of the power plant. In a meeting of around 35 people, on 11 March, 2019, several members of the community pressed UI to do more to save these vulnerable buildings, after the City of New Haven had recently announced a brick building on the site constructed in the 1890s would have to be demolished because bricks had begun falling from the façade onto the sidewalk below. Meeting goers questioned why there was not more being done as part of the remediation process to prevent such instances of decay and thus avoid further "demolition by neglect" (author's notes). Some lamented the loss of New Haven's history and built heritage, while others saw the potential for spectacular reuse, with one preservationist urging others to imagine the power plant transformed into a grand art museum like London's Tate Modern.

Nonetheless, UI officials have spurned the notion that it had any responsibility in preserving or stabilizing these structures, as they reminded the public that they were no longer the site owners and were only acting to fulfill their obligations outlined in the DEEP consent order. UI representatives did, however, state that there were no current plans to demolish or disassemble the primary 1920s power plant structure. Representatives of the firm that owns the property have not appeared at any public meetings about the site, incensing the preservationists, who are suspect of the owners because of their history of surreptitiously dismembering and scrapping materials from the main power plant. Initially it was the revelation that the plant was being piecemeal demolished by the owners in 2010–2011 that spurred the interest of the preservationists and forged the alliance between those and environmentalist concerns (Leff 2011), reinvigorating local public interest in and debate around the site.

Contamination as heritage: the legacy of English Station

The case study of English Station illustrates the challenges, potential and dominant narratives around postindustrial sites. It presents a view of how the meanings of postindustrial place, memory and heritage are made and represented. These places are the material embodiment of the arc of industrial cities, harkening to the era that created these cities, as well as a painful reminder of their decline (Apel 2015). When inquiring about the meaning and legacy of postindustrial place, this case study also stimulates interesting juxtapositions wherein the heritage and memory surrounding English Station is bound up not only in remembering the history of a place but also steeped in deep environmental contamination that has local and global implications. This site is not only the place that generated power, creating a modern electrified city but where that very activity created contamination that still threatens the local environment; of course, it is also a location where countless tons of greenhouse gas were emitted, contributing to the global climate crisis. So just as industrial heritage has been associated with the spectral and phantasmagoric (Kaika and Swyngedouw 2000; Edensor 2005, 2008; Hill 2013), it is the contamination of English Station that is haunting the site, serving as a link between past and present. Indeed, in local media reports on English Station, the site has been described in ghostly (Odermann 2016) and haunting terms, including one commenter writing, "perhaps every one-time industrial city in the United States will one day have its own English Station, a fenced in eyesore left to haunt residents for decades" (McGraw 2016).

English Station, as a site in the built environment and an architectural landmark in New Haven, can be interpreted as a text that speaks to postindustrial memory and heritage. Yet, environmental degradation and contamination are embedded within this place, polluting not just the soil but the memory and heritage of this site. From the beginning, when English Station was initially constructed, the threat of negative externalities influenced the public discourse, even influencing the station's architectural design. A local newspaper article in the *New Haven Independent* reminds us that the station's "cathedral-like structure was meant to assure residents that they wouldn't be zapped by the electricity coursing through their city" (Peak 2019).

So, in this way the narratives around the architectural value of this site and its contamination and environmental threat have been connected throughout the history of English Station. This provides insight into how we can interpret English

Station as a text about the postindustrial city, as it is a site that reflects the social and economic order and power of the time when it was produced and, by relation, how that time is remembered in the present. Just as English Station was created to look like a cathedral, I have often observed that the smokestacks of the industrial era are like the church steeples of traditional European or colonial cities – their tall structures visible on the landscape, marking place, for miles around. And just like the church steeples of traditional cities, smokestacks convey something about the social and economic values of their time period. While church steeples conveyed the power of the church and religion, smokestacks convey the power of industry and modernity. Today, I note this because of the fetishization of smokestacks in preservation schemes on brownfield sites. Everything of an old factory or plant can be torn down to be redeveloped, but the redevelopment almost always preserves the token smokestack as a nod to the former industrial use. As such, this chapter on English Station as a site of industrial heritage has contributed to scholarship on the fetishization of industrial buildings and ruins (Kaika and Swyngedouw 2000; Apel 2015).

This vignette on smokestacks allows us to consider contamination as heritage. While much of heritage and preservation concerns itself with built forms like smokestacks, let us pause to consider what these actually are: structures that facilitated the wide-scale dispersion of contaminants. In this way they, when viewed through the eyes of the present era of environmental degradation and climate catastrophe, communicate much more than just the power of industry and modernity – they also express the failures and faults of the modern industrial era. As such, these sites, smokestacks, and English Station more particularly provide a unique insight into the aspects of heritage that are not necessarily lauded by heritage makers and preservationists. They represent the contested side of heritage, its underbelly, the aspects of the memory of a place that are not necessarily positive but significant for their disastrous implications. If heritage is imbued with meaning through the lens of the present (Graham, Ashworth, and Tunbridge 2000), this offers a powerful understanding of post-industrial heritage: that it is not only the positive site of modern industrial creation or the memory of the value of labor that made the industrial city successful but also the site where urbanism and industry created far-reaching environmental contamination, both local and global. Local actors concerned with the fate of New Haven's English Station demonstrate this paradoxical remembering by lauding the architectural and historical merit of this industrial piece of the built environment while stressing the environmental degradation and threat the site presents.

Conclusion

When considering the meaning of post-industrial heritage and memory, the case of English Station presents two emerging narratives, one about contamination and one about preservation of the built environment. Do these two narratives and points of interest around English Station dovetail or diverge? Time will tell if the community interests driving debate around English Station will continue to collaborate and form a basis for community-driven outcomes in the future of this 'risky' brownfield site or whether their competing aims and concerns will drive them into separate camps, potentially weakening the power of community to influence the fate of this site. What is apparent now is that it has been community-based efforts that have propelled remediation of the site and are pushing for the site to be remembered and preserved. Importantly, these narratives reveal that history, memory, and meaning in sites of industrial heritage are of concern and interest, at least in New Haven. Moreover, they suggest that contamination is heritage: it is a central part of how people today view and interpret that site and how they make sense of it in today's post-industrial cityscape. In the Anthropocene, in an era of climate catastrophe, the polluting presence of this site is inseparable from the way industrial sites are remembered today. It is the moment when these industrial structures face deconstruction, demolition, ruin or rising sea levels that they leap back to the forefront of the urban environment and evoke remembering of industrial place and an awakening to their current situation in the urban landscape that links past with present.

This memory speaks to how an urban community operationalizes a sense of place and relationships of past and present. It demonstrates the way industrial places are understood from the view of the present – in this case a present overshadowed by environmental degradation and climate catastrophe – and how this is an indelible legacy of industrial heritage. It is also significant because it illuminates how memory and heritage of industrial places are contested and complex but that communities are engaging in this and wading through the messy pasts of these sites. Despite many urban dwellers seeing industrial sites as eyesores or blank slates in the landscape, the case study has shown there is also engagement, concern and activism on the part of communities to have a voice in remembering and possibly reimagining these spaces.

Note

1 Absent-presence here refers to the spectral elements of a form that is present but marks an absence. In this case, English Station is a large physical presence in the built environment, but being shut down and abandoned for three decades, as a place in the city no one can access, it also marks an absence, as well as the absence and decline of industry. Much of the work incorporating the idea of absent-presence draws from Derrida who writes:

> there is no ghost . . . without at least an appearance of flesh, in a space of invisible visibility, like the dis-appearing of an apparition. For there to be ghost, there must be a return to the body, but to a body that is more abstract than ever. The spectrogenetic process corresponds therefore to a paradoxical incorporation. . . . Not by returning to the living body from which ideas and thoughts have been torn loose, but by incarnating the latter in another artifactual body.
>
> (Derrida 1994, 126; original emphasis)

In this way English Station and other industrial ruins can be seen to incorporate a spectral sense of absent-presence. See also Edensor 2008; Wylie 2009; Maddrell 2013.

References

Apel, D. 2015. *Beautiful Terrible Ruins: Detroit and the Anxiety of Decline*. New Brunswick, NJ: Rutgers University Press.

Appel, A. 2019. "English Station's New Emissions: Anxieties." *New Haven Independent*. November 20. www.newhavenindependent.org/index.php/archives/entry/english_stationanxieties/.

Bass, P. 2015. "Harp Calls Jepsen English Station Hero." *New Haven Independent*. October 19. www.newhavenindependent.org/index.php/archives/entry/ui_english_station_deal/.

Bjelland, M. 2004. "Brownfield Sites in Minneapolis-St. Paul: The Interwoven Geographies of Industrial Disinvestment and Environmental Contamination." *Urban Geography* 25 (7): 631–57.

Castree, N. 2014. "The Anthropocene and Geography I: The Back Story." *Geography Compass* 8 (7): 436–49.

Crutzen, P. 2002. "Geology of Mankind." *Nature* 415 (January 3): 23.

Crutzen, P., and E.F. Stoermer. 2000. "The Anthropocene." *Global Change Newsletter* 41: 17–18.

Dawney, L. 2021. "Dramatising Deindustrialisation: Experiential Authority, Temporality, and Embodiment in a Play about Nuclear Decommissioning." In *Geographies of Post-Industrial Place, Memory, and Heritage*, edited by M. Rhodes, W. Price, and A. Walker. Abingdon: Routledge.

Del Pozo, P., and P. Gonzalez. 2012. "Industrial Heritage and Place Identity in Spain: From Monuments to Landscapes." *Geographical Review* 102 (4): 446–64.

Derrida, J. 1994. *Specters of Marx*. London: Routledge.

Duke, J.M., K.D. Messer, H.A. Michael, and D.L. Sparks. 2014. "The Joint Risks of Anticipated Sea Level Rise and Coastal Contaminated Sites: Economic and Scientific Evidence. University of Delaware." *Department of Applied Economics and Statistics Research Report*: 14–10.

Edensor, T. 2005. "The Ghosts of Industrial Ruins: Ordering and Disordering Memory in Excessive Space." *Environment and Planning D: Society and Space* 23 (6): 829–49.

———. 2008. "Mundane Hauntings: Commuting Through the Phantasmagoric Working-Class Spaces of Manchester, England." *Cultural Geographies* 15 (3): 313–33.

Frantál, B., and S. Martinát. 2013. "Brownfields: A Geographical Perspective." *Moravian Geographical Reports* 21 (2): 2–4.

Frisch, M. 1998. "De-, re-, and Post-Industrialization: Industrial Heritage as Contested Memorial Terrain." *Journal of Folklore Research*: 241–49.

Goss, J. 1988. "The Built Environment and Social Theory: Towards an Architectural Geography." *The Professional Geographer* 40: 392–403.

Gosselin, K.R. 2015. "United Illuminating, Iberdrola agree to $30 million English Station Cleanup." *Hartford Courant*. September 17. www.courant.com/business/hc-uil-english-station-cleanup-iberdrola-20150916-story.html.

Graham, B., G.J. Ashworth, and J.E. Tunbridge. 2000. *A Geography of Heritage: Power, Culture and Economy*. New York: Routledge.

Greenberg, M., K. Lowrie, L. Solitare, and L. Duncan. 2000. "Brownfields, Toads, and the Struggle for Neighborhood Redevelopment: A Case Study of the State of New Jersey." *Urban Affairs Review* 35 (5): 717–33.

Hill, L. 2013. "Archaeologies and Geographies of the Post-Industrial Past: Landscape, Memory and the Spectral." *Cultural Geographies* 20 (3): 379–96.

Kaika, M., and E. Swyngedouw. 2000. "Fetishizing the Modern City: The Phantasmagoria of Urban Technological Networks." *International Journal of Urban and Regional Research* 24 (1): 120–38.

Knox, P. 1993. *The Restless Urban Landscape*. Englewood Cliffs, NJ: Prentice Hall.

Leff, L. 2011. "Demolition Derailed; English Station in Limbo." *New Haven Independent*. August 19. www.newhavenindependent.org/index.php/archives/entry/english_station/.

Maddrell, A. 2013. "Living with the Deceased: Absence, Presence and Absence-Presence." *Cultural Geographies* 20 (4): 501–22.

McGraw, D.J. 2016. "America's Power Plant Problem." *Pacific Standard*. February 1. https://psmag.com/environment/what-to-do-with-americas-abandoned-power-plants.

Muehlebach, A. 2017. "The Body of Solidarity: Heritage, Memory, and Materiality in Post-Industrial Italy." *Comparative Studies in Society and History* 59 (1): 96–126.

O'Connor, D., X. Zheng, D. Hou, Z. Shen, G. Li, G. Miao, S. O'Connell, and M. Guo. 2019. "Phytoremediation: Climate Change Resilience and Sustainability Assessment at a Coastal Brownfield Redevelopment." *Environment International* 130: 104945.

Odermann, M. 2016. "Abandoned Buildings: Ghosts of Elm City's Past." *Yale Daily News*. October 31. http://features.yaledailynews.com/blog/2016/10/31/ghosts-of-elmcitys-past/.

Peak, C. 2019. "Dicey Deals Kept English Station Dirty." *New Haven Independent*. April 25. www.newhavenindependent.org/index.php/archives/entry/fishy_english_station/.

Rhodes, M. 2021. "Amgueddfa'r Gogledd: Slate, slavery, and transatlantic labor in the National Slate Museum." In *Geographies of Post-Industrial Place, Memory, and Heritage*, edited by M. Rhodes, W. Price, and A. Walker. Abingdon: Routledge.

Summerby-Murray, R. 2002. "Interpreting Deindustrialised Landscapes of Atlantic Canada: Memory and Industrial Heritage in Sackville, New Brunswick." *Canadian Geographer/Le Géographe canadien* 46 (1): 48–62.

Susilawati, C., and K. Thomas. 2012. "Perception of Brownfield Sites: Myth or Reality?" *Remediation Australasia* 11: 34–37.

Turmelle, L. 2001. "Blumenthal Enters Row Over Power Plant Use." *New Haven Register*. December 18.

———. 2014. "Oil Spill Cleanup Planned at New Haven's Former English Station Power Plant." *New Haven Register*. October 1.

———. 2015a. "Looney to UI, Iberdrola: Cleanup New Haven's English Station Plant." *New Haven Register*. August 5. www.nhregister.com/business/article/Looney-to-UI-Iberdrola-Clean-up-New-Haven-s-11350150.php.

———. 2015b. "New Haven's English Station to be Cleaned up Under New UIL, Iberdrola Deal." *New Haven Register*. September 17. www.nhregister.com/business/article/New-Haven-s-English-Station-to-be-cleaned-up-11345204.php.

Walker, A. 2021. "Everyday Resonances of Industrial Pasts: Considering Lived and Affective Memories in Ex-Coal Mining Landscapes in a South Wales Valley." In *Geographies of Post-Industrial Place, Memory, and Heritage*, edited by M. Rhodes, W. Price, and A. Walker. Abingdon: Routledge.

Wallace, A., and K. Wright. 2017. "Re/Dis-Membering Industrial Histories in the British North." *lo Squaderno* 43: 43–48.

Wylie, J. 2009. "Landscape, Absence and the Geographies of Love." *Transactions of the Institute of British Geographers* 34 (3): 275–89.

12 Amgueddfa'r Gogledd

Slate, slavery, and transatlantic labor in the National Slate Museum

Mark Alan Rhodes II

The National Museum of Wales is both a unique expression of the Welsh nation and key to the development of Welsh national identity, history, and increasingly economy. With seven museums across the country, each with its own narratives, communities, and visitors but linked by a singular institutional framework, National Museum Wales operates as a memory consortium to symbolize understandings of the Welsh nation.

Focusing on the National Slate Museum, the only national museum remaining in North Wales, I demonstrate how the critical theories emerging from Black geographies, memory studies, and landscape geographers mesh with the historic and ongoing practices of capitalism, colonialism, and nationalism in the industrial heritage of Wales. Dubbed the "roofer of the world," the slate industry was a substantial part of the British, and particularly North Walian export economy. As the nickname infers, the majority of the slate was either quarried from the side of the mountains or mined from within the mountains, hand-split, dressed, and used for roofing and other building materials in Wales and throughout the British Empire.

This chapter adds to a growing literature of Welsh studies. Having only devolved from the British Parliament in 1998, the new Welsh Assembly (now Welsh Parliament) and the Welsh Government gained democratic control over the cultural and heritage industries in Wales. This chapter reflects upon these institutional processes of memory work and national identity in the context of a complicated and pluralistic past. Asking how the National Slate Museum's memory work shapes history into national identity through a series of archival, personal, intangible, and tangible landscapes, I establish the foundation for a comparison across the Welsh heritage institutions, as well as similar bodies in the United Kingdom, Europe, and the world.

Memory work and the memorial landscape

Introducing the term "transoptic landscape" as landscape beyond – yet still including – the visual, I offer yet another "way of seeing," which grasps greater meaning stemming from the more-than-representational while maintaining flexibility (Cosgrove 1998; Lorimer 2003). Further, the utility of transoptic landscapes allow for greater incorporation of critical geographies, such as what some may call an Indigenous understanding of landscape from a Welsh perspective. Thus, transoptic indicates the significance of observable sensory elements of sound, touch, smell, and emotion as well as "dynamic, embodying characteristics associated with the sublime such as multi-sensory experience, non-human agency, and emotional and affective impact" (Cole 2015, 49). Not only do landscapes reveal "social worlds of the past," but they represent continued values of the present (Doss 2010). Cosgrove (1998, 15) clearly states that the role of landscape is not only a method but an ontology, again transoptic: a perspective that comprehends "territorial space as both subject and object of human agency." In this way, landscape and its embedded memories are both subjective and objective; rooted in people, place, and space; and thus understood through the combination of material, archival, and experiential epistemologies and methodologies.

Cymraeg, the Welsh language, contains multiple words for the English "landscape": *tirwedd* and *tirlun* are most common. *Tirwedd* means land (*tir*) face or land appearance (*wedd*) and is used when describing topography, while *tirlun* translates directly to land picture (*lun*) and has historically been used when describing landscape painting. A third term, *Cynefin* is an arguably untranslatable concept, but in general combines *tirwedd* and *tirlun* with history, identity, and home. Its literal translations include acquainted, accustomed, familiar, haunt, and habitat, placing it firmly into a more-than-representational understanding of landscape. The Welsh landscape artist Kyffin Williams (1998, 16) describes *cynefin* as "not just landscape but a landscape with everything in it."

Osmond's (2007) book, *Myths, Memories and Futures: The National Library and National Museum in the Story of Wales*, discusses Welsh memory on a national scale yet does not discuss the National Slate Museum as one seventh of the overall museological narrative. Likewise, Howell (2013a, 2013b, 2016) and Mason (2007) engage with the post-devolution heritage of the national museum but do not include any extensive overview of the National Slate Museum. This chapter, as part of a larger project examining multiple institutions of heritage in Wales, including National Museum Wales, provides an in-depth overview of the National Slate Museum in the context of landscapes of memory work and Welsh national identity.

Geographers specifically have focused their attention in memory work on scales from the local (DeSilvey 2007) to the municipal (Till 2005), but attention to national memory work across a broad scale of representative institutions of the state continues to develop (Osborne 2001). Paasi's (2015) research into Finland's "geohistory" similarly reveals the relevancy of memory work to current debates of national identity, nationalism, and independence movements. Particularly tying territory, sovereignty, and memory together, Paasi (2015, 3) encourages a conceptualization of state territory "as a geohistorical *process* that becomes institutionalized" (c.f. Sack 1983). Taken together, history or memory may be utilized, shaped, or created by the national or state institutions of a governing territory or organization, in order to shape the very nation, state, or territory itself. Established research on Wales acknowledges these processes yet tends to focus on historic accuracy rather than examining the *work* that historical (re)creation and memory does (Williams 1985; Curtis 1986; Gruffudd 1995; Howell 2013a).

Industrial heritage, museum, and method

Symonds (2005, 33) writes,

> If Marx were alive today, he might well muse that a spectre is haunting Europe, the spectre of industrial archaeology. How delicious it might seem to him that the modern-day bourgeoisie is earnestly engaged in an activity that maps the decline and failure of its own capitalist forebears, and moreover seeks to preserve individual monuments, and even whole landscapes, in homage to the generations of workers that struggled to create the modern world.

Consistently compared economically to Eastern European states, Wales' economic standing consistently sits at the bottom of all UK nations. The average annual 2019 earnings in Wales are below all other regions, and in 2011 the district of Dwyfor Meirionnydd (directly south of Llanberis and covering the majority of the North Wales slate region) saw the lowest annual earnings of all 619 districts in the United Kingdom.[1] Underemployment accompanies these post-industrial landscapes in the economic spectre, haunting the economic, historical, and cultural geographies of Llanberis, Blaenavon, and other industrial landscapes of slate in North Wales (Figure 12.1).

Figure 12.1 Ruins of Dinorwig Quarry's slate splitting and dressing sheds high above the town of Llanberis

Source: Mark Alan Rhodes II

This research, in implementing a transoptic landscape analysis, draws from Schein's (2009) landscape methodology to address four themes with the National Slate Museum as a case study for national heritage institution and industrial heritage particularly through Welsh contexts. First, to understand the historical layers embedded within the landscape, archival research undergone in the National Museum Wales Library and the National Library of Wales provided historical context (Osmond 2007; Rhodes 2019).

Second, landscape meaning came through a series of interviews. Part of these interviews drew from Drozdzewski's (2016, 20) "memory-methods" implementing a vox pop (short, on-the-spot) interviewing style. Over the course of two days in late July and early August 2017, utilizing convenience sampling, I interviewed 53 visitors as they were leaving the museum. Each semi-structured interview consisted of 11 questions, primarily asking participants about their experience of Welsh history, and lasted approximately three minutes.

Third, approaching landscape through a lens of performance and performativity opens the rich possibilities of landscape's navigation of actors, scripts, and the affect, agency, and structures embedded within landscapes of heritage, memory, and identity. Dewsbury et al. (2002, 438 as cited in Waterton 2013, 67) reiterate that landscapes are not "'codes to be broken,' but instances, events, and practices that are 'performative in themselves; as doings.'" Performativity links the position of the body, "as both produced by and a product of the world" (Waterton 2013, 68). Performance provides a key component to a transoptic understanding of landscape, breaking down the traditional landscape barriers of the tangible and material.

Landscape performance further understands landscape itself as able to perform and, in line with the Welsh *cynefin*, acknowledges the agency of memory and history to embed into a layered and haunted inhabitance. Through personal observations, field notes, audio and visual recording, and the broader context from landscape archives, interviews, and discourses, I engage the multidimensional landscape performances of self, place, and staff at the National Slate Museum (Dittmer and Waterton 2016, 177; Longhurst, Ho, and Johnston 2008, 215).

Finally, landscape as discourse wraps history, meaning, and performance up with tangible and intangible ways of knowing (Schein 2009, 383). This framework builds upon the strong foundation established by Schein (2009) to provide a comprehensive method of understanding our cultural, historical, and memorial landscapes as transoptic in origin. Drawing from the "more-than-representational" understanding of cultural landscape from Lorimer (2003) and Waterton (2014), this approach recognizes the role of the body and practice within the creation of landscape meaning. Recognizing that assemblages treat the landscape as "expressing multiple, overlapping, and sometimes contested meanings" allows discourse analysis to be employed with the necessary tactics for interpreting these meanings (Smith and Foote 2017, 133). Including attention to soundscape (Lowenthal 1976; Smith 1994; Faudree 2012; Devadoss 2017; Leadley 2011) and performative methods (Dittmer and Waterton 2016, 177), this discourse-focused analysis of memory tools centers on the collective memory in particular and how politics find their way into nation-building via memory work. Employing these understandings of landscape, the discourse analysis employed later moves beyond Schein's (1997, 2009) landscape as "discourse materialized" and takes the next step by understanding the cultural, historical, and memorial landscape as something including – yet beyond – the material.

Archives of the National Slate Museum[2]

At one point, the National Slate Museum in Llanberis was part of a trifecta of national museums in the north. In an informational conversation with Keeper Dafydd Roberts (personal conversation 30 July 2018), he relayed much of the history of the National Museum in the north. For more than a decade, about 1980–1994 National Museum Wales operated what became the National Slate Museum, the Segontium Roman Museum, Oriel Eyryi, a mud steamer harbored in Caernarfon, and the Garland Stone moored in Porthmadog.

After several years of little change to the underfunded Snowdon Gallery named Oriel Eyryi, Dafydd Roberts arrived in the north as head of the Slate Museum *and* the gallery, which then changed its name and directive. Now named Amgueddfa'r Gogledd or the Museum of the North, the goal was to provide a space to show off the very best of the museum's collections to the people of North Wales. On a rotating basis, departments in Cardiff would put together exhibitions for display in the museum. During a period of museum contraction in 1994, National Museum Wales sold the gallery/museum and the ships. Segontium was handed over to CADW (the Welsh Government's heritage authority) in the mid-2000s, so that only the National Slate Museum remained in the north as part of National Museum Wales. Upon selling Amgueddfa'r Gogledd for £375,000, that money was matched from national lottery and European Union funds to significantly redevelop the National Slate Museum into the museum it is today.

Established in 1972 as the North Wales Quarrying Museum, the National Slate Museum occupies an old slate quarry engineering workshop (Gilfach Ddu) as part of the Dinorwig Quarry. The site and situation of the National Slate Museum challenges the academic and historic nature of the museum. With by far the lowest numbers of individual Welsh visitors (only 28% according to National Museum Wales (2016) or 9% from my own survey – my data indicated 58% at St. Fagans National Museum of Welsh History; Rhodes 2019), the museum now functions as a default "Amgueddfa'r Gogledd" or a gateway for international visitors experiencing Wales from the north. The National Slate Museum sees coach-loads of primarily English tourists arrive daily, particularly in the summer to enjoy a weekend or day out in Wales (see Figure 12.2).

This all being said, my interviews and experience with the directors, staff, and visitors show that the significance of authenticity is not taken lightly. Instead, I found a substantial diversity of historical contexts and meaning embedded into the landscapes in and around the de-facto National (Slate) Museum of the North.

Figure 12.2 Remains of the Anglesey Barracks for Dinorwig Quarry workers. The mountains of Snowdownia National Park can be seen in the distance

Source: Mark Alan Rhodes II

Table 12.1 Total visitor response to the question: "Have you experienced Welsh history . . ."

Museum	*Yes*	*Percent Yes*	*No*	*Percent No*	*N/A*	*Total*
National Museum Cardiff	23	49	18	38	6	47
St. Fagans National Museum of History	42	84	5	10	3	50
National Roman Legion Museum	24	51	18	38	5	47
Big Pit National Coal Museum	37	79	6	13	4	47
National Waterfront Museum	40	80	7	14	3	50
National Wool Museum	37	76	4	8	8	49
National Slate Museum	34	64	12	23	7	53
Average	34	69	10	21	5	49
Total	237		70		36	343

Landscape meaning

Visitors to the National Slate Museum were the smallest in both number and percentage in terms of Welsh identity to all the National Museum Wales sites, with only five claiming Welsh ethnicity or nationality and an additional five living in Wales but not claiming Welsh identity. With this information, it is not surprising that the visitors I interviewed felt that they had experienced Welsh history at a much smaller rate than at the other national museums.

Figure 12.3, a word cloud created using the software Nvivo, illustrates positive visitor responses to their experience of Welsh history in the museum. Certain visitor narratives jump out:

- Artifacts: houses, tools, slate
- The impact of the film
- The role of the slatesplitters
- The geography, geology, and landscape of the area
- Labor and life

Figure 12.3 Word cloud of visitor responses to how they have experienced Welsh history at National Slate Museum

Source: Mark Alan Rhodes II

While there were many visitors who broadly commented on "how life was back then," many others seem to apply that to a deeper level:

> Oh yeah, what working life was like, and also how the local landscape affects workers' lives, cause obviously the slate is local. So how they used the geography around them to make their living.
>
> (Interviewee #10)

> It's been great. It's really opened my eyes to everything. How they worked the mines, how they got it out, how they lived with the support of it, how Health and Safety never interrupted their jobs. . . . When you're not in the slate business (the mining and that), you just don't really realize what they had to do and how it was transported, how they dug it up and split it, and just everything to do with it.
>
> (Interviewee #40)

> Yes, their [the people who worked here] lives, their history, their independence, their struggle. The hardships.
>
> (Interviewee #27)

This last individual also connected on a personal level through his use of the tools and machines found throughout the museum and commented at the end of the interview:

> I find it very interesting, actually. Just in the way the whole place was set up, the workshop, the library, the different people. The different exhibits, too. The machines, and the water, having a big waterwheel, the way they lived.

In addition to vox pop interviews with visitors, semi-structured in-depth interviews with museum staff, such as Keeper of the National Slate Museum, Dafydd Roberts (personal conversation 27 July 2017), made it very clear that the museum is "a full part of Amgueddfa Cymru. . . . We are bound together closely and quite effectively." From operational to curatorial decision making and support, the various branches and administrations across National Museum Wales work together in each museum's development. He continued by saying "[i]t is important that they understand that we are members of a family and that we tell a national tale." Nonetheless, low numbers of visitors having visited another national museum in Wales (17%) indicate a disconnect between the museum and the broader system (National Museum Wales 2016, 114).

No doubt, from my interviews, slate itself in the context of a national memory is a significant point of experience, but that does not necessarily translate into broader engagement beyond the museum into the surrounding localities. While there may also have been deeper engagements, at least the one quote (#40) earlier demonstrates a disconnect between the experience of the quarriers and the wider labor movement. The comments on health and safety and independence indicate a misunderstanding and possible romanticization of the violent cycles of capitalism at play. These cycles include slavery – which brought in the capital for Lord Penrhyn to forcibly purchase, develop, and displace people in the northern Cambrians – and the later dead labor of the slate industry as Penrhyn and others aggressively fought against unionization and labor rights.

Performance

Direct acting also plays (no pun intended) a part in the National Slate Museum. Once a week during school holidays, Rhian Cadwaladr performs the role of the engineer's wife, Hannah, as she tells the many stories associated with the house, the time, and slate. Rhian does not just perform an abstract idea of place and identity but rather performs part of herself displaced in time yet rooted in place. Her brother, grandfather, and great-grandfather all worked in Dinorwic or the workshops of Gilfach Dde. Because of this, she says, "[S]o, I feel as if the place belongs to me."

Additionally, quarrymen conduct slatesplitting demonstrations. Carwyn Price and John-Jo Jones are both "demonstrating craftsmen" at the museum, and while they indeed have a total of 60 years of experience in Penrhyn Quarry and Bethesda and use that for slate demonstrating, they also play a pivotal role in the maintenance and upkeep of the museum.

I spoke with both of them to better understand how they not only engage with Welsh history and connect the museum into a national narrative but how their performance/demonstration makes an impact in that process of visitor experience. In both cases, slate factors into this national narrative, and their performance of that story impacts the memory work of the museum. In their own words . . .

> John-Jo: Most of the people when you go on TripAdvisor mention this, so it's a big part of the museum in a way. And they can feel. They can touch. They can listen to the noises made by working the slate. . . . So I tell a bit of the history of the actual quarry and how the villages are here and everything. Cause when you go back to the early days of the quarry, these people hereabouts with money. They took the land off the local people in a way, in a bad way. So that's the idea. So you try and mix it up with different people in a way.
>
> Carwyn: Well this is quite an important industry in Wales, because you have the slate industry here, the coal and steel works, and those were basically the main industry in Wales at the time, but I think it is very very important especially in North Wales where they've got so many quarries and we tell, well we actually show people here how slate had been made.

Once again, we return to the discourse of the museum and the national narrative that extends beyond that material to the processes of crafting that product and even the sensory experiences that these performances bring.

What I found in Llanberis was a community of ex-quarriers, their families, and their descendants, performing themselves in such a way as to not only engage with the performances of the working class and labor relations of the time but bring about a very real *embodied* experience (c.f. Walker 2021). The following quote comes from the National Coal Museum but is easily transferable across the Welsh industrial museums: "he (any miner) [sic.] won't see a museum artifact, he'll see something real, part of his body, part of his craft, part . . . of his pride." This "autobiographical working-class performance," as Dicks (2008) describes, allows John-Jo, Carwyn, and Rhian to bridge those connections, go "off script," and begin drawing connections that the more hegemonic-based institutions of the museum either cannot or will not acknowledge.

Discourse

The discourses encountered at the National Slate Museum reflect a series of absences and presences of various Waleses. The push and pull of minority voices and the power of capitalist structures seems at an impasse between critical academic reflection by staff and the typical Anglo-American tourist seeking an "authentic mining" (sic.) experience (c.f. Coupland and Coupland 2014; Prentice 2001; Price 2021). The heritage economy in Llanberis goes part and parcel with the broader economic, cultural, political, and environmental landscape. The impacts of capitalism through both a continued industrial heritage economy and continued industry is reflected through the National Slate Museum and the surrounding community very much in line with Walker's (2021) work on the South Wales Valleys in Chapter IV of this text. History, meaning, performance, and discourse combine to present the contexts of museological memory work.

That being said, there are three additional themes that emerge beyond the more quantitative visitor survey assessments provided previously. The first is a general fracture in meaning somewhere between topic and structure. While the slate industry in North Wales certainly brought in jobs and, at times, significant wealth to areas of Wales, it also functioned as a key imperial praxis.

Within the multiple layers of primitive accumulation at work in Britain and in Wales, in particular, the extraction of Welsh resources for the benefit of English companies, through the wealth acquired via the British Empire, remains absent in the meaning interpreted by visitors to these historical spaces. Echoed across my broader study on the doorsteps of the coal exchange in Cardiff and in the quarries of North Wales stripped of their sustainable family agricultural and slate work by the accumulated wealth of Lord Penrhyn's Jamaican sugar plantations, this imperial presence remains absent. Slavery in Jamaica (and throughout the empire) bequest labor exploitation in Wales, and while many visitors acknowledge the hard work and exploited nature of miners or other common laborers throughout Wales, only in rare instances did an interviewee mention the broader impacts of the British Empire and Wales' active role within such processes, despite widespread knowledge among institutional leadership.

Vital to the national and memorial discourses of the National Slate Museum are those discourses of community and regional legacy from the scales of the newly nominated Slate Industry of North Wales UNESCO World Heritage Site, to Snowdonia National Park, the Electric Mountain Visitors Center in the old Amgueddfa'r Gogledd building, and Penrhyn Castle in Bangor. These transoptic and transnational connections start with the fact that the only national museum in the northern half of Wales *is* the National Slate Museum. After Amgueddfa'r Gogledd was sold, the prominence of slate to the national narrative of Wales only intensified. Locked into this narrative are the discourses at work from Penrhyn Castle and Penrhyn Quarry, which made their fortunes both on the backs of slaves working in the Jamaican sugar industry and the quarriers at the forefront of the British Labour Movement. The Great Strike of 1900–1903 remains the longest industrial walkout in British history (see Figure 12.4).

As in many aspects of Welsh national identity and memorialization, socialism, labor, and the impact and lasting legacy of worker organization stand strong within national narratives within and without the National Slate Museum. Penrhyn Castle, 20 miles north of Llanberis, is mentioned multiple times throughout the discourses of the slate museum, particularly in the film "How to Steal a Mountain":

> In the world of heritage, it is easy to be romantic about the past. There was very little real romance in the lockouts which marked the quarrymen's fights against rules, which rightly or wrongly, hurt their freedoms. . . . Didn't lord Penrhyn deserve to spend the fruits of their labor on a castle by the sea?

In the 1832 painting "The Penrhyn Slate Quarry" by Henry Hawkins in Penrhyn Castle "men and muscle are pitted against the slate." As the film at the slate museum states, "even today, the workshops of Gilfach Ddu can remind us of those primitive forces which stole a mountain." The trouble with this statement, however, remains that visitors are only reminded of one-half of those primitive forces: those that stripped the land from subsistence and peasant agricultural workers to capitalize upon labor and landscape in North Wales. The capital necessary to develop these landscapes and construct the vast infrastructural projects to extract, transport, and ship the slate originated in the primitive accumulation generated through the Pennant's sugar plantations and slave labor in Jamaica.

While much of the Welsh-British primitive accumulation of the slave trade remains obfuscated, the Pennants and later Lords of Penrhyn are one of few distinct examples where the wealth generated through 8,000 acres of sugar plantations and 600 slaves clearly and directly funded the industrial development of the North Wales slate industry (Morgan 2007; Evans 2010). Described by Marx as capitalism's "original sin," primitive accumulation in the form of colonization by the British *both* in Wales and in Africa and the Caribbean drove people from the means of production. Slaves were taken from their land and forced to extract wealth for the benefit of their owners, the Indigenous peoples of Jamaica were either killed or enslaved to make way for that land, and once profits had accumulated, farmers who had been working the land and the slate since at least the time of the Romans were then driven from their land in Wales, as well.

The film continues: "[t]hese workshops and quarries are their proud memorial. These walls echo with their memories. These lakes mirror their endeavors. These

Figure 12.4 A sculpture in memorial to the workers and communities impacted by the Great Strike of 1900–1903 created by artists Zoe Walker and Neil Bromwich for a temporary exhibition inside Penrhyn Castle

Source: Mark Alan Rhodes II

mountains celebrate their skills." These national institutions, such as the National Slate Museum and all the institutions that embrace it, like Snowdonia National Park and Penrhyn Castle, are indeed memorials to the lives and communities sacrificed and sustained by the North Wales slate industry. Particularly as this region looks ahead towards a UNESCO World Heritage Site status, these institutions must remain cognizant of such deeply integral labor relations in the heritage of the region. As Price and Ronck (2019, 3) comment,

> Designation on the World Heritage List will provide a prestigious international validation of North Wales slate heritage. It will also potentially yield important economic benefits in an area that has experienced loss of income and jobs to accompany the decline in slate production. While one desired outcome is increased awareness and demand for slate as a roofing material, a more vital income source for the region is elevated tourism demand.

With any heritage region, economy and memory are delicately balanced. I fear that with so little conversation about the legacy of slavery currently within the Slate Museum (and other institutions) further magnification of the memories of the slate industry will simply amplify these absences. As the UNESCO bid goes before UNESCO in 2021, the community and commercial stakeholders continue to coalesce around a single master plan for the site. My hope is that under the leadership of the National Slate Museum, in particular, the transatlantic linkages of labor may also be amplified by UNESCO alongside their other archived, meaningful, and performative discourses of memory.

Conclusion

The National Slate Museum holds memory embedded in place and space, and that memory spans beyond the text or even the narratives of the museum. Just as Griffiths (2014) ties together "hydropolitical memory" in North Wales through the intersection of the flooding of the Tryweryn Valley and its subsequent commemoration in the landscape of North Wales (and now in the global Welsh diaspora) and the poetry and literature of Wales, this work links the heritage of the slate industry, its commemoration, and its various discourses and performances. The walls and stones and slates do have a voice, and the people who visit and work within these spaces carry meaning and performance with them.

As in most locales, identity, memory, and landscape transcend one another through iterative everyday practice. Performing Welshness in the national institutions takes on a variety of forms from descending into a coal mine, woolen mill, or slate workshop to tapping into an historic and ethnic idea of Celticity. Lewis (2018, 25), who focuses on Welsh museums, festivals, and theatre as performances of memory, place, and culture, situates this performance of touching the artifacts in the museums or dwelling in these institutional spaces as intrinsic to Welsh culture as a "relationship with place that is often profoundly embodied."

The agency of artifacts and landscape of the National Slate Museum, even when not bringing about the greater structural understanding identified here, engage the collective memory embedded within them. At times that touch, thinking through the ideas of *cynefin* and a transoptic landscape, may be in the form of haunting. *Cynefin* – and the broader more-than-representational modes of understanding landscape – presents the National Slate Museum to the researcher, staff, and visitors as intangible and tangible, haunted and lived, and cultural and historical landscape. The National Slate Museum is part of a haunted landscape divorced of its historical context yet retaining the scars of its past (Hill 2013; Edensor 2008). Overall, the National Slate Museum in Llanberis reminds us as scholars and those interested in industrial heritage that the economic legacies and structures of the state (and sub-state) of Wales, the United Kingdom, and the British Empire have deep socioeconomic impacts on the memory work of the nation.

Notes

1 Data derived from the Office for National Statistics Earnings and hours worked reports by place of residence by Parliamentary constituency and by UK region by industry by two-digit SIC for 2011 and 2019. The 2011 data reflects the lowest median gross annual pay. The 2019 data reflects the lowest mean gross annual pay.
2 These included The National Museum of Wales Records in the National Library of Wales and archival materials, books, and reports in the National Museum Cardiff and St. Fagans National Museum of History Libraries.

Works cited

Cole, E. 2015. "Impetuous Torrents: Scottish Waterfalls in Travellers' Narratives, 1769–1830." *Scottish Geographical Journal* 131 (1): 49–66.

Cosgrove, D. 1998. *Social Formation and Symbolic Landscape*. Madison: University of Wisconsin Press.

Coupland, B., and N. Coupland. 2014. "The Authenticating Discourses of Mining Heritage Tourism in Cornwall and Wales." *Journal of Sociolinguistics* 18 (4): 495–517.

Curtis, T. 1986. *Wales: The Imagined Nation*. Bridgend, Wales: Poetry Wales Press.

DeSilvey, C. 2007. "Art and Archive: Memory-Work on a Montana Homestead." *Journal of Historical Geography* 33 (4): 878–900.

Devadoss, C. 2017. "Sound and Identity Explored Through the Indian Tamil Diaspora and Tamil Nadu." *Journal of Cultural Geography* 34 (1): 70–92.

Dewsbury, J.D., P. Harrison, M. Rose, and J. Wylie. 2002. "Introduction: Enacting Geographies." *Geoforum* 33: 437–40.

Dicks, B. 2008. "Performing the Hidden Injuries of Class in Coal-Mining Heritage." *Sociology* 42 (3): 436–52.

Dittmer, J. and E. Waterton. 2016. "Embodied Memory at the Australian War Memorial." In *Memory, Place and Identity: Commemoration and Remembrance of War and Conflict*, edited by D. Drozdzewski, S. De Nardi, and E. Waterton, E, 169–88. Abington, UK: Routledge.

Doss, E. 2010. *Memorial Mania: Public Feeling in America*. Chicago, IL: University of Chicago Press. Nook e-book.

Drozdzewski, D. 2016. "Encountering Memory in the Everyday City." In *Memory, Place and Identity: Commemoration and Remembrance of War and Conflict*, edited by D. Drozdzewski, S. De Nardi, and E. Waterton. Abington, UK: Routledge.

Edensor, T. 2008. "Mundane Hauntings: Commuting Through the Phantasmagoric Working-Class Spaces of Manchester, England." *Cultural Geographies* 15: 313–33.

Evans, C. 2010. *Slave Wales: The Welsh and Atlantic Slavery 1660–1850*. Cardiff: University of Wales Press.

Faudree, P. 2012. "Music, Language, and Texts: Sound and Semiotic Ethnography." *Annual Review of Anthropology* 41: 519–36.

Griffiths, H. 2014. "Water Under the Bridge? Nature, Memory and Hydropolitics." *Cultural Geographies* 21 (3): 449–74.

Gruffudd, P. 1995. "Remaking Wales: Nation-Building and the Geographical Imagination, 1925–50." *Political Geography* 14 (3): 219–39.

Hill, L. 2013. "Archaeologies and Geographies of the Post-Industrial Past: Landscape, Memory and the Spectral." *Cultural Geographies* 20 (3): 379–96.

Howell, D.R. 2013a. "The Intangible Cultural Heritage of Wales: A Need for Safeguarding?" *International Journal of Intangible Heritage* 8: 104–16.

———. 2013b. "The Heritage Industry in a Politically Devolved Wales." PhD diss., University of South Wales. 20468211.

———. 2016. "Selection and Deselection of the National Narrative: Approaches to Heritage Through Devolved Politics in Wales." In *Heritage and Tourism in Britain and Ireland* edited by G. Hooper, 161–76. London: Palgrave Macmillan.

Leadley, M. 2011. "Soundscape and Perception: Reconfiguring the Acoustic Environment for Experimental Purpose." *SoundEffects* 1 (1): 118–38.

Lewis, L. 2018. *Performing Wales: People, Memory, and Place*. Cardiff: University of Wales Press.

Longhurst, R., E. Ho, and L. Johnston. 2008. "Using 'the Body' as an 'Instrument of Research': kimch'i and Pavlova." *Area* 40 (2): 208–17.

Lorimer, H. 2003. "Telling Small Stories: Spaces of Knowledge and the Practice of Geography." *Transactions of the Institute of British Geographers* 28: 197–217.

Lowenthal, D. 1976. Tuning into the Past: Can We Recapture Soundscapes of Bygone Days?" *The UNESCO Courier* 29 (November): 15–21.

Mason, R. 2007. *Museums, Nations, Identities: Wales and its National Museums*. Cardiff: University of Wales.

Morgan, K. 2007. *Slavery and the British Empire*. Oxford: Oxford University Press.

National Museum Wales. 2016. *Visitor Profile Survey 2015–2016*. Cardiff: National Museum Wales.

Osborne, B. 2001. "Landscapes, Memory, Monuments, and Commemoration: Putting Identity in Its Place." *Canadian Ethnic Studies* 33 (3).

Osmond, J. 2007. *Myths, Memories and Futures: The National Library and National Museum in the Story of Wales*. Cardiff: Institute of Welsh Affairs.

Paasi, A. 2015. "Dancing on the Graves: Independence, Hot/Banal Nationalism and the Mobilization of Memory." *Political Geography*. doi:10.1016/j.polgeo.2015.07.005.

Prentice, R. 2001. "Experiential Cultural Tourism: Museums & the Marketing of the New Romanticism of Evoked Authenticity." *Museum Management and Curatorship* 19 (1): 5–26.

Price, W. 2021. "Unearthing Community Identities at the National Coal Mining Museums of Great Britain." In *Geographies of Post-Industrial Place, Memory, and Heritage*, edited by M. Rhodes, W. Price, and A. Walker. Abingdon: Routledge.

Price, W., and C. Ronck. 2019. "Quarrying for World Heritage Designation: Slate Tourism in North Wales." *Geoheritage*. doi:10.1007/s12371-019-00402-0.

Rhodes, M. 2019. "The Memory Work of Welsh Heritage: Multidimentional Landscapes of a Multinational Wales." PhD diss., Kent State University.

Sack, R. 1983. "Human Territoriality: A Theory." *Annals of the Association of American Geographers* 73 (1): 55–74.

Schein, R. 1997. "The Place of Landscape: A Conceptual Framework for Interpreting an American Scene." *Annals of the Association of American Geographers* 87 (4): 660–80.

———. 2009. "A Methodological Framework for Interpreting Ordinary Landscapes: Lexington, Kentucky's Courthouse Square." *The Geographical Review* 99 (3): 377–402.

Smith, S.A. 1994. "Soundscape." *Area* 26 (3): 232–40.

Smith, S.A., and K.E. Foote. 2017. "Museum/Space/Discourse: Analyzing Discourse in Three Dimensions in Denver's History Colorado Center." *Cultural Geographies* 24 (1): 131–48.

Symonds, J. 2005. "Experiencing Industry." In *Industrial Archaeology. Contributions to Global Historical Archaeology*, edited by E. Casella and J. Symonds, 33–57. Boston: Springer.

Till, K. 2005. *The New Berlin: Memory, Politics, Place*. Minneapolis: University of Minnesota Press.

Walker, A. 2021. "Everyday Resonances of Industrial Pasts: Considering Lived and Affective Memories in Ex-Coal Mining Landscapes in a South Wales Valley." In *Geographies of Post-Industrial Place, Memory, and Heritage*, edited by M. Rhodes, W. Price, and A. Walker. Abingdon: Routledge.

Waterton, E. 2014. "A More-Than-Representational Understanding of Heritage? The 'Past' and the Politics of Affect." *Geography Compass* 8 (11): 823–33.

———. 2013. "Landscape and Non-Representational Theories." In *The Routledge Companion to Landscape Studies*, edited by P. Howard, I. Thompson, and E. Waterton, 66–75. Abingdon, England: Routledge.

Williams, G. 1985. *When Was Wales? A History of the Welsh*. London: Black Raven Press.

Williams, K. 1998. *The Land and the Sea*. Llandysul: Gomer.

Index

For Product Safety Concerns and Information please contact our EU representative GPSR@taylorandfrancis.com
Taylor & Francis Verlag GmbH, Kaufingerstraße 24, 80331 München, Germany

www.ingramcontent.com/pod-product-compliance
Ingram Content Group UK Ltd.
Pitfield, Milton Keynes, MK11 3LW, UK
UKHW020006200926
475702UK00015B/2502
* 9 7 8 0 3 6 7 6 2 8 3 1 4 *